Caravans and Wedding Bands

Memories of a Romany Life

EVA PETULENGRO

with Claire Petulengro

PAN BOOKS

First published 2012 by Pan Books
an imprint of Pan Macmillan, a division of Macmillan Publishers Limited
Pan Macmillan, 20 New Wharf Road, London N1 9RR
Basingstoke and Oxford
Associated companies throughout the world
www.panmacmillan.com

ISBN 978-1-44720-944-7

1 3 5 7 9 8 6 4 2

A CIP catalogue record for this book is available from
the British Library.

Typeset by Ellipsis Books Limited, Glasgow
Printed in the UK by CPI Group (UK) Ltd, Croydon CR0 4YY

Visit **www.panmacmillan.com** to read more about all our books
and to buy them. You will also find features, author interviews and
news of any author events, and you can sign up for e-newsletters
so that you're always first to hear about our new releases.

For my beloved Mummy,
my husband Johnnie and my brother Eddie.
Thank you for a wonderful life!

And to our dear friend Geraldine Mary Clarke,
who has now joined them in heaven.
You were always a true rawney (lady).

Contents

Prologue

I lay awake in the dark, alert for sounds. It was quiet, too quiet. I waited for something to break through the silence, but nothing came. For so many years my home had been a caravan, where the sound of the wind or rain hitting the roof could always be heard. My thoughts drifted back to comforting childhood nights spent in Granny's traditional Romany vardo, her painted caravan. Perhaps I would never quite get used to a life where bricks and mortar did such a good job of shutting out the elements.

I turned to look at the figure sleeping by my side. Johnnie, my husband of less than twenty-four hours, lay with an arm draped across me. I loved him more than I ever knew it was possible to love someone, and now I was his wife and his little Brighton bachelor pad was home. I felt like the happiest woman in the world, so I should have been enjoying a peaceful, contented sleep, but the unnerving silence nagged away at me and kept me awake. Even the sound of the boiler coming on would have helped, or the clink of milk bottles being left outside our door. I listened hard, but could hear nothing. You'd think I would have got used to living in a house in the four years since my family had left behind their travelling life to settle in Brighton. But at home, someone would always leave a radio on or a window slightly open to let nature's sounds in. I needed some sort of background noise before I could sleep.

I eased myself carefully out from under Johnnie's arm, crept out of bed and switched on the radio, tuning the dial until I found something to reassure me that I wasn't the only person awake at such an ungodly hour. I went back to bed, slipping under the satin sheets. As I laid my head on the pillow, I lifted Johnnie's arm and placed it around me again. Perfect now, I said to myself, closing my eyes, the warbling of Johnny Mathis soothing me and giving me the sense of security I needed.

I knew that, next to me, Johnnie was oblivious to the radio. His steady breathing told me he was lost in deep slumber, probably dreaming of his speedboat rides or the impulsive drives we would take when the mood took us. Now I too was being taken away into dreams, dreams of the past, of lying in Granny's feather bed in the painted caravan, the sound of rain dripping from trees beating a gentle rhythm on the roof, a sense of wonder at the shadows cast across my window by the branches moving above us.

ONE

Wedding Bells

I woke with a start, and for a moment lay still, replaying the previous day's excitement. On 3 November 1964, I had put on my smart black suit and pink chiffon blouse and tiptoed down the stairs and out of the home I shared with my family in West Street, Brighton, clutching the black cartwheel hat I'd last worn a few weeks earlier at my cousin's wedding. Now I was about to wear it at my own wedding. I had raced down the road in my high heels, my stomach churning as the enormity of what I was about to do sank in. I had not told Mummy or Daddy I was getting married; I had said nothing to my younger brothers Nathan and Eddie; nor had I breathed a word to my little sister Anne, Eddie's twin.

In true Romany tradition, I was eloping, and it was my secret. A secret Johnnie and I shared. At the register office in Brighton, just a few streets from my parents' home, Johnnie and I made our vows. I couldn't believe I'd had the nerve to go through with it.

Immediately after the ceremony, Johnnie had called my mother.

'Hello, Mrs Petulengro,' he had said. 'I'm John Tullett. I've just married your daughter.'

Johnnie got straight to the point, while I sat in the background biting my nails, dreading my mother's reaction to the fact that I had just married a non-Romany. By this point in time it was relatively common for Romanies to marry 'gorgers' (non-Romanies), but my family was still very true to its roots and quite traditional in many ways. I sat there with bated breath. Would I have disappointed her? Nothing in the world could keep me away from my Johnnie, but I couldn't stand the thought of upsetting Mummy.

I needn't have been so worried since she wasn't in the least bit surprised. She had guessed what was going on and had left it up to me to make the right choice; all she wanted was for me to be happy. There were no recriminations, just plenty of champagne to celebrate the marriage of her eldest child. 'Get round here now,' she ordered. 'We've got some celebrating to do!' Although Mummy did interrogate Johnnie for ten minutes in the kitchen when we first arrived!

We had drunk, danced and sung into the early morning, and my head felt heavy now. As I lay there, my mind whirling at the thought of how different my life had become in such a short space of time, I realized that Johnnie and I could have tied the knot three years earlier if I'd said yes to him then. I was being a good girl and doing what I felt my mother would approve of, but what a waste of time and life! Still, all's well that ends well. I was with him now and that was all that mattered.

In the dim early-morning light, I looked around the flat, taking in the curtains and the furniture. This was where I now lived – a bachelor pad! As I lay in bed, I realized I actually hated the satin sheets I had insisted on getting for when we were married, as they were too slippery and they slid all over the place and weren't nearly as luxurious-feeling as they had seemed when I bought them. I vowed to buy some good old-fashioned cotton sheets.

From somewhere in the flat came the sound of Johnnie singing: 'She wears red feathers and a huly-huly skirt.' Where the hell was my husband anyway?

'Johnnie,' I called.

He suddenly appeared at the doorway, bright-eyed, a cup of PG Tips in his hand. 'I didn't want to wake you,' he said. 'You had a lot of excitement yesterday, and a lot of champagne!' We laughed together at the memory.

Johnnie sat on the edge of the bed. 'Here's your

cuppa tea, duck,' he said, a phrase he had picked up from me and which I had learned from my time in Nottingham in my teens.

His eyes sparkled. How could anyone be so happy at this early hour? Surely he needed more time to acclimatize? It was beyond me. I had never been good in the mornings. My brother Eddie could leap up and resume a conversation from where he'd left off the night before, with a spring in his step and a smile on his face, anywhere, any day of the week. I, on the other hand, could not. My family knew not to phone me or bother talking to me until gone eleven, as that's when my batteries turned on. At this stage of my life, I have come to the conclusion that I will never do mornings! Thank goodness Johnnie worked that out fairly early on.

'What would you like to do now then?' he asked.

We had told everyone we were going off on a honeymoon because we wanted to be left alone, but we hadn't made any proper plans.

'If you like,' he said, 'we can go to Gatwick and take a flight somewhere hot?'

I gazed up at him. 'What do *you* want to do?'

'As long as I'm with you, I don't care what we do or where we are.'

We had both always been direct, saying exactly what we meant and meaning exactly what we said. 'I can't lie on a beach thinking about what needs to be done to this flat,' I said. 'You don't own a single pot or pan, only a grill which you use to cook the only thing you can – a bacon sandwich. I want to cook you some real food.'

Johnnie had never experienced my cooking, and I'd always loved to cook.

He laughed. 'Tell me what you want and I'm at your service.'

'OK, I want to go shopping, but not in Brighton. I don't want to run into anybody we know yet.'

In the days before the wedding, we had bought a few things to make Johnnie's flat a bit more homely – there was a new dark-blue three-piece suite and rugs and curtains to complement it – but we had not yet got essentials like pots and pans and all the other things that make a home.

'London would be nice,' Johnnie said with a smile and a twinkle in his eye.

'Oh yes,' I said, delighted at the thought of a shopping spree in the capital.

Johnnie got a pen, a piece of paper and a tape measure. 'Where would you like to start, madam?'

'Kitchen – *definitely* kitchen.' I threw back the bedcovers, jumped up and ran past him.

Johnnie's kitchen was a very sparse room with a sink and only one shelf. I stood for a second or two, working out what was needed to brighten the place up.

'Curtains for the window,' I ordered. Johnnie made a note. 'Oh, and cupboards and shelves for pots and food.' He started taking measurements, the two of us quickly moving around the bare space, working well together.

'How about a nice room divider that can serve as a breakfast table where we can sit and eat?' he said. Johnnie used to build boats for a living and was great at woodwork. Having served his apprenticeship as a young man in a boat yard, he was not afraid of a challenge. He quickly sketched what he had in mind for the room divider, then began measuring the walls, asking where I wanted everything to be placed.

I was now on fast-forward, ideas taking shape one after another. 'I'd like a copper top on the room divider, please.'

Johnnie gave me a questioning look. 'You won't like it,' he warned.

I insisted I would. I could picture it already.

He laughed and wrote it on the list. 'What colour shall I paint the walls?' he pondered.

'Bright orange,' I said excitedly. As a child, I had always loved the rich jewel colours in Granny's vardo: the ruby red of the old gas lamps, the emerald of the leaded lights and the deep amber of the doorknobs. 'It will go lovely with copper and I've seen some old Victorian copper saucepans I'm going to buy to hang on the wall.' There had been copper trim on the vardo too. My imagination was running wild and we were both revelling in designing our first home together.

We headed to the station and up to London. Shopping as a pair of newlyweds was great fun – and very expensive! It was then that I realized my husband was colour blind. I'd thought I'd like the bathroom to be cream and brown, and had spotted some lovely striped towels and flannels and a mat for the floor. Johnnie suddenly pointed at a pile of grey and white towels and said, 'Is that what you're looking for?' My mind flashed back to an oil painting he'd done of me. When he gave it to me, the only problem with it was that he'd painted my eyes brown. Surely he had noticed I had blue eyes? Now, with the mix-up over the towels, I knew for sure. Colours would definitely have to be my department! I selected my cream and brown towels and, laden down with parcels and bags, we headed for Victoria station. We were going home. To *our* home. I couldn't wait to hang my new towels on the rail in our bathroom.

Every aspect of our lives was good, and we worked well together, quickly adapting to married life. I was twenty-five and Johnnie was nine years older. I had become well known as a clairvoyant and was busy seeing my clients and writing a regular horoscope column for the *Evening Argus* in Brighton and several other newspapers and magazines. At the same time, I was producing my quarterly horoscope guide, which had proved hugely popular. Johnnie worked in a boat yard in Newhaven, and in the summer he ran a speed-boat from the West Pier in Brighton. He had begun working with boats at the age of sixteen, when he went to work as an apprentice in a boat yard where there were lots of office girls. He told me that on his first day at work they made an excuse to get him into one of the sheds, where there was some molten tar that was used in the boat-building process. They had cooled some off, so it wasn't hot, but still sticky. The girls rolled up his trousers and held him whilst one of the women painted the tar onto his legs and arms from the elbows down. Then one of the girls produced a bag of feathers. They held onto him until the feathers were well and truly glued on. Apparently, this was what they did to all new people, especially if they were young. Shortly after this, he was offered a well-paid job in a wet-fish shop.

'I only lasted two weeks,' he told me. 'I couldn't get rid of the smell, so I went back to the boat yard. In the summer I started working on the speedboats in Littlehampton – did that for a few years – then one winter I got involved in yacht deliveries. I'd be back working on the speedboats in the summer months.'

At the time of our wedding, he'd also taken a job in an off-licence in Brighton. When I could, I would take him lunch and we would sit in the back room, where I would write my horoscopes for the newspapers.

We loved spending as much time together as we could, but we also had our own loves and passions that we stayed true to after we tied the knot. In between writing for my horoscope columns and guide, I would put aside some time each week to make notes for the book I'd been planning to write since I was a child. And Johnnie could spend hours locked away in a room painting.

Since Johnnie had worked out that I was not at my best first thing, we fell into a daily routine where he would bring me a cup of tea and then sneak out of the room, so as not to have to listen to, or reply to, whatever grumpy comment came out of my mouth. Instead he headed downstairs to read the paper – the 'rag', as he liked to call it.

I would never feel like eating until after 11.30, but always made breakfast for Johnnie. One of his friends had told him that when you look at a woman over your paper in the morning, you've got to love her. I knew that would always be the case for me and Johnnie; I couldn't imagine either of us ever looking at each other with anything other than a loving smile. As he ate, we would discuss what we wanted to do with our future, coming up with all sorts of new and exciting plans – some of which would come to fruition and others that would always remain pipe dreams. I loved moving around, whereas Johnnie loved living on a boat. He had lived on a barge for a while when he was single, but we both knew it wasn't for me.

'You couldn't do it, Jewel,' he said. Jewel was the nickname he had given me. Although my real name was Julie Eva, I used Eva, my granny's name, for my horoscopes and readings, but I was always Jewel or Jules to Johnnie. He went on, 'Barges on rivers attract rats.' He saw me shudder and grinned. 'That's a definite no, then?'

'If and when we have children,' I said, 'and I want *six* children by the way—'

Johnnie cut in. 'What I was going to say,' he said with a smile, 'is what about a floating home? A boat we can actually live on, a bit like your vardo. The difference being, that instead of travelling the roads, we could travel on the water and go abroad, or anywhere you fancy, for the winters and come back for the summer seasons.'

Now this idea appealed to me. 'The only thing is, what about schools?' I said. 'By law, the children –

when we have them – will have to go to school, unless we home-school them.'

Johnnie was laughing. 'Now you really are getting ahead of yourself.'

He was right, I was. I started laughing too.

We occasionally chatted about that idea of living on a boat as the years passed, but nothing ever came of it. There was no way I would ever really consider living on a boat when I couldn't swim!

A lot of people have asked me what it was like to have to adapt to a house after living in a vardo for so many years. I have always been a big film fan and one of the things I envied, when watching films, was the sight of a glamorous star lying in a bubble bath. It was a luxury not afforded to those of us who lived in caravans. We had to put up with a top-to-toe wash in a hand bowl, and our idea of a luxury bath would be one of those tin baths some house-dwellers used, which were not big enough to completely immerse your body in. You'd have to sit up, which was fine for kids, but for adults that meant your knees were up against your chin. Not very comfortable, but nonetheless preferable to the hand bowl. Having bathed, you then had the problem of disposing of the water. You would use a jug to fill a bucket, which you would then have to empty before filling it again with more of the bath water, and repeating the process several times. Hardly relaxing after a soak with your knees tucked up beneath your chin! I remember dreaming about turning on a tap and seeing water flow into the bath, rather than having to fill up cans from taps I had trekked up hill and down dale to find. So, you can imagine my delight at the thought of having running water on tap – and not only cold water, but *hot, hot, hot*. Delicious bubbles in which I could actually stretch out my legs and even dip my head under, should I so desire, and to top off this heavenly experience, all I had to do when I was finished was pull the plug. Even today, I still appreciate my baths because the memories of the hard work involved in my early ones are still etched on my mind.

Throughout mine and Johnnie's courtship, the Sussex public house in the heart of Brighton had been our main venue to meet, and now we were married we still went there for a drink. The landlord and landlady were such colourful characters, and we liked them enormously.

I first met Harry and Cath Taylor in 1960, when I started going out with Johnnie. They were a glamorous couple with three lovely sons. Harry had a wonderful moustache and a persona that made you feel as if you should curtsey in his presence, while Cath always had a beaming smile on her face, sparkling eyes and a great sense of humour. Before she was a landlady she used to be the Queen's hairdresser; she was an incredibly creative lady.

Johnnie and I would meet our friends in the Sussex if we were going out, and the pub drew many wonderful and outrageous people. Many people from the theatre world went there. I remember one lady, Betty, who was always two sheets to the wind and kept us entertained with her antics.

Cath and Harry were wonderfully friendly people, forever making everyone laugh, and we always had a great time at their lock-ins. At closing time they would say, 'Don't go anywhere, you two. Stay where you are.' When the pub had emptied we would find ourselves in an elite little group with the likes of the TV and radio personality Gilbert Harding, who on one occasion actually walked down from his home in Clifton Terrace in his dressing gown and pyjamas with his pet Pekinese to join us! Among the other regulars were actors Nigel Green, who appeared in *Jason and the Argonauts* and *Zulu*, and Robert Coote, who starred in *My Fair Lady* on Broadway, playwright Alan Melville and singer John Leyton, who topped the charts in 1961 with 'Johnny Remember Me'.

I recall one evening in particular. I didn't want any more to drink, but one did not refuse a drink at these handpicked lock-ins and everyone had to stand their round.

'Oh no, I don't want any more,' I said, and John Leyton, who was next to me, beckoned me over to the window, where we stood with our backs to the others.

'This is what you do with the drinks you don't want, Eva,' he said. He pulled the curtain to one side to reveal four large gin and tonics lined up on the windowsill.

In future, that was where my unwanted drinks would go too.

Later that same evening as we were all standing round chatting and laughing, drinks in hand, Cath called for everyone's attention. 'Quickly, everyone upstairs, the police are at the door. We're being raided!'

We all piled into the lounge upstairs like naughty schoolchildren, giggling. One or two of us were slightly the worse for wear. Anyone who's ever been in a lock-in will know that the drinks do seem to taste better after hours. It must be something to do with that naughty, illicit feeling of having a drink when you're not supposed to. Thankfully, Cath and Harry didn't lose their licence, which, without mentioning any names, was a lot to do with the fact that one of the senior police officers was also one of the main after-hours drinkers there. They were good times, filled with laughter.

*

Although I had been in daily phone contact with Mummy, after a week of married life it was time to go and visit, to find out what was happening in the family. I had never been away from my mother for such a long time before and I was desperate to see her. Johnnie and I walked into the flat to see a beaming face.

'Hello, Mummy,' I said.

She hugged me tighter than usual, before pushing me and Johnnie into the lounge. 'Sit down, you people,' she ordered. 'I've got something to tell you.'

My brother Nathan had recently moved out and the twins were at school, so we were the only ones there. I could see the worried look on Mummy's face and began to feel quite concerned.

'I'm sure you know, Eva,' Mummy continued, 'that things haven't been right between me and your father for some time. And now that you and Nathan have both left home, I don't need to put up with your father any longer,' she said. 'He was never really around much anyway, so I told him to just pack up his stuff and go.'

She said the words as quickly as she could, and then seemed to stand there holding her breath, gazing at me intently to see what my reaction would be. I stood up and looked at her. I knew it must have taken an enormous amount of courage to make such a decision, especially for a Romany woman who firmly believed that marriage was for life, but he had only ever made her unhappy and I couldn't have been more pleased for her now. 'It's about time, Mummy,' I said.

She let out a huge sigh of relief, and we both hugged, tears of happiness rolling down our cheeks. Before we knew it, we were laughing.

'If it hadn't been for you,' she said, 'I would have kicked him out years ago, but you thought the world of him.'

'Oh no, I didn't,' I said, determined to let her know that wasn't the case. The only reason I had never complained to her about my father's manipulating ways was because I didn't want to hurt her or make things difficult. 'I've always thought the complete opposite. I just didn't want to upset you,' I said.

Now Johnnie began to laugh too.

She decided not to tell me that day, but it came out soon afterwards that Daddy had been having an affair for quite some time and that Mummy had found out about it. It was with this 'other woman' that he was living, in a flat on the other side of Brighton.

Mummy still had the twins, Eddie and Anne, now fifteen and very lively characters, living with her. They had inherited her dry wit and ability to look at life as if the glass was half full. In a sense, I never really left home, even though I was married, because at that time, our dukkering (palm-reading) place was actually Mummy's flat, so we found ourselves together most of the time. She also felt as though she had inherited another son in Johnnie, who was round at Mummy's as often as the rest of us. Within hours of meeting on our wedding day, my mother and Johnnie became like two of the musketeers, so much so that whenever she phoned up, it was Johnnie she asked to speak to, to tell him her latest joke or adventure, and he was the same with her. They got on wonderfully and shared the same dry sense of humour. It seemed as if he'd been part of our family forever.

Johnnie and Eddie would play football together, and he and Nathan shared a love of cameras. Often, when we were at Mummy's flat, Johnnie and Nathan would go off for a pint together. Anne had her own pals, and across the road from the flat was an ice-skating rink which was great fun for her and her friends. She also now had her own bedroom since I'd moved out, where she and her friends would disappear to play games, watch TV and do homework. In Brighton, the twins had two years at school, between the ages of fourteen and sixteen. It was late to be attending school for the first time, but at least it showed them that a gorger's life was very different to ours and prepared them for the changing times. Eddie used to lock himself in his bedroom for hours to paint pictures that no one was allowed to see. So all in all, life continued much as it had before, except that my father's absence made for lighter spirits and the house was always full of laughter now. And Mummy especially looked like a huge weight had been lifted from her shoulders. Looking back, I realized Daddy had never joined in with us, never really wanted to be part of the family, and in fact had cast a grey cloud over the rest of us.

Shortly after he moved out, Daddy called to say he was having a party and he wondered if I would come along. I couldn't think of an excuse quickly enough, so I had to agree. But then he said, 'Would you bring along your friends too? All of them, as many as you can.'

'How strange,' I thought. But I did as he asked and invited a few of mine and Johnnie's friends along. When we arrived at the party, Daddy asked me what I wanted to drink. 'Brandy and coke, please,' I replied. When he came back with the drink, one sip told me there was absolutely no brandy in there at all! I spotted him swanning round the room with everyone patting him on the back, telling him how generous he was, and I realized then that he had used me once again, just as he always had. The whole thing was an elaborate attempt to make himself out to be a wonderful, generous fellow, opening his pockets to all his friends and family, when in fact the 'party' was probably costing him just pennies. And as he didn't have any friends of his own, he'd asked me to bring mine along instead! I thought back to all the times he had used me as a child, giving me all the horrible jobs he considered himself to be too high for – sorting the rotten fruit outside his shop at 6 a.m. every day, getting up even earlier to feed his chickens, making hot dogs and toffee apples and scrubbing his fairground stall at all hours of the day and night, while he stood around chatting – all while I was doing my palmistry apprenticeship with Mummy and looking after the twins. But that was my daddy; some things would never change.

I would regale Johnnie with stories of my childhood and how us Romanies used to live, and he loved the cookouts which took place in Mummy's back garden as they brought all those tales to life for him. By the time we all arrived, the stick fire would already be lit and we'd sit around it and talk about our day. At one of these gatherings, Johnnie said he had something important to tell Mummy. 'I've just met up with a guy I used to know years ago,' he said. 'He's a butcher and he provides the meat for the royal kitchens. I hope it's all right, Eva,' he added, looking at my mother, 'but I've invited him to pop round and say hello.'

Mummy looked at Johnnie quizzically. 'There's more to it, boy. What is it?'

'I thought you could do with some meat and fowl that he'll let you have for the wholesale price.' Johnnie looked a bit nervous, not knowing if he'd been too presumptuous. But he'd thought it was worth the risk as he knew how much Mummy loved a bargain!

Mummy was beaming at this. Ten minutes later, a dapper, well-dressed little fellow came through the yard. He was introduced to everyone as George. Mummy asked him to sit down.

'Now then, young man, before we go any further, would you like a drink of any kind?'

'Oh, I could kill a cup of tea,' he replied.

'Anne, go and make this man a cup of tea.' With this, Anne ran up the spiral staircase that led from the garden into the kitchen.

George was soon chatting to Mummy about different cuts of meat. He got out his notebook and pen and proceeded to take her order.

'I would like a sirloin of beef, a leg of lamb, fillet steaks and some sweetbreads.'

I loved Mummy's sweetbreads. She would gently fry them in butter with a little salt and pepper, and they tasted delicious.

So the next time I saw George, I ordered some steak and some sweetbreads. He looked at me and said, 'Do you want the sweetbreads from around the heart or the throat?'

I stared at him in horror. 'Cancel it!' I said.

Although I had eaten sweetbreads for years, I'd never

known which part of the animal they came from. In one minute flat, he had put me off for life. It doesn't take much to put me off something!

Romanies are indeed a strange lot. Things like a dog drinking or eating from our plates aren't tolerated at all, whereas I know that many gorgers are happy to let their dogs finish what they don't eat straight from their plates. In the old days, I remember that if a dog took food from a plate, the plate would be smashed. A waste, you may think, but it is our way. But we like to eat with our fingers when around a fire, as gorgers do with fish and chips. Food cooked on a stick fire tastes better eaten that way than with a knife and fork off a plate. I saw a film about Henry VIII once, and they were all at a big banqueting table, eating with their fingers. If it was good enough for him . . .

That evening after George left, Mummy began to boil a big ham on the bone in a boiler over the stick fire, while Johnnie watched her in awe, completely fascinated. When it was cooked, she cooled it, then cut all the fat from it. She spread English mustard all over it, then brown sugar, patted it and took it upstairs into the oven in the kitchen, until the sugar melted. Before it burned, she removed it and let it cool. I remember Granny doing the same thing when I was a child. She brought it back down and we all tore strips off with our fingers, savouring every delicious morsel.

This was a recipe my family had made for generations, and any ham that was left over would be re-cooked in the boiler with dried peas, which had been soaked the night before, slices of onions, carrots, leeks and potatoes, which were put in last, just after the ham had drifted from the bone. The peas disintegrated and the vegetables cooked. We'd add a dash of black pepper, and you would have a pea and ham soup to die for.

I can remember Granny singing 'Roses of Picardy' as she cooked, which was her favourite song, her head waving back and forth, her long grey hair plaited each side and pinned into what was called 'earphones', a popular hairdo when I was a child. I can still see the white pinafores she always wore when cooking, which she would wash and then soak in 'blue', little blue blocks of ultramarine and baking soda wrapped in cellophane. They didn't turn blue, but instead came out whiter than white. I'm still often reminded of Granny and her ways.

All of a sudden there was a clatter on the spiral staircase and we turned round to see Eddie and Nathan coming down into the garden with their guitars, to play our favourite tunes. Nathan pulled out a table top, which was laid on the ground, and Mummy and I tap danced on it together while they played 'I Got Rhythm', 'Top Hat' and 'Isn't This a Lovely Day?' Johnnie loved it all – it was so new to him.

That night, as we returned home to our flat, Johnnie said, 'I wish I'd been born a Romany; it's a totally different world.'

I looked at him and smiled. 'You are a Romany now, boy!'

TWO

Stick Fires and Red Faces

It was May 1965, and Johnnie and I had been married for seven months. Everyone was looking forward to a peaceful bank holiday after what had become known as the Battle of Brighton over the Whitsun weekend the year before, when rival gangs of mods and rockers poured into the town. Something like 3,000 of them had gathered on the seafront – the mods with their suits and parkas and scooters, the rockers in leathers on powerful motorbikes. When they clashed, it was mayhem: holidaymakers running for cover, deckchairs flying off the end of the Palace Pier and windows smashed. It took hundreds of police officers, many on horseback, to restore anything like order. The same thing had gone on in other seaside towns that weekend. It was the worst, most violent bank holiday anyone could remember.

One lovely hot evening over the bank holiday weekend, we had been invited to a dinner party by a gorger friend of Johnnie's. His name was Kenneth and his wife was Angela, and they owned a lucrative local business. Johnnie had done some work on Kenneth's yacht for him, and in the process they had discovered a mutual love for boats and life on the sea.

Kenneth proposed to sail over to France with some friends, with Johnnie as skipper, and we were invited to the dinner party in order to meet the friends who would also be making the trip. Forgive me, but I disliked the group as soon as I laid eyes on them. They seemed to me to be pretentious, *nouveau riche* and imagined they were the cream of society. Kenneth, blond-haired and a big, strapping bloke, was nice enough – until he opened his mouth! He gave the impression that he knew everything and everyone, and had been everywhere. He had the beginnings of a beer belly and his shirt strained across his middle and hung out the back of his trousers.

Looking round, my heart sank, until I was introduced to Angela, a quiet girl who certainly didn't fit in with any of her husband's friends. She was in her late twenties, about ten years younger than Kenneth, and was very slim, with glasses. I observed that she could be a real good-looker if she had a makeover. Her hair, in particular, needed attention – she wore it tied up in a ponytail. I was interested to know where she'd met Kenneth.

'I worked for Kenny as a secretary in his head office,' she said. 'After work, he'd drop me home, and after a few weeks, we started dating.' He had introduced her to a new and affluent way of life. 'He's ever so generous,' she said.

As everyone sat in the garden, drinking Pimms and airing opinions and so-called knowledge on various subjects from the sublime to the ridiculous, Angela and I retreated to the kitchen. I had taken an immediate liking to her.

'You've got some interesting friends,' I said.

She pulled a face. 'They're not my friends, Eva. It's Kenneth's crowd really. It's difficult. He loves having them round and I don't dare say I don't want to mix with them.'

I felt for her. 'Can't be easy,' I said.

'Oh well, it's easy enough to slip away when it all gets a bit much. I don't suppose they notice whether I'm there or not.'

I thought that Angela suffered from low self-esteem and I decided to make it my job to help her. I talked to her, emphasizing her good points and telling her how pretty she was, and I suggested what she might do with her hair. I gave her a proper pep talk. Gradually we bonded and in no time we were allies, laughing together like old friends.

As the two of us chatted, Richard, one of Kenneth's friends, appeared at the kitchen door with an empty Pimms jug.

'Can we have a refill, please, and a lager for John?'

I took the jug from him. 'We'll bring it out for you.' I winked at Angela as I tipped almost a full bottle of vodka into the jug.

Her jaw dropped open. 'Eva, what are you doing?'

I gave her a mischievous grin. 'This will relax them,' I said. 'It's obvious they're playing one-upmanship out there, showing off and trying to outdo each other. Well, give them a minute and once they've got this inside them, watch them let their guards down and you'll see them for what they really are.'

By now Angela and I were having a great time. Nervously, but with a large grin, she took the jug and carried it out into the garden to a crowd that was getting louder by the minute.

When she returned, she pulled out a very large platter of fillet steaks from the fridge. 'Can I help you?' I asked.

'Thanks, Eva. I've already made the salads and the desserts. All that needs doing now is to fry the steaks. I'll get on with that if you don't mind taking the salads out.'

As I placed the salads on the large table that was

already set, a distressed cry came from Angela in the kitchen.

'Noooo!'

I rushed in, to see her most upset. 'Whatever's wrong?'

'The cooker won't work,' she said, almost in tears. 'Can you get Kenneth to come and help me?'

I went and found Kenneth, who checked all of the switches and fuses. 'Nope, damned if I know what's wrong,' he said, baffled.

Soon three of the other men were in the kitchen, all determined to fix the cooker and have their steaks, but to no avail. Not even Johnnie, who was a genuine Mr Fix-It, could work out what was wrong.

Kenneth put a reassuring hand on his wife's arm. 'Don't worry, we'll have a barbecue instead.'

Angela looked stricken. 'We can't,' she wailed, defeated. 'I've loaned it to my sister.'

Seeing how upset she was at not being able to cook a simple steak for her arrogant guests, I came up with an idea. 'I know, how would you like me to cook them for you Romany-style?' Seeing that Angela was about to have a coronary, I directed the question at Kenneth.

Kenneth looked both relieved and a bit embarrassed. I'm not sure he liked the idea of a female guest stepping in to save the day.

'Anything you say, Eva,' he said eventually.

'I must warn you though, it's going to make a mess of your lawn,' I said.

'Eva, darling, I'm past caring. Make all the mess you like!'

Now, there was an invitation! 'OK,' I said, 'I'm going to need some wood.'

Excitedly, Angela chipped in, 'We've got some logs in the garage – will they do?'

'Absolutely ideal,' I replied. 'But I'm going to need a nice strong man to chop them up.' I looked at Kenneth.

'I'll come with you,' Johnnie said. 'I know how she needs them to be cut.'

Johnnie and Kenneth trotted off to the garage like two schoolboys on a homework assignment.

'I'm going to need some newspaper,' I told Angela, 'and a very sharp knife.'

I rooted around in the garden, found some straight sticks and sharpened both ends with the knife. I prepared the steaks by covering them with sea salt and cracked black pepper and picked what herbs I could from their garden. There was some fresh rosemary, which was perfect, and I made small slits in the meat and pushed the sprigs inside, along with some garlic. Now we were in business! Finally, I threaded the steaks onto the sticks and screwed up the newspaper Angela had found.

Johnnie and Kenneth emerged from the garage with

the chopped logs. Since Johnnie had seen Mummy and me make stick fires before, he knew just how thick I needed them to be. I criss-crossed some small ones on top of the newspaper to start the fire off, then I lit the newspaper with a match and, to my relief, the fire caught almost immediately and the logs began to burn. I watched with pride as my fire came to life. Piling on some more logs, I waited until it was all alight and then allowed the fire to die down, so that grey ash replaced the flames. The heat was just right. I pushed the pointed sticks into the lawn around the fire and we sat watching the meat sizzle, me twisting the sticks so the steaks would cook evenly.

'Oh, how very primitive,' bellowed one woman, a redhead with tracks of black mascara running down her cheeks. She had downed several of my 'special' Pimms and was obviously feeling the effect. She seemed oblivious to the fact that she was sitting much too close to the fire and the smoke was making her eyes run.

Angela appeared from the kitchen with another big tray of drinks. I noticed she had taken off her glasses.

'Your recipe, Eva,' she said gaily. It was lovely to see her looking so happy and loosening up a bit; it was such a contrast to the way she'd been earlier in the evening, feeling uptight and acting as if she was walking on eggshells.

The conversation was now all about the forthcoming trip to France. 'Once we get over there, we might have a couple of nights in Paris,' someone suggested.

Everyone started talking at once, mentioning restaurants and places they had been to. Johnnie and I had our own special restaurant in Montmartre, La Mère Catherine, which served the best French onion soup we'd ever tasted and in the evenings had a live singer who would sing all of Edith Piaf's songs. We looked at each other with a sly, secretive grin. There was no way we were telling this lot about our special restaurant. I looked up to see Kenneth tottering towards me with a bottle of champagne in one hand and two glasses in the other.

'I haven't seen Eva and Angela have a drink yet,' he said, slurring his words slightly. 'I know this is Angela's favourite.'

'Mine too!' I said.

Angela and I had been drinking coffee and it was our first proper drink of the evening. I looked around at the other guests, who were by now very drunk. Angela and I exchanged grins and toasted each other.

It was obvious to me that no one was in a fit state to drive home – not after several jugs of my special-recipe Pimms! It would have to be taxis all round. I was very naïve in the ways of gorgers and innocently asked the men to hand over their car keys. All at once, their expressions changed – some seemed bemused, but a few seemed surprisingly quick to do what I'd asked.

A man with a face flushed from a combination of booze and the heat of the fire perked up straightaway and dangled his keyring in front of me. 'Happy to oblige,' he said, with what I could have sworn was a drunken leer.

The tipsy redhead watched wide-eyed. 'Now it's getting interesting,' she said.

One by one, the men dug their keys out of their pockets and passed them across. Johnnie was almost hysterical, trying hard not to laugh. He knew how innocent I was and that I was just trying to do the right thing.

'It's taxis home tonight, boys,' I said, depositing the keys into Angela's hands. 'Hide these,' I told her. 'I'm not going to be responsible for accidents and drunk drivers.'

Angela beckoned me into the kitchen, practically doubled up with hysterics. She could hardly talk for laughing. 'Don't you know about car keys and parties?' she managed to splutter.

I shook my head. What on earth did she mean? 'No, what?'

She went on to explain that in certain circles they had 'car key parties' and what I had just done made it look as if I wanted to get one going.

'Once everyone has thrown their keys into a hat or a bag or whatever, the women each pull out a set of keys and whoever the keys belong to is supposed to be their bed partner for the night.'

I didn't have a clue about such parties, nor had I ever been anywhere near one. I had never been someone who flushed easily, but instantly my cheeks began to burn. I'd never felt so embarrassed in my life. Needless to say, I didn't stay more than five minutes after I'd learnt of my mistake.

I called Johnnie over. 'Quick, let's go.'

'I think we'd better, before anyone starts trying to swap keys!'

'I didn't know that's what it meant!'

'I know, Jules, that's the best bit about it.'

'You've got some funny friends, that's all I can say.'

'Not as funny as you, darling!'

Johnnie laughed all the way home. 'I know they weren't our kind of people, Jules, but it was worth it just to see your face when you realized what you'd done.'

He stopped laughing when I announced that there was no way I was about to go anywhere on a boat with a crowd like that. The looks on a few of the men's faces when I'd asked for their car keys were enough to ensure I was not going to allow myself to be marooned in the middle of the ocean with any of them.

35

As Johnnie digested this, I sneaked a look at him and saw the disappointment on his face. 'How about we go to Paris on our own?' I said. 'Have a nice big bowl of that lovely French onion soup. What do you think?'

He broke out in a large grin. 'La Mère Catherine, here we come! It wouldn't have been any good going with that mob anyway. You know what they say: two's company, three's a crowd, but *sixteen* . . .'

The next day Johnnie phoned Kenneth to say he couldn't skipper his boat after all.

'What a shame, John,' Kenneth said, his head probably still fragile from all the alcohol consumed the night before. 'Hey, they were nice steaks, but have you seen the state of my lawn?'

Needless to say, this was not a friendship either party pursued, although Angela and I did go on to meet for lunch occasionally and I learned I'd had a lucky escape. Two of the couples had gone on to swap partners on a permanent basis!

Johnnie and I didn't go out a lot, and spent most of our time getting our flat shipshape and going to the shops together. When we went to the supermarket, I would pick up the same staple items each time. Due to my upbringing, I was always wary of running out of certain things, as when my family had been on the road, we would sometimes pull into places where there were no shops. We also often had unexpected visitors when others would park up their caravans nearby, so there were certain things you always kept in the cupboard, such as tins of John West salmon and Ye Olde Oak ham which would come in handy if anyone came round and you needed a quick meal. Making sure I had back-ups like this was a habit I got from my mother.

'Time we started inviting people up for one of your lovely meals,' Johnnie suggested one day.

It sounded good to me, now that the kitchen was the way I wanted it, with my copper pans and fully stocked cupboards. He made a list of the people he thought we would like to invite. As I didn't really know any of his old friends, I left it up to him.

He decided to invite his friend Anita Perilli, her partner Gordon – whom she later married – and her mother. I made a steak and kidney pudding and Johnnie's favourite dessert, cherry pie with fresh clotted cream.

Johnnie had known Anita for many years, from his time in Littlehampton, where he ran a speedboat. Apparently, lots of the women who came for rides would come back again and again . . . because they fancied the skipper! Anita's mother ran the coffee bar where Johnnie would go for lunch and Anita often had free rides on the boat. Johnnie could never have imagined that in a few years' time his friend – by then Anita Roddick – would enjoy huge success with her company, the Body Shop. He was so proud to see her achieve so much.

The meal went down very well, as did the wine. The evening was going with a swing until Anita began to tell us about her latest project.

'How does it work then?' I enquired.

'Well, if we find an empty house, we put a new lock on it and allow homeless people to live in it.'

'Is this with the consent of the people who own it?' I asked, naïvely.

'Oh no,' Anita said.

This disturbed me somewhat and I said to her, 'So if John and I decide to go on holiday for a few days or weeks, you'd change our locks and allow homeless people to live here?'

'Yes, that's right,' she replied.

'Well, how do you stand with the law?' I continued.

'There is no law at the moment preventing us from doing it,' she grinned.

I was horrified and my face clearly showed how I felt. 'I think that's totally despicable, out of order and wrong.'

Anita's mother and partner could sense the warning signs in my attitude. Her mother said, 'Time we got going now, I think.'

'Jolly good idea, good night.' I got up and walked out of the room to the bedroom, leaving Johnnie to let his friends out.

Once they'd gone, I apologized. 'I'm sorry, I didn't mean to spoil the night.'

Johnnie shook his head. 'There's nothing to apologize for. I don't agree with what she's doing either, Jewel, so let's not worry about it.'

Personally, I couldn't see the difference between stealing a house and stealing a car. Why should one be legal and the other one not? It has never ceased to amaze me what some people think is acceptable behaviour!

THREE

Skating on Thin Ice

The Eva Petulengro Horoscope Guide is something I started in 1963. The *Brighton Evening Argus*, with whom I had a regular daily column, was raising money for a children's charity and I suggested to the editor, Mr Gorange, that I could write and produce a booklet of horoscopes for the year ahead, which could be sold in newsagents in Sussex, with all of the proceeds going to the children's charity. He agreed, so we went ahead and had 10,000 printed and distributed, and they were sold out within one week. I then realized that if I did this little magazine myself, it could be quite profitable and I decided to produce one every three months for a year.

Johnnie encouraged me and by the time we were married in 1964 the magazine was already doing very well. We bought a van and Johnnie arranged for a sign-writer to spray it white, with the name of the magazine and the phone number prominently displayed. We wanted it to be eye-catching, so we gave him carte blanche to paint the signs of the zodiac all over it too! One evening Johnnie answered the phone to find a frantic woman on the other end of the line.

'Please help me,' she said, sounding desperate. 'My husband has been locked away in our garage for ten days, and most of the nights as well. I can't get him to come out.'

Johnnie was baffled. 'What has that got to do with me?'

The woman's voice thundered down the line. 'He can't stop painting the bloody zodiac signs on your friggin' van! *That's* what it's got to do with you!'

Trying not to laugh, Johnnie said, 'Well, tell him I'm on the phone and it's urgent.' When she eventually managed to persuade her husband to put down his paint brush and come to the phone, Johnnie came up with the excuse that we needed the van double-quick.

'Asap,' he said. 'Soon as you can have it done.'

The signwriter got the message and completed the paint job. And so all was well. The frantic wife got her husband out of the garage and we got a fabulous-looking van, which no one could fail to notice.

It was quite amazing how popular my magazine became. We had orders from all over England, Scotland and Wales, and these were mainly delivered to the wholesalers in bulk. WHSmith and Surridge Dawson were two of the main distributors that we used, but certain areas used different distributors, and Johnnie would fill up the van and deliver lots of copies on a sale or return basis to those who had not placed orders. He returned from Birmingham late one night.

'The manager refuses to take them for the Birmingham shops. He said there is no call for this type of thing.' There was a glint in his eyes. 'Fancy a trip to Birmingham, Jules?'

We set off early a couple of days later, and I remember it was very cold; it was just before Christmas and our breath was like little white puffs of smoke in the chilly air. We had an appointment with the manager who'd turned Johnnie down earlier that week.

'There's no call for this sort of thing,' he said once more with a bored look on his face.

I was wearing a full-length mink coat. I stood up and pointed at the gold bracelets on my arm and my gold hoop earrings. 'Sir, if there was no call for my magazine, I wouldn't be dressed like this,' I said. 'I'll tell you what I'll do. I'll leave you 2,000 copies and if you don't sell them I will take you and your partner to the restaurant of your choice – anywhere you like – and I'll pay for everything.'

His face was a picture. It was obvious he was convinced the stock would remain unsold, but he couldn't lose. We left the magazines with him and went home, confident they would prove as popular in Birmingham as they had everywhere else. The manager never got to take me up on my offer, because – as we predicted – he sold out!

As Christmas came closer, orders for the next issue of the magazine were flooding in. I was working for the *Sunday Mail* in Scotland, writing the horoscopes as well as a 'Dear Eva' column, where I answered readers' problems with the aid of astrology. It was so popular, they were receiving approximately 2,000 letters a week. One of the first letters I answered was from a gentleman who said, 'I am building a spaceship to go to Mars. I know a lot about the Romany people and I wonder if you and some of your people will join me on this journey to start a new colony?'

My answer was, 'You obviously don't know much about Romanies. Didn't you know we suffer from space sickness?'

'I've had a lot of orders from Scotland,' Johnnie said worriedly one afternoon in mid-December. 'I don't know how I'm going to be able to get them up there, as well as the deliveries to other towns.'

'Well, I need to go to Edinburgh and Glasgow on business, so I could always ask Nathan to drive me up and we can drop off the orders for Scotland for you.'

We agreed that that was the best plan, and Nathan

was happy to take me. But on the day we set off the weather took a turn for the worse. It was cold and windy, and north of the border, it began to snow. We dropped the books off at Glasgow and as we left the city to join the road to Edinburgh, the snow began to come down thick and fast, making it difficult to see anything and creating treacherous conditions. We got about halfway to Edinburgh and Nathan was clearly worried.

'Open the door of the van,' he said. 'You may have to jump out and guide us because the wheels aren't gripping. There's too much snow on the road.'

The sound of the slush churning and slapping against the underside of the vehicle as we made our way along the road was constant. Then all of a sudden, the noise stopped and I saw Nathan's jaw tighten. His face was grim. The slush had turned to ice and the road was like a skating rink. At that point, we began to notice at least half a dozen accidents, both ahead of us and behind, where other drivers had lost control of their vehicles. It was like a scene from a disaster movie, and a sense of horror coursed through me. We were on a dual carriageway and all I could think about was getting off it and finding another route. We had to get away as soon as possible before something ploughed into us. Suddenly an articulated lorry coming from the opposite direction crossed the motorway, completely out of control, and careered into a car right in front of us. Later we learned that the driver of the car had been decapitated. We could see three or four other cars sliding sideways, their drivers desperately trying to regain control. We had to get out of here now.

'There's a little lane across the road,' I said. I pointed towards it and noticed that my hand was shaking. 'Go through the gap in the barrier and down the lane.'

Nathan was loath to steer the van over the central reservation. 'I don't know if it will take it. We could get stuck,' he said, frightened.

'Well, we don't have a lot of choice. We're nearly out of petrol anyway.' I stared with trepidation at the gauge, which was hovering just above empty.

'Hold tight,' he shouted as he swung the van, hitting the barrier with a bump. He kept his foot down and the van slid and slithered as it made its way back down off the barrier. We both sighed with relief as we skidded into the lane and felt the van regain some control. In front of us was a little sign that said 'Shotts'.

I began to feel hopeful. 'Look, there's a village up here, follow the sign.' We got about 200 yards up the lane and, to our great relief and joy, on the right-hand side was a big hotel. We drew into the car park and walked in, immediately ordering a large brandy each. We were freezing and had been frightened by the sight of other less lucky travellers. We clinked our glasses with big grins on our faces, our fear turning to nervous laughter.

'Cheers,' we said in unison, with a hint of triumph.

Before we could even take a sip of our drinks, a man in a black suit came over to us. 'You're not booked in.' His tone was harsh and scolding. 'It's ten thirty. We don't serve non-residents at this hour.'

'That's all right, I'd like to book a twin room please. We're not going out in that again tonight,' I replied. I could see from the look on his face that we would have to convince him that we actually needed a place to stay. 'We're almost out of petrol,' I went on.

This was a most unpleasant man, who clearly had no compassion for our woes. 'We're fully booked,' he barked. 'Not a bed in the house.'

I looked around the bar and spotted two armchairs in front of a window, through which it was plain to see that the snow was coming down even heavier than it had been before. I pointed at the chairs. 'That's OK, we'll sleep on those tonight,' I suggested.

'It's not allowed,' he barked at us again.

'Please,' I said, trying to soften my tone in the hope of finding some common ground and a small shred of sympathy from this hard character. 'I'll pay the full rate for a room,' I pleaded.

Again, the answer was a firm no. People who know

me well know that I can have a very aggressive attitude when the situation warrants it, and seeing how dire the weather was outside and thinking about Nathan having to get back behind the wheel, my instincts as protective older sister took over – as well as my confrontational instincts, of course!

Nathan, sensing that I was about to show this side of my character, stepped forward and, placing his hand gingerly on the man's shoulder, suggested they have a quiet word. What went on was one man begging another to help him in his plight, to avoid what could have quite easily become a suicide mission should we have ventured out. With virtually no petrol in the van and a snowstorm raging, even the best driver would struggle to survive unscathed.

Nathan might as well have saved his breath. It was like talking to a brick wall and we were asked to leave. Well, we were virtually thrown out.

'Sell us a bottle of brandy,' I said, as we were being ushered out.

I had to try to come up with something that could help us and, having heard many years before that you could run a car on spirits should an emergency occur, a bottle of brandy really did seem like our only option.

The man was physically pushing us out the door when Nathan's shoulders suddenly went up and he turned around, fronting the man square on, growling slowly in a low voice, 'Sell the lady the brandy.'

The man took a step back. By now he could see the situation was about to turn very ugly and, as I saw Nathan pull his fists into balls, I could certainly guarantee it was. The man backed away again and took yet another step back towards the bar, where he went behind the counter, grabbed a bottle of brandy and handed it to Nathan.

'I'll want paying for it,' he muttered.

Nathan stuffed his hands into his pockets and, without even looking at what he was pulling out, threw a bundle of notes at the man and uttered a string of swear words, some of which I'd never heard before.

As we set out into the icy night, the wind and snow whipped at our faces, giving us a sharp shock.

'Give us a swig of that brandy,' Nathan said, defeat and the realization of the situation we were in finally hitting him.

'Silly bugger,' I said, pushing him in the shoulder as we trudged through the snow. 'It's for the *van*, not you!'

He looked at me with bewilderment, before saying 'Are there two Ls in bollocks?', a cheeky grin spreading across his face.

'Oh, go on then,' I said, opening the bottle. 'I think we could both do with a swig after that horrible piece of work in there, don't you?'

We got back into the van, after very carefully making sure the key didn't break off in the frozen lock and completely ruin our chances of leaving this scene of madness. Nathan used his cigarette lighter to melt the ice.

Once in the driver's seat, he said, 'Well, I'm not putting the brandy in the van if it's not going to start in the first place. We may need it to keep us warm.'

I nodded in agreement and after we'd both silently said some prayers, he turned the key in the ignition. Nothing. We sank down lower into our seats. He tried again. A splutter, there was definitely some sort of a splutter.

'Come on!' I called out.

Third time lucky. The van started and as Nathan put the gearstick into first, slowly but surely, we started to move. Nathan began to steer us off down the road, muttering more to himself than to me, 'Let's hope this slope doesn't turn into a slide.' I pressed my face to the glass, keeping an eye out for somewhere else to pull in.

We turned a corner and, lo and behold, right in front of us, lights ablaze, was a pretty little public house. The door to the pub swung open and bright, cheery light spilled out into the night. We stared at it like rabbits caught in headlights, wondering what sight would greet us next. Out of the door came a little old man in a striped old-fashioned nightshirt and a hat with a bobble on the end. He looked like something from another era, as if he had stepped straight off the pages of *A Christmas Carol*. He was a dead ringer for Ebenezer Scrooge and even had a Tilley lamp in his right hand to complete the look.

Nathan pulled up and opened the door. The man marched right up to us, lamp in hand, shouting, 'What are you children doing out in this?' He was squinting at us and using his free hand to wave us inside. 'Get inside immediately; you'll catch your death of cold out here.'

We didn't need to be asked twice.

Inside were half a dozen men, who were obviously the worse for wear. 'Everyone, I've found some more for the party!' the old man announced. He turned to us. 'This lot can't get home tonight and they only live nearby, so there's no chance you'll be going anywhere. We're well and truly snowed-in.'

Actually, it was hard to make out exactly what he had said, with his strong Scottish accent and slightly inebriated drawl, but we got the message all right. We were safe. We were going to be fine after all.

We sat up drinking, laughing and singing songs. It didn't take long to warm up, especially with the stiff brandies the landlord was pouring us. When we told him of our encounter with the other landlord, he nodded.

'Forget sleeping on a chair, lassie, you two can have my bedroom tonight. I can't have you thinking that no-good piece of shite up the road is what all we Scots are like, now can I? Besides, boys,' he said, with a wink at his locals, 'we're not going to bed anyway, are we?' And with this, they broke out into song again. I looked at Nathan, who was asking one of the men for his guitar, and I could see that we too would probably not be going to bed that night.

In the morning, the roads had been cleared and we continued on our journey to Edinburgh, although not before having to unfreeze the lock on the van with Nathan's lighter for the second time in the space of a few hours.

FOUR

The Way Things Were

Johnnie and I spent a lot of time talking about the past, and when I described my time as a child living on the site at Bedworth, he was intrigued.

'I'll take you back there one day,' he said. 'I'd like to see it.'

The idea really excited me. We had moved to Bedworth, a mining town about five miles from Coventry, when I was eleven. I had so many memories of living there, all the fairground people coming to the site as summer drew to a close, bringing the place to life. In many ways it had been a magical time.

One Friday evening, Johnnie said, 'Pack a bag, we're going on an adventure.'

I'd learned not to ask questions, so I packed with no idea of where we were heading. I did not care where he was taking me. As long as I was with him, life was exciting and there was nothing I liked more than to sit in a car meandering along the highways and byways, looking at the wonders of nature. It may sound nuts, but I loved old farm gates: there was just something about them. I would wonder how long they had been there, who had built them, who had gone in and out over the years – the generations of farmers, or perhaps even travelling people, pulling in for rest. It was strange, but just one of the many things I found fascinating on our trips.

We passed a house, and in the garden was an old bow-top vardo.

'Is that what you used to live in?' Johnnie said.

'Certainly not. Pull up and I'll show you.'

We got out the car and took a closer look. 'You've seen the photographs of the vardo I lived in,' I said. 'Now, look at the difference. You can see that this vardo was once an old farm cart. Its wheels are all the same size and have tyres. People turned old farm carts into caravans by bending big pieces of metal round to form the arch and fastening them at each side, then covering them over with canvas.'

'Oh, I see.' Johnnie's chin rested on his hands as he took it all in. 'Well, who lived in these ones then?' he enquired.

'I don't really know, but what I've been told is that in Ireland, in the nineteenth century, when the potato famine struck, all the people that used to pick potatoes for a living suddenly had no jobs. A lot of them came over to England to try to find work, and they would live in these caravans and travel around looking for someone to take them on.

'I remember years ago, when we were at Coventry on the bomb site, some Irish travellers with three of these caravans, each pulled by two horses, stopped and pitched on the other side of the field. I think they must only have been passing through. We'd all gone to bed that evening and all of a sudden there was a lot of shouting and screaming.

'Mummy went outside to see what was going on and I quickly followed her in my nightwear, with no shoes on. Two women were fighting, stripped bare to the waist. It was like watching a bizarre comedy film. They had built a fire and the light from the fire and the street lamps on the road by the side of the field made it appear like a flickering movie. The women were screaming and swearing in thick Irish accents. You could hardly make out what they were saying because of the racket their companions – men as well as women – were making. It was as if they were cheering them on. It was fascinating to watch, but I remember suddenly feeling my mother's hand on my shoulders as she shouted, "Get inside, girl." She pushed me into our vardo and locked the door behind us. After making a cup of tea, she sat down and I asked her, "Mummy, what is that, what is going on?" She said, "They could be fighting over a dog, a man, they could just be fighting because they're drunk, but you listen to me, we don't mix with those people."

'When we awoke the next morning, every man, woman, dog and horse from that group of travellers had disappeared. They must have left during the night. What I'd seen certainly warned me off and hat is why I didn't try to get to know them or mix with them.' I looked across at the vardo Johnnie had spotted. 'So, maybe this vardo was used by travellers like them.'

We got back on the road and all of a sudden I realized where we were headed. We were going through Coventry and I thought, 'He's taking me to Bedworth, to old Malcolm's fairground.' I had told Johnnie all sorts of stories about our time here, such as how I used to lug cans of water down to where our vardo was resting, making two or three trips for supplies for cooking and making tea, washing up, bathing and washing the clothes.

I was really becoming excited now, wondering if the Malcolm family would still be there. I thought, 'Will I see anyone I recognize?' and 'Will the shops still be the same?' An image came to me of the bakery on the corner and just across the road the wool shop that kept me in supplies so I could knit for absolutely hours on end. Oh, and the ground behind the public house with the chicken farm my father won in a game of cards. I had been forced to feed the little critters, which put me off eggs and chicken forever.

However, as we drove into Bedworth, my heart began to sink. All kinds of emotions were running through me. The entrance to Malcolm's fairground had disappeared, as indeed had the fields behind it. It was now one big council estate, with houses as far as I could see. We then drove along the high street, where I saw that the bakery and wool shop had both been replaced – one by a Costcutter and the other by a discount shop. It instantly made me cry and wish I had never gone back. I didn't even bother to try to find out if the Malcolms were still there, as I couldn't stand any more disappointments that day. Johnnie put his foot down and sped towards Stratford-upon-Avon, where he booked us into a lovely hotel, took me out for a slap-up dinner and plied me with champagne – in order, he said, to wash away the memory of my disappointment.

It was a rarity for my trips to end in disappointment. I remember when I met the singer Frankie Vaughan on a train. I'd been up to London on business and on the way back I walked into a first-class compartment where two men were sitting. When I recognized one of them as Frankie Vaughan, I apologized and started to leave the compartment. Frankie stopped me.

'I recognize you,' he said. 'Please come and sit down and join us, Eva. My mother is a big fan of yours!'

Just imagine, one of my big, *big* heroes saying that to me! His song 'Green Door' was one of my favourites. Anyway, we got talking and he asked me who my agent was. 'I don't have one,' I said. I had always done all right without one.

Frankie suggested I went to see his agent, Paul Cave, and gave me his number to keep in touch with him. A couple of weeks later I went to meet Paul and he got me an audition for Eamonn Andrews' new Saturday sports programme. The television company took me to the races, where they put me in front of a camera, gave me a newspaper listing all the runners and riders and told me to predict who was going to win. I ask you! When I finally stopped laughing, I told them that if I could do that I'd be a millionaire. As a clairvoyant, it was people I read, not horses. That was the end of my TV career with Eamonn Andrews.

I decided that agents were not for me. I didn't want to be under anyone's orders. I wanted to do what I wanted when I wanted, and TV work didn't interest me anyway.

In the meantime, Frankie Vaughan had sent me two tickets to see his show at the London Palladium. My mother adored him too and she and I went together. We were seated in the first row and Mummy was thrilled at the way he seemed to be singing solely to her. We went backstage after the show and he introduced us to Tommy Cooper, another of Mummy's favourites, and Cilla Black, who was just starting out in her career. Tommy Cooper did a trick and managed to make a scarf appear from Mummy's handbag, while I read Cilla Black's palm and saw a long and phenomenally successful career.

I was mixing a fair bit in showbiz circles by then. An agent client friend of mine had started using my services to pick out talent, and brought the band the Commodores to meet me long before they made it. I knew straightaway that there were big things ahead for them, and the rest is history.

Around the same time, my friend, John Cook, asked me to see a group called Pickettywitch, which I again recommended and told him he should handle. Shortly after, John put them forward for *Opportunity Knocks*, which they won, and this was followed up by six hits! Who could have guessed that the young girl running bare-footed through fields, picking wild herbs, before returning to watch her mother read people's palms in the back of their small but beautifully painted caravan, would one day move in such circles! My life really had taken on a speed of its own.

FIVE

Destination Unknown

It was coming up to our first wedding anniversary and, behind my back, Johnnie had booked a weekend away for the two of us. He told me to pack an overnight bag and that we were going up to Gatwick Airport, but he absolutely refused to tell me where he was taking me.

'How exciting,' I said, although the impatient aspect of my star sign, Pisces, urged me to say, 'Oh, come on, Johnnie, tell me where we're going.'

He must have had an idea of what was going through my head. 'Don't spoil the surprise for me,' he pleaded.

We were in the lounge, sitting in front of the departures board, when all of a sudden a voice over the tannoy announced, 'All passengers for Amsterdam, please go to Gate 12.' With that, Johnnie grabbed my bag.

'Now you know, don't you, nosy?' he said, grinning.

I was thrilled. Amsterdam was a place I had always been curious about. It was the home of tulips and made me think of Lincolnshire, where I had spent so much of my childhood. The area around Skegness was known as Little Holland because the tulip fields there splashed great swathes of vibrant colour across the landscape. As we walked towards the gate, I vowed that we would take some tulips back for our friend Winnie, the landlady of the Cricketers, in Black Lion Street. She was a really wonderful woman, very knowledgeable and cultured and always taking her favourite customers and friends on trips to the opera, theatre, Royal Ascot, Glyndebourne and other wonderful places. When Johnnie and I first started going to her pub, one day, as it was coming up to closing time, Winnie leaned over towards us and said, 'Would you two mind hanging on for a few minutes, while I clear the bar?'

In those days the pubs would close at two thirty in the afternoon. Johnnie and I were deep in conversation and before we knew it, the doors were locked and Winnie approached us. By then, we'd been going to the Cricketers for about a month or so.

'I have to tell you,' Winnie said, 'that most married couples who come in here either just sit and ignore each other or chatter to their friends, but you two are always chatting to each other and constantly laughing. I would like you two to have a drink on me, because I think you're a lovely couple!'

She was right about us being wrapped up in one

another. Sometimes when we were together it was as if no one else existed, like the only two people on the planet were us.

It wasn't long before we were firm friends with Winnie and had formed a mutual admiration society, for she was the kindest and most thoughtful person we had ever met. Our friendship went on for many years. She was the kind of person who opened up on Christmas morning, when she didn't have to, because she felt sorry for those who had nowhere else to go, and she would make sure they had a little bit of Christmas cheer, with good music, free food and drinks. She was a devout Catholic and had visited the Vatican many times. In fact, Johnnie came up with a joke about standing in St Peter's Square, looking up at the spot where the Pope appeared to wave to his people, and the man beside him asking, 'Who's that on the balcony?' to which he replied, 'That's Winnie Sexton. I don't know who the fella is.'

The people Winnie helped without others knowing about it are too numerous to mention. There would not be enough space to list her good deeds in these pages. I found out later that she'd had one love in her life and kept a portrait of him on the stairs of the pub leading up to her restaurant. When I asked who it was one day, she explained, 'That was my fiancé. He was killed in the war, Eva, and he's the only man I've loved in my life.' Each year, her late fiancé's two sisters would come down to Brighton and spend the day with Winnie, in memory of their brother and her lost love. It was a ritual.

Winnie had moved to the coast from London, where she had been running a very successful public house, the Zetland Arms, with her parents. She had many followers, who all trooped down to Brighton at odd times to see her. When she opened the Cricketers, she also brought many of the staff with her from London, including Joan, who was her bar manager, and Dennis, the potman, whom we nicknamed Dennis the Menace after the character in the *Beano* comic. Lord Boothby, who had been Winston Churchill's secretary, was her friend, and became one of ours. Numerous actors and public figures, as well as people from ordinary walks of life, all mingled under her roof and wanted to be in this charismatic lady's company.

Winnie was the first person I thought of when I realized we were on our way to Amsterdam, and when we were seated on the plane, Johnnie told me that he had discussed the trip in great detail with her.

'I told her I'd like to take you away for a break for our wedding anniversary, and she told me she remembered that you had said you'd always wanted to see Amsterdam but never had,' Johnnie said. 'She suggested this would be a great place for us to go.'

'She was right,' I gushed, full of excitement.

Johnnie never failed to surprise me with his actions. 'What I thought,' he began, 'is that we'd go straight to the Hilton, where I've booked us in, leave our stuff and then head into Amsterdam to find somewhere nice for lunch. We can have a look round and come back to the hotel for a rest. In the basement of the hotel there's a nightclub called Julianna's, and I know you've never been to a proper nightclub, so I thought we could go together?'

I laid my head on his chest. I'd certainly picked the right guy in Johnnie. He had been worth waiting for, and I could not wait for the day ahead.

It was the first time I'd been on a plane and I wasn't looking forward to the landing, but luckily it was smooth – phew! – and before we knew it, we were on the ground and making our way into the terminal. We went straight to the Hilton, checked in, got a taxi into Amsterdam and found a little bistro, where we ordered fillet steaks. When they came, they were served with a pear poached in red wine. It was a delicious accompaniment to the steak. I vowed that if ever I had a restaurant, this would certainly go on my menu.

After the meal, we wandered along the canal and got on a cruise boat for a sightseeing trip, taking in the narrow little house on the Singel Canal which was squeezed in among others and, according to the guide, was supposed to be the smallest house in the world. It couldn't have been more than a metre across.

After the cruise, Johnnie led me to one of the infamous sights of Amsterdam, the red-light district. To my astonishment, there were windows all along the road and in each window was a prostitute, posing. Apparently, they were not allowed to beckon the men in and if the curtain was closed that meant they had a client in! I was especially intrigued by one particular window that had a leopard-skin curtain pulled across it and a queue of about twelve to fifteen men outside.

'Wait, Johnnie, I want to see what she looks like. She must be something, judging by her queue.' I was overawed, as I never knew that sort of thing was allowed to go on.

Johnnie laughed. 'This is also the district where all the little coffee bars legally sell drugs.'

I dragged my gaze away from the leopard-skin curtain and gave him a suspicious look. 'Have you ever been into one of those windows?'

He laughed again. 'Darling, I've never had to pay for it!'

We decided to head back to the hotel, so we went to a square where there was a taxi rank and I tugged on his arm. 'Wait, I need to use the ladies'. There's a hotel across the way. Let's just nip in there, before we get a taxi.' As we walked in, there was a bar to the left.

'I'll wait in there for you,' Johnnie said. 'I'll just have half a lager.' He knew full well I would be reapplying my eyeliner and lipstick before I returned and that he was in for a bit of a wait.

When I went into the bar to collect my husband, he was sitting with three men and the barman, all huddled together, deep in conversation. When I arrived at his side, Johnnie said, 'Let me introduce you to the three Hs. This is Harold, Harry and Hank. They're over from America on a business trip and they've just invited us to play a game of brain's trust.'

I'd never heard of it. 'What's that?' I asked.

Johnnie whispered in my ear, 'Jules, it's what we call Spoof.'

We played Spoof all the time in the Cricketers, and of course I knew it very well.

'Gee,' Harry said, 'I'll explain, little lady. You take three coins each and hold them behind your back so no one can see what's going on. Then you put none, one, two or three coins in one hand and put it on the bar, firmly clenched, and the other players take it in turns to guess how many coins you're holding. The person who guesses right drops out and the remaining players continue until there are only two players left. When there are only two players left, the one who loses the round pays for all the drinks. Think you can handle it?'

I looked at him and said, 'I guess so. I'll give it a go.' We sat in the bar until ten o'clock that night, not having bought a single round of drinks. The game is all about luck so I presume I'm just a very lucky person as I've never lost at it. Or maybe my clairvoyant instincts played a role. I suppose I'll never know for sure. Finally we decided to put them out of their misery and go.

'Goodnight, fellas, we've got a date with a nightclub. Oh and by the way,' Johnnie said as he turned back, 'in England, we call this game Spoof.' Their mouths fell open and, thank goodness, they laughed.

The barman shouted after us, 'Hey, you two, thank you for the lesson.'

We went back to the hotel, by now very tired.

'We'll have an hour's sleep,' Johnnie suggested, 'and then we'll head back down to the nightclub.'

We lay on top of the bedcovers fully dressed for our power nap, all set to hit the nightclub later. After a good sleep, I opened my eyes ready for the next chapter of our journey and saw light streaming in through the window.

'Johnnie,' I said, as I shook him awake, 'I think Julianna's is closed. It's seven in the morning, darling.'

SIX

Roses are Shining in Picardy

Because I was writing for so many newspapers and magazines, I was receiving lots of mail from different areas of England. One of the places where I was very popular was Bristol, and I'd received requests from lots of people there who wanted readings, so I arranged a visit.

Johnnie could not take me, so I asked my brother Eddie. He arrived at our house the night before for dinner, so he could stay the night and we could set off early the next morning. I did a double take when he came out of the bathroom the next morning, as he was dressed so beautifully. He had on a white polo-neck sweater and smart white trousers, topped with a navy blazer.

'Ready, kid?' he asked.

I looked him up and down and came out with the phrase our family always used when anyone looked 'the business'.

'If you don't get a woman in that outfit, you'll never get one,' I said, full of admiration.

Eddie gave me a wink. 'Only one?' he asked.

Eddie picked up my suitcase and led me to the zodiac van, as we would also be delivering some magazines to that area. As we covered the miles to Bristol, my head began to drift elsewhere, taking me back to my Romany childhood when I was being coached in the art of palmistry. I had a picture in my mind of us children sitting around Shunty, Mummy's youngest sister, who would ask us which line was which on the hand, testing us with endless questions. We were all very competitive, shouting out the correct answers at the same time. I was immersed in these fond memories when all of a sudden the van started smoking and choking from under the bonnet.

'Damn it,' Eddie exclaimed, 'I didn't check the water.'

'Where are we?'

'We're on the outskirts of Bristol, and I don't think there's anywhere nearby to get any water. You've got your first clients at half eleven, girl, time you were awake anyway.'

We stood on the grassy bank of the motorway, waiting for the engine to cool. Cars were whizzing past and after about twenty minutes a police patrol car pulled up behind us. 'Thank God,' we both said in unison, relieved.

The policeman climbed out of the car and walked very slowly towards us. 'You can't park on the motorway,' he growled.

Eddie's glance at me was a signal not to speak. 'We're out of water,' he said. Although I'd been warned not to, I couldn't help but chime in. 'We have appointments in Bristol – can you help us?'

Before I could say anything else, he retorted, 'We're not a taxi service. I can't help you.' With that, he turned on his heels and headed back to his car.

'You mean you *won't* help us,' I muttered under my breath. I ran to catch him up. 'Wait,' I shouted.

He turned and looked at me, frowning. 'There's a ditch at the side of the road that's got water in it,' he said ungraciously.

'Have you got something in your car that I could fill up with water?' I asked, still optimistic he might help us out.

'No,' he said coolly.

'Well then,' I said, hoping he might have a sense of humour, 'lend me your hat? I'll use that.'

Obviously he wasn't in the mood for a joke as he jumped in the car and drove off without a backward glance at me and Eddie.

Eddie and I simultaneously lit cigarettes and began walking up and down the grass verge, looking for a bottle, a tin, anything thrown from a passing car that we could use. All of a sudden, I looked round and Eddie had disappeared. 'He must be in the ditch,' I thought, and gingerly tried to peer over the edge, but could not see a thing. I was scared to go too close in case I fell over in my high-heeled shoes. Quick as a flash, Eddie appeared with a grin on his face that said, 'Success!' – holding up a Coca-Cola can. He spent quite a while scampering down into the ditch to fill his Coke can with muddy water and back up again to pour it into the van radiator.

'Get in the van,' he said, after several of these trips.

I got into the passenger seat, touched up my lipstick, checked my eyeliner and we were on our way. About half a mile up the road, we found a slip road leading to a village, with a pub on the right-hand side. Eddie ran in and asked the landlord for more water, who appeared carrying two full watering cans. Then we jumped back into the van and off we went.

We arrived at the hotel almost two hours late. 'I expect our first clients have given up on us,' I said.

I hurried ahead, with Eddie behind me, and that was when I noticed the looks on the faces of my waiting clients. They were all staring at Eddie. I turned to see what they were looking at and immediately burst out laughing. His beautiful white outfit was covered in mud, as were his face and hair. In our desperate rush to get here, I hadn't even noticed!

'Ladies,' I announced, 'I think we all need a cup of tea or coffee.' I called the concierge over. 'Eddie, you'd better get the keys to our suite and go and look in the mirror,' I said with a smile. 'Now then, ladies, we are running very late.' I quickly explained what had happened. 'I'm quite happy to stay an extra day in order to fit you all in. Who would like to see me tomorrow morning?' Nobody wanted to take me up on the offer; they all wanted to be seen that day. I could see that at least two of them were taken with Eddie and were casting glances at him.

I waited until he had cleaned himself up and appeared from upstairs, then I ushered my first client in for a reading. The ladies came in one by one, and while I was giving readings, Eddie was having a nice little party with the others. Each time I came out to collect my next client, they all appeared to be having a whale of a time. They had been joined by other clients, who were also having a ball. One of the ladies asked me if it was all right for her to have a cigarette in the consulting room. I didn't usually smoke in front of clients unless they did, so I joined her. It turned out this particular lady was the matron of a breast cancer hospital.

'Doesn't it bother you, being in that job?' I said. 'Surely it would have put you off smoking by now?'

'No, Eva,' she said. 'Out of all the patients we have in that clinic, only two out of ten are smokers.'

This made me feel much better, as by now I was becoming quite a smoker myself.

We worked all the way through the day, without stopping for anything to eat, although we were well supplied with coffee and tea. By the time the last client left at ten o'clock that night, Eddie said, 'Right, let's hit the dining room.'

This sounded good to me, and off we went. It had been quite a day. Again.

'Why is it that nothing ever runs to plan with me?' I said.

'I've no idea,' Eddie said, 'but things like this don't happen to other people as often as they happen to you. It's because you're you, Eva. That policeman must have known who you were because it's written all over the van. You've probably been giving him some bad forecasts in the local paper!'

We started to laugh. By eleven we were both what I call shopping for Dracula – out for the count.

It was late in 1965 when I realized I might be expecting a baby. Excitedly, I explained my symptoms to my mother. She confirmed that these were indeed the things to expect when you are first pregnant. To make sure, I booked an appointment with my doctor, who had only ever treated me twice, both times for food poisoning from dodgy oysters. This, I had a feeling, was going to be an entirely different and perhaps life-changing visit. However, when I reached the surgery, I learned that my doctor, Doctor Roe, was on holiday and a locum was seeing her patients, a young man of about thirty years old. When I told him of my symptoms, he examined me and was most emphatic.

'No, you're not pregnant,' he said, making out a prescription for what he said were blocked ducts in my breasts.

I left the surgery feeling quite perplexed as I had been certain I was pregnant, and something told me not to have the prescription filled. I was ill at ease enough with the fact that a strange man had examined my breasts rather than doing a pregnancy test. But there it was. He was the doctor and he'd said it was blocked ducts, so that must be the case. This didn't explain the other pregnancy symptoms which I'd tried to inform him of, but he was the expert after all. Even so, I couldn't believe what he had said and found it impossible to take myself into a chemist to get something I felt was not the answer to my condition. I was sure my mother would not have been wrong, since she herself had been pregnant three times!

Doctor Roe was back the following week, and I made an appointment to go and see her. My first words to her were, 'Doctor Roe, am I pregnant?'

She gasped and replied, 'Eva, are you in a position to be?'

'Well, I am married,' I spluttered.

'Thank God for that,' she laughed. With that, she examined me and declared I was indeed expecting a baby.

'I think you're about three months, Eva,' she said.

With this wonderful news, I then produced the prescription her locum had made out for me. 'What would have happened if I'd taken what he prescribed?'

Her face was grave. 'You'd have lost the baby, Eva,' she said.

'Don't let that man see your patients again,' I said, looking her straight in the eye. But my excitement at the confirmation that I was indeed expecting overshadowed my anger and I left the surgery with thoughts and plans for the soon-to-be new arrival filling my head.

'We're going to need a nursery; we've got to move,' I told myself. My head was spinning with how drastically life was about to change for us. I was so excited. 'I want a Silver Cross pram,' I thought dreamily, the same as the twins had had when we were little. I wanted my child to have the sort of happy childhood I'd had, only better. And I hoped I could be just as good a mother as my mum.

There was a perfectly timed life-changing advancement that took place in 1966, the year my first child was due to be born. The one thing I had hated when the twins were little was washing their soiled nappies time after time. In those days, I would do it by hand, and it really was not a pleasant task, but one which I duly did to keep them comfortable and clean. Now, however, someone – a genius! – had invented disposable nappies. Heaven! I could not believe it, and being impulsive as I am, I went straight out and bought a packet. I also bought knitting needles and some balls of the softest white wool. I was a good knitter. I never worked from a pattern and liked to make it up as I went along. I walked into our flat, or rather glided in, and threw the bag with the wool and needles at Johnnie. He grabbed it and peeked into it. He looked slightly confused when he saw the wool, but when he moved it to one side and saw the pack of nappies underneath his face was a picture. He leapt up and put his arms around me.

'Jewel, Jewel,' he said, his grin stretching from ear to ear. It was the most fantastic news, for both of us. He spun me round then gave me the biggest kiss. 'Let's go and tell your mother,' he said. He knew me so well – that's exactly what I wanted to do.

I suffered from morning sickness throughout my whole pregnancy and constant heartburn, for which I would take swigs from a bottle of milk of magnesia. I never left home without some in my bag! But even when I felt rotten I still imagined I was floating on air as I thought about the little baby growing inside my belly. I would dream of holding my little bundle in my arms and imagine how perfect life would be when he or she arrived.

My sister Anne had also married a non-Romany, Mac, when she was seventeen and had chosen a gorger way of life. She was expecting her first baby at the same time as I was, and we both went for tea with Mummy a few weeks before we were due to give birth. Mummy's clairvoyant instincts had never let her down, so when she gave us each a parcel, mine containing a set of baby clothes in blue and Anne's a pretty outfit in pink, we both knew at that point what we were having!

Johnnie and I had decided that we needed a larger flat, and after inspecting half a dozen or so, we found the ideal one, with two large bedrooms, in Lansdowne Road, in Hove. But we could not move in until late February 1966. Our baby was due to be born in March, but my impatient child decided to arrive ten days early, before we had the flat ready. The day he was born, at around one o'clock in the morning, I started having contractions. An hour later our doorbell rang. Johnnie answered it to find Mummy on the doorstep, looking confused and muddled.

'What's the matter?' he asked as he ushered her in.

'No, you tell me,' she said firmly. 'I've been thinking about Eva for the last two hours. Now tell me what's going on.' She took one look at me and turned to Johnnie. 'Phone for an ambulance, silly boy, she's having the baby.'

'But it's not due for ten days,' Johnnie said.

'Well, it's on its way now,' Mummy said, laughing.

The ambulance duly arrived and the three of us got into it and headed for the maternity hospital, which was in Buckingham Road, near Brighton station. I refused to allow Mummy or Johnnie into the delivery room with me. Labour is considered a very private female thing by Romanies, and men are not allowed into the room in which their wives are giving birth. I also had a feeling I was going to be in for a rough time and didn't want Johnnie or my mother to witness it.

Once the baby was on the way, he arrived in a hurry. It was all a bit of a blur, but I remember hearing a voice say, 'It's a little boy.' But before he could even be placed in my arms, someone was ringing a bell and a medical team had rushed to the side of my bed. 'The placenta has stuck,' I heard someone say. I thought, 'I couldn't just have a normal birth, could I? That wouldn't be me.' They told me they would have to operate to remove it and that it would need to be done immediately.

'Where's my baby?' I asked, desperate to see him. I could hear him crying on the other side of the room, but could only see the nurse who stood in front of him cleaning him up.

'Your baby's fine, Mrs Tullett,' a kind doctor with white eyebrows and thick, horn-rimmed glasses replied. 'You'll be able to see him as soon as you're out of theatre.'

The bed had begun to be wheeled out of the room, and past Johnnie who had been waiting in the corridor. A nurse had already told him what was happening, so he kissed my head and squeezed my hand, telling me everything would be fine. But I could see the look of concern in his eyes. Then we turned the corner and went through a set of double doors where I was lifted onto a bed in the centre of a room. Someone appeared with a mask that they pulled over my head, and before I knew it everything went dark.

I woke up feeling groggy and it took me a minute or two to realize where I was. Then I saw Johnnie sitting in the chair next to my bed, my beautiful baby cradled in his arms.

'Hello darling,' he said. 'Meet our perfect little boy.' Johnnie placed him in my arms and I was utterly mesmerized. I couldn't take my eyes off him, my own little miracle. The matron appeared a short while later and stood at the side of the bed saying something, but whatever it was I couldn't take it in. I was completely captivated by my baby.

'Mrs Tullett,' the matron said eventually, teasing me, 'you do know that if you take your eyes off that child, he won't disappear, don't you?'

It was no good – I couldn't tear myself away from my perfect little boy.

By this time, my own doctor, Doctor Roe, had arrived. She stood there looking down at me. 'Eva,' she explained, 'I must make you aware that after this you will not be able to have a home birth. This situation is very unlikely to happen again – there's only a million to one chance, in fact – but any future births will have to happen in a hospital.'

'Am I all right now?' I asked her.

'Yes, but you need to rest, dear.'

'Right, I'm going home to rest,' I said.

The day our baby boy was born was the very day that Johnnie moved our stuff into the new flat. He arrived at the hospital that evening carrying a roll of carpet under one arm and a Chinese meal under the other. He unfurled the carpet on the floor of my room and said, 'What do you think of this one?' It was a two-tone grey, good-quality Axminster, and I loved it immediately.

'Right, get that on the stairs and we'll have the same in the front room and landings,' I said. 'We'll decide on the bedroom carpets once I get home.'

I didn't want to wait until the next day to go home, so I discharged myself there and then, on 1 March, the same day I gave birth, despite all of the arguments the hospital tried to put up. I didn't like being in hospital and I had Mummy and Johnnie to take care of me. After all, when Mummy had the twins in the caravan at Coventry we had coped together without a team of doctors and nurses, and I didn't see why this situation could not be the same. I would rest better at home than in a hospital, I knew. So we took our beautiful little boy home, whom we had decided to name John Warren.

The day after he was born, the doorbell rang. I opened it and there stood a midwife.

'Good morning, I've come to show you how to bathe your new baby.' This idea rather amused me, as I knew full well how to bathe and change a baby. After all, I had been nanny to the twins since they were born. Nevertheless, I welcomed her in. I thought that I mustn't be off with her – after all, she was only trying to do her job. We went into my bedroom.

'Do you have a baby bath?' she asked.

'Yes, it's in the bathroom,' I replied. A few minutes later, the nurse came out of the bathroom carrying the baby bath containing water and placed it on my oak table underneath the window. She pushed the window up and I could feel the cold March air circulating in the room. I didn't say a word at this point, just watched her, waiting to see if she intended to do what I thought she would. She took off my newborn baby's clothes and nappy and wrapped him in a white towel. She laid him on the bed, went over to the bath, rolled her sleeves up and dipped her elbow in the water to check the temperature. The air coming in through the open window was glacial.

'What's your name?' I said.

'Janet,' she replied.

'Well, Janet,' I said, as kindly as I could, 'I am not about to let you strip my newborn son off and attempt to bathe him in front of an open window when the March winds are blowing in. It'll give him his death of cold. Now put him back on the bed and I suggest you get your things and leave me to it, thank you.'

A few days later, my doctor gave John Warren his first injection. Within minutes, my little baby son had turned purple and was screaming his lungs out.

'Pick him up, Eva, quick, let's get him to my car,' Doctor Roe ordered. 'We haven't got time to wait for an ambulance.'

I grabbed my baby in a state of panic, my insides churning. We arrived at the hospital and before I knew what was happening, Doctor Roe disappeared into a room with another doctor. I couldn't stay outside not knowing what was happening, so I walked in and said, 'What the hell is going on? What's wrong with my baby?'

She said, 'Did you or your brothers and sisters have inoculations when you were babies?'

'No, of course not,' I replied. 'Romanies don't have inoculations.' As I said it, it hit me. How could I not have thought of that? I was told that I needed to get my baby vaccinated so that was what I did. Why hadn't I thought to tell her before? I couldn't believe I'd been so stupid. I stared at my helpless little baby boy, who was, thankfully, now back to his normal colour. He had stopped screaming and was looking rather angry at having been taken from his blanket cocoon and thrown into such disarray. I picked him up and held him close.

'Will he be all right?' I asked, frightened.

'He's fine now.' Her voice was soft and reassuring. 'But, Eva, we could have lost him, and I would not advise you to give him or any other children you have inoculations. It has obviously not agreed with him. Maybe it's to do with your culture and race?'

And so began life with John Warren, who became

known as simply Warren. It seemed to suit him better somehow, and he never responded when we called him John, so Warren it was!

When Warren was two weeks old, I started seeing clients and giving readings again. I kept working at the same pace as before and didn't find it difficult to fit in everything I had to do around a new baby. I was always full of energy and Mummy was a wonderful help, doing all the cooking for the first week. Warren was a very good baby too and seemed to operate like clockwork – he would sleep for three hours, wake for a feed and then sleep again – so I had plenty of time and would write when I felt like it, often in the evenings, between seven and midnight, which suited me down to the ground as I had always been a night owl and often did my best work after 11 p.m. When he was a couple of months old, I also did what had always been done in my family with newborn babies and gave him boiled water instead of milk when he woke for his 3 a.m. feed, the idea being that he would soon get used to not needing milk at this time. And it worked a treat: after four or five nights, he slept right through.

We decided to take him to Whaplode, in Lincoln-shire, to meet Granny. It would be the first time Johnnie had met her too. 'I think it's about time I met this magical granny of yours,' he said, as we packed for a flying visit. Mummy had decided to come with us as well.

Granny was ninety-two by then and was no longer living in her old painted vardo. Instead, she had a lovely modern caravan on the old bakery site that had been her home in the winter months for many years. Mummy's youngest sister, Shunty, her husband Frank and their children were living in a neighbouring caravan which was a blessing as, although Granny was still very mobile for her age and as quick-witted as she had ever been, Shunty and Frank were able to do so much to help her. In the summer months, they'd hook up and all of them would head to Skegness for the summer season, which Granny loved but would never have been able to do on her own.

As soon as we arrived, Granny appeared in the doorway of her caravan, a tiny figure with her hair plaited and pinned at the sides of her head in the earphone style. She had her gold hoop earrings on and a smart pinafore dress. She stepped forward, took the baby from me and began crooning to him. 'Roses are shining in Picardy,' she sang, cradling Warren in her arms as he gazed up at her, content. Johnnie grinned at me. I could see he had been instantly won over by Granny.

It was a wonderful visit, with Granny regaling Johnnie with all sorts of tales of our ancestors, many of which I hadn't heard since I was a child. But before

I knew it, it was morning and time for us to head back to Brighton. Sadly, that was the last time I ever saw Granny.

Johnnie and I had gone for lunch at the Cricketers. Looking over the bar, I noticed that Winnie's slip was showing beneath her dress. When we were younger and used to go to the dances, it was well known that if you saw a girl – even one you didn't know – whose slip was showing, you would simply speak the words 'Charlie's dead!' She would immediately know her slip was on view and rectify things without her date or dancing partner realizing there had ever been a problem. I leaned discreetly across the bar, thinking that Winnie would know what this expression meant.

'Charlie's dead,' I whispered.

Winnie's face was a picture. 'Oh, I'm so sorry, Eva, how old was he?'

I explained that this old saying was code for something else. She burst out laughing. Winnie explained that she hadn't gone out dancing much when she was young.

'At least Charlie's all right then, that's the main thing,' she giggled. 'I was worried there for a minute, Eva.'

Back at the bar, we were all chatting away and I said, 'Come on, you two, tell me where I'm going on my wedding anniversary this year.'

Winnie said, 'Well, I'm not going to tell you, but if the monkeys leave the island, it'll sink.'

'That's it,' Johnnie said, exasperated, 'I'm not taking you now.'

As uneducated as I was, I did know about the old saying that if the monkeys ever left Gibraltar, it would sink. Winnie knew Johnnie was a man of his word. She'd blown the surprise so that was that; I wouldn't be going to Gibraltar.

'Well, don't tell me next time, then I can't ruin it,' Winnie said, trying to smooth things over. 'If you're not taking her anywhere, Johnnie, then I'll throw a party here upstairs for you both.' God love her. To be honest, I was relieved: Gibraltar was not a place I really fancied going to.

At this point, our good friend Howard Taylor walked in. Immediately, Winnie blurted out, 'We're having a party on 3 November, Howard, bring the gang!' Johnnie, Winnie and Howard huddled together and made a guest list, which unbeknown to me included all of my family from far and wide.

He contacted some of my relations from Lincolnshire and Blackpool, who now that their season had finished were ready for a trip down south, and it was such a wonderful surprise when my cousins Honour and Daisy turned up. It was wonderful to see them as it had been months since we had all got together.

I was all dressed up in a green, blue and black print silk dress that was draped at the hip and had a square neckline and little cap sleeves. Johnnie was in a sharp grey suit with a blue shirt and a black tie with grey and blue stripes. He looked so stylish. We drank champagne and mingled with our guests, now and then catching one another's eye across the room. No words needed to be spoken; we each knew what the other felt.

There was singing, tap dancing and all sorts of musical instruments were brought out and played. As I sat taking in all the fun, I thought to myself that there was nowhere else I'd rather be. The scene around me was not the same as the family gatherings of many years before, but it was just as merry, and my past and present were all merged into one.

SEVEN

Hello, Goodbye

When I told Johnnie I wanted a Silver Cross pram, he didn't seem to share my enthusiasm.

'No, Jewel,' he said. 'We can't fold up a big pram like that and put it in the back of a car.'

I don't have to tell you that I got my own way on this, do I? I would leave the big pram at my mother's in West Street, as I was still using the consulting room there for my palm-reading. But we had a smaller fold-up one in the car, for when we wanted to go further afield. In my mother's garden, Johnnie had built her a trellis, as she wanted climbing flowers like roses and sweet peas. He'd also given her some plant pots which held various herbs to be used for making remedies and for cooking with.

One day, when I had popped over to Mummy's to pick up the pram, I was chatting to her in the kitchen as she chopped some herbs she had just gathered from her pots when a young lady appeared outside the door at the top of the winding staircase that led down to the garden. She was dressed as a hippy, in wide bell-bottom jeans, with a bright scarf tied bandana-style on her head. The glazed look in her eyes told us immediately that she was under the influence of drugs. Mummy stood up at once.

'Who are you looking for, dear?'

'I'm looking for my mother,' she said dreamily.

'And who's your mother?' Mummy said.

The girl said, 'My mother is Joan Baez.'

'Oh yes,' Mummy replied. 'She's on the beach with the others. Now, careful how you go down those steps.'

The girl obediently turned and went on her way, and we both burst out laughing.

By then, the mods and rockers had given way to hippies, who congregated on Brighton's pebble beach. They wore their hair long and favoured bright colours with clashing prints, waistcoats and faded jeans with bell-bottoms that flapped as they walked. Jazzy head-scarves done up bandana-style and lots and lots of beads were also popular with the young hippie crowd. Some made the beach their home, sleeping there throughout the summer. They seemed peaceful enough, although their calm, laid-back attitude may have had as much to do with being spaced-out on illegal substances as anything else.

*

I loved being a mother, and had always wanted a big family, so decided not to hang around! Thirteen months after Warren was born, my second baby was due and I got busy making things for our new arrival, crocheting a white shawl with soft tassels. Again, my sister Anne was also expecting, and we both went round to see Mummy. A parcel was produced for each of us, mine with a baby outfit in blue and Anne's with a pink set of clothes. I had no doubt Mummy was right in her predictions again and was delighted to think I'd have two boys close enough in age to be great pals.

The night I went into labour, Johnnie drove me to the hospital and I was examined by a nurse.

'You're not going to have a baby tonight, Mrs Tullett,' she said. 'Go home and get some rest.'

I was sure I *was* going to give birth that night, so Johnnie and I sat outside in the car with the radio on as my contractions became more and more frequent. After sitting there for half an hour, I turned to him and said, 'Come on, time to go.'

Sure enough, I was right: my baby was on its way. And guess what? If I'd been able to bet £1 on my placenta getting stuck again, I would have become a millionaire as, despite it being a million to one chance that it would happen again, I ended up back in theatre in exactly the same situation as when I'd had Warren. Once again, as soon as I could, I discharged myself from the hospital and went home with my brand new beautiful son, Lee Bradley.

After I'd fed and winded him, Johnnie wrapped a blanket round him and paced about the room, humming and singing to him, just as he had with Warren.

Bradley was a good baby, sleeping most of the time, waking only every four hours for a feed. He had a way of wrinkling up his face, just like my brother Eddie, that made me think of the slapstick actor Oliver Hardy, so I nicknamed him Olly. Just like his brother, he was amazing and I couldn't believe how lucky Johnnie and I were to have been blessed with two such perfect little boys.

I was planning to take Bradley to see Granny when he was a bit older, but sadly it wasn't to be. When Bradley was just ten days out, there was a knock at the door and Johnnie opened it to find Mummy standing there, her eyes red and puffy from crying. She had come to tell me that her mother, my beloved granny, had died.

Mummy and I sobbed as we held onto each other. I never learned any details of her death – I couldn't face knowing. All I know is that she died in her sleep at the grand age of ninety-three, a thought which has comforted me on many occasions. I like to picture her warm in bed, a little smile on her face as she dreamed of times long gone.

EIGHT

The Queen of the Romanies

Travelling in the car to my Granny's funeral in May 1967, I rested my head back on the seat and closed my eyes. I was very tired, as Bradley was just three weeks old. We had had to leave for the funeral very early, so, just like any mother with a new baby, I had not had a chance to have any proper sleep. We had wanted to get going as soon as possible to meet with the other members of the family.

All of the family was meeting at the Lamb and Flag public house in Whaplode. The pub was a popular spot with Romany men and was the focal point for gatherings whenever there was a funeral. Landlords came and went, but there was always a warm welcome for anyone from our community. Johnnie and I had rented a vardo, to be parked in the yard of the pub, that we would use as a base and for us and the children to sleep in that night. But we had a long way to go to get there. The two children were in the back of the car, Warren all strapped in and Bradley in his carry cot, both sound asleep.

My mind went back to Granny – known by all as the Queen of the Romanies due to her wisdom, knowledge and natural Romany instincts, which were second to none. I thought about how, as a child, I had always shared her comfortable feather bed when we were parked near her, and she would tell me of the olden days when she herself was a child. She told me one night that one of our ancestors was burnt at the stake as a witch because she knew so much about people and made so-called magical potions, which were actually herbal remedies. Whether this tale was true or not I'll never know, as our people kept no written records.

'There was a lady who used to come and see me who lost her life when the *Titanic* went down, Eva,' Granny told me one night, when we were snuggled up together having one of our chats. The liner sank in 1912, the same year my Aunt Adeline was born.

'Some of the passengers managed to get into lifeboats, but not my client. She was one of the unlucky ones,' Granny said. 'Someone else in her family also came to me for regular readings and after the *Titanic* disaster, she came to see me and told me what had happened to her. It was the most terrible tragedy, so many lives lost.'

I was dozing in the car, but woke suddenly as we braked hard and the horn in our vehicle and many others around us started blaring. I saw a big green lorry overtaking us and noticed the words 'Gordon's Gin' on the side. The lorry was out of control and swerving all over the road.

My instincts sent me scrambling over the back of the seat immediately, to get to my two babies. The commotion had woken them both and they were screaming and crying. I gathered them up and held them to my chest, one in each arm, trying to cover their faces and shield them from whatever was about to happen to us. We had a large estate car, with lots of room. It shuddered to a halt, as did the car behind us, which held Mummy, Nathan and the twins.

The Gordon's Gin lorry skidded across the motorway. All the cars as far as we could see had come to a violent halt. Horns continued to sound. 'Don't they know there's been an accident?' I thought to myself. 'Why the hell are they blowing their horns? Do they think the skies are going to open up and lift them out of it?' Why couldn't they stop all the racket so we could think and work out if anyone was hurt and what was going on? At least it had missed us and I could see from looking through the back window that Nathan's car and everyone in it was OK. My heart was beating so fast. We could have all been killed.

Nathan jumped out of his car and rushed up to our window.

'Are the tickneys sort tache?' he demanded. (Are the babies all right?)

Mummy came up behind him. 'John, lead the way and get us off this motorway. I can't have this.'

'Up the way, about half a mile, there's a turning to a village,' Johnnie responded. 'Follow me there!'

After what seemed to be an eternity, the traffic was allowed to move again. To my surprise, I had been able to very easily calm the babies and they were safely fastened back into the seat and carry cot. Before we arrived at the village, a thought suddenly struck me and I started to giggle, which quickly turned into a very loud laugh. Winnie Sexton, at the Cricketers public house in Brighton, was a gin drinker and I would occasionally have the odd one with her. I had suddenly imagined news reaching the pub that I had been squashed by a Gordon's Gin lorry. Winnie would have thought that would be the perfect way to go! Luckily, that had not been the ending to this tale and, happily, we later found out that no one had been hurt. When I got back home, the first gin I had in the Cricketers would have a tale to go with it, and a toast would be made with thanks to the heavens above, that was for sure.

Meanwhile, back in the car, we turned a corner and

suddenly saw the village we had been aiming for. It comprised a little row of shops, a pub and a restaurant with a car park conveniently adjacent. We all got out of the cars with relief, Mummy and I giving each other a hug, and the men respectfully patting one another on the back for their handling of the dramatic situation we had just been through. Taking my babe in arms, and Johnnie taking Warren, we entered the restaurant.

'Hello, darling,' I said to the waitress who greeted us. 'I wonder if we could have a table for six and two babies. Do you have a highchair?' She showed us to a large table. 'Could I have a jug of hot water to warm my babies' milk, please?' I asked.

Bradley gave out a loud cry.

'I'll do that first.' The waitress smiled. 'I can hear he's ready for his lunch.' As she went to walk off, she turned around and asked, 'Did you see anything of the lorry incident on the motorway?'

We were obviously not the first to arrive at the restaurant from the chaos on the motorway. We quickly filled her in on what we had experienced and said, 'We're all pretty shaken up.' With that, the waitress called the manager.

'Come and help me out, please. These people have had the same experience as the ones on table two. It's going to be busier in here today than we thought.'

The manager came over and asked us if he could

give us a drink to steady our nerves, which we had to refuse as we still had to make it to Granny's funeral and the men were driving.

After our meal, Mummy said to the waitress, 'How far away are the shops?'

'Just a little further down the road. There's a bakery and general shops, everything you need, I should think.'

Mummy excused herself and said, 'I'm going to walk down and get a few things I need.' And with this, off she trotted.

I finished feeding Bradley and gave him to Johnnie to get his wind up. 'I've got a few things to get from the shops as well,' I said, and off I toddled. As soon as I got outside I lit up a cigarette and sighed out loud. What a way to start a trip to a funeral!

The first shop I encountered as I walked down the road was actually an off-licence. I went inside, purchased half a bottle of brandy and slipped it into my bag. With the way things had begun, we might need it. Better prepared than not, I decided.

Next door was a draper's shop. Some towels in the window immediately caught my eye and I decided to buy one and two flannels as they're always handy on a journey. On the other side of the lane was a grocery and bakery, where I bought ham, cheese, rolls and butter, and then popped into a kitchenware shop to buy a knife.

When I returned, Mummy was already back in the restaurant, sipping a cup of tea. 'What did you buy, Eva?' she enquired.

When I told her, she started laughing and couldn't stop. She dug into the bags at her feet and pulled out towels, brandy, ham, cheese, rolls and even the knife! The only difference between the purchases we'd made was that her towels were green and mine were white. At this sight, the entire group erupted into hysterical laughter, including our waitress, who by now was a friend to all round the table.

'Do you want to make your sandwiches here, rather than in the car?' the waitress offered. Mummy nodded gratefully. With that, the waitress went into the kitchen and returned with a chopping board and a roll of grease-proof paper for us to wrap them in.

We had a long way to go and, realizing this, she also gave us an entire packet of paper serviettes. Eddie gave her one of his notorious winks and she gave a beaming grin back and then a flirty downward smile as she waved her wedding ring at him. We realized that she was actually the wife of the manager and not just a waitress. Needless to say, we gave her a hefty tip.

Eddie flirted with every woman, regardless of age, size, looks or marital state. It was a natural instinct with him. He meant no harm; he enjoyed it, and so did the people on the receiving end of his attentions. We always said that Eddie could flirt with a lamp post and make it sway at his charms. We had even seen husbands allow their wives to be flirted with as he was such a professional at it. I'm sure they picked up a few tips after the reactions they had seen from their partners.

What the manager of the restaurant didn't know – nor we until after we'd left – was that Eddie had a little secret. Outside, he slid his hand into his pocket and pulled out a napkin, the same as the ones we had been given for our journey, the only difference being that on his was a number written in lipstick. It was the waitress's number! Mummy tutted, deftly took it off him and gave him one of her looks.

'Wafedi chore,' she muttered under her breath – bad boy!

We were on the road again, each one of us deep in thought about the near miss that we had just had with the gin lorry. I was also thinking about Granny and about one night in particular, when I was in her bed. I must have been about seven years old. She would always tell me the most wonderful stories and that night she was telling me how we were related to a famous movie star.

'His name was Charlie Chaplin,' she said. 'Charlie's mother was a Smith and was your grandfather's cousin.'

My grandfather, Naughty Smith, had died before

I came along. 'Granny, I wish I had met Naughty,' I said.

She laughed and said, 'Well, he was a character, girl. We don't talk a lot about him being related to Chaplin though, as Charlie's mother was a *dindlo* [crazy] and ended up in a mental home. Her husband wasn't much help to the poor woman. He was a real *motsi mingre* [drunken man]. They parted when Charlie was only three years old, but he did well for himself, that boy, and was a credit to every Romany in the land.' Granny gave me a big smile. 'It's the blood that counts, girl.'

This always gave me great pride over the years, when I saw one of Charlie Chaplin's films, as it made me think back to what Granny had said.

My daydreaming was interrupted when I spotted a sign for Spalding. We were nearly at our destination. Whaplode was only six miles away.

When we arrived at the cute, old-fashioned village and turned into the car park of the Lamb and Flag, there were already lots of Romanies gathered, all talking in little groups. At the side of the hedge that separated Granny's piece of ground, known as the old bakery site, stood the caravan we had hired, and in the doorway was the young travelling girl we knew who was to be our babysitter during the funeral.

'Millie,' I called to the girl as I walked towards her, 'this is Warren and this little one is Bradley and they've come to play with you for the day.'

Johnnie followed me with a box of toys and Millie immediately started getting them out.

'Hello, little boys,' Millie said. 'We're going to have some fun today, and I've got a lollipop for you, Warren.'

I instructed her on the care and feeding of the boys, then went outside to look for Mummy.

People had come from far and wide to honour my Granny. There were Boswells, Greys, Taylors and lots of Smiths. Many had towed their vardos to the site and planned to stay over. Granny's nickname was 'the Bird'. This was because when she was talking she would tilt her head left and then right, just like a bird.

There were four big farm trucks filled to capacity with wreaths, which would later follow us to the grave-side. I couldn't see Mummy in the yard so, leaving Johnnie with the men, I walked into the pub, where I assumed most of the women would be. At these occasions, the women and the men would separate, the men to talk men's talk and the women to talk women's talk. The men in our family welcomed Johnnie with open arms and treated him no differently from any Romany man. He had proved he could be one of them and it was clear that he and I were made for each other.

Sure enough, there was Mummy at a big table with her sisters, Vera, Adeline, Shunty and Lena. They were drinking tea and talking very sensibly as I sat down. I picked up on what they were discussing. It seemed that

Granny had left everything, including the old bakery site, to be divided between all of her children equally. Something had been said among the women that had Shunty protesting.

'No, it's what she wanted,' she said, insistent.

'Listen, Shunty,' Mummy said, 'we've all gone off and led our own lives. You never left her; you stayed with her the whole way through. *You* deserve to have the ground and that's the end of it.'

The others all nodded in agreement. 'That bit of land is your home, girl,' Aunt Vera said. 'Do what you want with it – build on it, sell it, dig it all up if you want – but it's yours.'

'You've earned it, and that's the end of it,' Aunt Adeline said with authority.

The conversation was broken up with the arrival of the hearse covered in flowers. The realization that Granny had passed on hit us all again. Mummy put her arm round me. 'Don't cry,' she said in a trembling voice. I could see that she too was overwhelmed by memories and emotions. 'Your granny had ninety-three good years and enjoyed every one of them. No one has a bad memory of her and she enjoyed good health throughout.'

The hearse turned right and started on up the road from the yard, to make its way slowly to the church. The sides of the road were lined four deep with gorgers who had known the family, not only from Whaplode and Spalding, but from miles away, many from Skegness. Behind the hearse, the family walked slowly and silently, in rows of six. I turned to see who was beside me and was amazed. The sight reminded me of soldiers in their regimented units, moving in columns. There were people on foot behind us as far as I could see.

Once inside the church, we all took our places. One thing about our people that was different from the gorgers was that we didn't sing hymns and for occasions like funerals we would hire a choir. The reason for this, I believe, is that we sang when we were happy, and a funeral was not a happy occasion. Also many Romanies were illiterate and couldn't read the hymn books. Having said that, the hymns played at our family funerals were taught to us as children, and we knew them by heart. Usually, we started off with the Lord's Prayer, followed by 'Abide with Me', then 'The Old Rugged Cross' and finally 'Amazing Grace'. The church had been filled with flowers and you could have heard a pin drop, as we waited for the service to begin.

When the service drew to an end, everyone made their way outside and again we followed the hearse to the other little church where our burial ground was. This church was almost next to the old bakery site where Granny had lived. I remember one Romany family that attended the funeral, a mother and daughter, had a big American car and a chauffeur in uniform. These two were not very popular with the Romanies, although they were related. As we walked towards the second church, we could hear Elvis Presley singing. Their chauffeur had the radio in the car on full blast and was parked right outside the gates to the entrance of the churchyard. Some of the men went over to order him to move and turn the radio off.

After the burial, we all trooped back to the Lamb and Flag, everyone now animated and talking to each other. The pub was ours for the rest of the day and well into the evening, and we caught up on gossip and reminisced. Every now and then a laugh would break out when someone was relating a story about Granny.

My cousin Daisy said, 'Remember when we were little and Granny would give us syrup of figs if we hadn't been to the toilet?'

I made a face, thinking back. Granny would also give chase with a bar of green soap and a knife if you hadn't 'been' and she would slice off a sliver of soap and stick it where the monkey puts his nuts. Daisy and I were in fits of laughter at the memory.

A feast was laid out, including lots of joints of meat. Traditionally, the Romany doesn't eat red meat after a death until the burial has taken place. Every woman in the place was dressed in the black of mourning, although nine times out of ten we wore black anyway. There wasn't enough room in the building for everyone, so most of the men went outside to eat and drink. The Romany women didn't drink – well, at least not as far as their menfolk were concerned. The female members of the close family sat down with teas and coffees while the men crowded into the main bar to get their drinks to take outside. I motioned to my mother across the table and discreetly pulled out the half bottle of brandy I'd bought on the way there from my handbag. As I showed her the top of the bottle, she immediately put her hand in her bag and drew hers out, and several of the other women produced theirs. It was all very discreet, I must add, as we laced our coffees, not letting the men see in case we got into trouble.

Very early the next morning, we set off home back to Brighton, Mummy and I exchanging stories and scandals the family had told us and commenting on how everyone looked and how much people had changed.

Mummy said, 'Did you ever hear the one about Lillian, a traveller who worked in a café in the amusement park?'

'Who's Lillian?' I asked.

'No, you wouldn't have,' Mummy said. 'You weren't even born. Well, she had a plump thirteen-year-old daughter whom she'd named Jill. Jill didn't go to school but walked around the amusement park all day long.

No father, and a mother who let her do as she wanted. They were in their caravan one night, Lillian just dozing off to sleep, when all of a sudden Jill started screaming, "Mummy, Mummy, Mummy."

'"Whatever is the matter?" Lillian said. "Are you having a nightmare?"

'"There's something in the bed, Mummy," Jill cried. Lillian quickly snatched the blanket and pulled it off her daughter, to find a newborn baby. Lillian did not, as you might expect, call a doctor, but instead simply cut the cord herself, cleaned up her child and her child's child and swaddled the baby in a sheet.'

One of Lillian's friends had been married for five years and told her she could never have children. Cunning Lillian contacted her and told her that she might be able to get hold of a newborn child that was unwanted, but said the parents were very hard up and wanted money.

'She did not want the bother of bringing up another child when she couldn't cope with the one she already had,' Mummy said.

The childless couple jumped at the chance of a baby and gathered up every penny they could find. They had £500, which Lillian said she would take straight to the parents of the child.

'Don't ask who they are or the deal's off,' she said. 'This has to stay a strict secret or the couple will be shamed. You're doing each other a favour here.'

She then interrogated her daughter. 'Who's the father?' she demanded, hoping it might be one of the owners of the amusement park, so she could put pressure on him and strike yet another lucrative deal.

Jill cried and cried and in the end confessed she didn't know who the father was. Apparently, she was known as the park 'bike', available to any of the grease-rags, the men who worked the machines. After this, mother and daughter headed for London, where Jill, even though she was very large in size, took up the oldest profession in the world, with Lillian as her madam.

'After all, Jill,' her mother told her, 'if you're going to give it away, they may as well pay me.'

I was wide-eyed with amazement. 'Never,' I said to Mummy.

'Yes,' she replied, 'and from what I've heard on the grapevine, she did very well in London.'

I could just imagine how Granny would have laughed at this story! With this, I closed my eyes and realized, as I drifted off in the back of the car, what an important chapter in all our lives had been closed with the journey to bury my beloved granny. Both Mummy and I knew that this really was the end of an era, and the Queen of the Romanies was no more.

NINE

Pickles

Our expanding family meant we had moved from the flat in Hove to Ship Street Gardens, in Brighton Lanes. It was a quaint, 300-year-old fisherman's cottage, and within the first five months of being there, Johnnie had used his building and decorating skills to turn the downstairs into an amazing office, waiting room and consulting rooms for me to cater for my growing business needs. The upstairs was our living accommodation and we had another very large room downstairs, beneath the palmistry place, which we turned into a bedroom for the boys to share. It had a small kitchen, which we called the galley, where I loved to while away the hours cooking for my family.

Every Sunday Johnnie would take the children down to the seafront to ride their tricycles, while I cooked Sunday dinner, but on one particularly sunny day I also decided to pickle some onions while they were out. I was wearing Warren's swimming goggles, hoping they would stop the strong fumes from the onions from burning my eyes. I agree, I must have looked quite a sight, but to me it seemed a very logical thing to do. Mind you, we all know by now that I am not normal! I was in the middle of pickling when the phone rang.

'Hello, Eva Petulengro's office,' I said.

'It's me,' Mummy said. 'Shunty's here. She's come down to see us for a few days as her season's over, so I'm taking her down to the Cricketers for a drink – will you come and join us, girl?'

The last time we had seen Shunty, Mummy's youngest sister, was at Granny's funeral a few months before. 'I'd love to see her, but I'm a bit busy at the moment, Mummy,' I replied with a slight sniff. The goggles were not working quite as planned. 'You'll be coming over for lunch with her afterwards though, I hope?'

'Of course. Dick you in a bida.' (See you in a minute.)

I stood there with my goggles on, pickling my onions, pondering whether to join my mother and Shunty. I decided I wouldn't and thought I would call Mummy back to confirm I wouldn't be coming, as I knew she'd think I'd be tempted and would probably just turn up at the pub. Knowing her, she would order a drink for me and have it sitting on the bar, waiting. I picked up the phone, proud of my determination to become the pickle-making champion, even though the goggles were starting to fail miserably at their onion-repelling job.

I dialled my mother's number, heard the receiver being picked up and, with gusto, said, 'Fuck the pub, have you got any pickle jars? I'm on a pickle mission!'

A very posh voice, which I instantly knew was not my mother's, said, 'I *beg* your pardon?'

'Sorry, wrong number,' I whispered, before putting the phone down firmly and dissolving into hysterics. The tears came, as did the laughter, which began in my stomach and formed a sound more like a cry than a laugh. I began rocking back and forth, thinking what on earth the posh voice on the other end of the phone must have thought.

I turned and glanced through my kitchen window, still crying pickled onion tears of laughter, and there, staring back at me with shocked expressions, were four faces in the building next door. It must have been a sight for them, this crazy woman, only her head and shoulders visible, wearing children's swimming goggles, rocking back and forth, crying and laughing to herself. But that only made me laugh even more.

I decided that being in my own company was turning into a rather dangerous experience, so decided to take off my apron and the swimming goggles and join my mother and Shunty in the pub after all. And do you know what? As I walked in, Mummy already had a gin and tonic waiting for me on the bar.

'What took you so long, Eva?' she asked innocently.

I looked around the bar for Shunty's husband. 'Where's Frank?'

'He's busy decorating, fixing our places in Butlins in Skegness,' Shunty said. 'He's not been out of Lincolnshire for years and he hates trains, so I've left him to it.'

We had a good laugh and caught up on family news in the pub before heading back to our new house in Ship Street Gardens. When Johnnie and the children arrived home from their Sunday seafront jaunt, we all sat down and enjoyed a big roast beef lunch.

After lunch, we set off to show our cousins from Skegness around Brighton. Shunty had two girls and a boy. John, the eldest, a very witty and elegant young man, was wise beyond his years and very close to his mother. They seemed to be able to read each other's minds. Then followed two very beautiful young daughters, each quite different from the other. The youngest we called Baby Adeline and she was very dark and petite, a real head-turner. In sharp contrast was Carol, a striking, leggy blonde, who could hold her own with anyone; a very determined girl and a born businesswoman.

We walked them down the Lanes, looking in all the antiques shops. It was late November, the end of the season, and the chance for all of us to recover after the seven-day weeks we'd worked all summer. Now we could actually hold whole conversations with each other, rather than having to cut each other off halfway through, when a client walked in for an appointment, at which we'd curtly say to one another down the receiver, 'Kekka rocker, gorger akai, mandy jaw, owly.' (Can't talk, non-Romany here, I've got to go, OK.)

We were getting peckish with the sea air, and Mummy suggested we go to a wonderful bakery and teashop near the seafront. We were lucky enough to get a big table and on the table next to us was an old-fashioned cake stand laden with iced buns, pink and yellow fondant fancies, éclairs, cream horns, custard slices and all manner of mouth-watering treats.

'Oh, we'll have some of those,' Mummy said. As usual, we ordered lots of pots of strong tea. 'An extra teabag in the pot, please, dear,' Mummy would always say with a wink.

The waitress, dressed in black with a white frilly apron, took our order and went into the kitchen. When she returned she lifted the cake stand from the table next to us and put it in the middle of our table.

'Just a minute, dear,' Mummy said. 'I don't want those. The people on that table have been touching them and breathing all over them. Would you please bring us a fresh tray of cakes?'

We looked at each other with absolute determination, agreeing one hundred per cent with Mummy. The waitress shrugged, promptly picked up the cake stand and returned with a fresh selection. We all smiled now and she looked relieved. 'Thank you, my dear,' Mummy said with a satisfied grin.

Shunty was giving us all the latest news from Skegness. They were all staying with my mother and I decided to take John, Carol and Adeline to the cinema, to give Shunty a break so she could talk 'grown-up gossip' with Mummy.

After the cinema, I took the children to our favourite Chinese restaurant, Nang King, where food was very good and the staff knew us well. I'd never eaten Chinese food until I started dating Johnnie, but it had since become a firm favourite and I'd introduced many of my lot to this restaurant over the years. It would always be the same for Johnnie and me: a 59 (chow mein), a 79 (sweet-and-sour prawns) and half a portion of fried rice, all for ten shillings.

Young John declared he'd never tried Chinese food before and was a little bit wary of it, so I ordered extra tasty bits, such as spare ribs with a sticky sauce and steak in black bean sauce. The waitress placed a finger bowl with a slice of lemon next to John's plate. As we chatted, I watched John pick up the bowl and draw it towards his mouth, the lemon floating towards his lips.

'Kekka, kekka,' I muttered in a hushed tone. 'That's not to drink, it's to wash your fingers in after you've eaten the ribs.'

An embarrassed John said defensively, 'Well, I've never been in a Chinese restaurant until tonight. You should have told me.' He set the bowl back down on the table, looking around to see if the staff had rumbled his mistake. They had not, or if they had they didn't let on, and we went on to enjoy a real slap-up meal, the first of many Chinese meals we were to have together. The memory of the water bowl stuck, though, and from then on there was not a meal we shared in a Chinese restaurant when I did not ask John if he would like a finger bowl to drink from with his food.

Shunty and the children only stayed for three days, but it was wonderful to see them and we were all very sad when they left.

TEN

Love and Legends

Nathan and Daddy had opened a café together near the train station in Brighton, but unfortunately they could not work together and had had a big falling out. It had only been open three months, but after many arguments over who was the boss Nathan realized it was not for him and decided to move on and branch out on his own. Someone had told him about an advert for a catering manager on the pier at Bognor Regis. Being impulsive, just like me, he jumped into his Mini and drove down to investigate. He went to see the pier manager, a nice man he immediately got on with, who explained that they had previously had two managers for the restaurants, but neither had worked out.

Surprised, Nathan said, 'Restaurants? You mean there's more than one?'

'Yes, there are three – the Wimpy bar on the front of the pier and, on the very end of the pier, there's a yachting café. You'd also be in charge of the bar upstairs, where you'd have to provide food.'

Nathan couldn't believe it. *Three* outlets for food! By now, he was determined. He wanted this job and he was going to get it. 'Will you do me a favour? Can you get through to the actual owner? Could I talk to them?'

The manager had taken a liking to Nathan, admiring the boy's spirit and determination. 'Good idea, lad,' he said. 'Get in there before someone else does.'

He led Nathan to the office, dialled a number and after a few words to the person on the other end, handed Nathan the receiver.

'Hello,' Nathan said. 'Thank you for taking my call. I've had a look around your restaurants, and I think I know what needs to be done. If you give me the chance, I'll work for free for a week and if you don't like what I've done, I'll leave without any wages and we'll call it a day.'

There was a slight pause and a woman's voice said, 'Let me speak to the manager of the pier again, please.'

Nathan handed the phone over and after a brief conversation the manager passed it back to Nathan. To his absolute astonishment, the owner of the restaurants agreed to his terms. Nathan was extremely happy.

'You realize you have eighteen staff to manage too?' the manager said.

'Not a problem,' Nathan said with a smile, even though his stomach was doing somersaults.

'I'm glad about this,' the manager said. 'I've had to let the staff in and let them out and lock up after them. Now it's all your responsibility, mate.'

Nathan realized what he had taken on and decided to start immediately, that very afternoon. He went to each restaurant and introduced himself to all the staff and, because many of them were much older than him and had obviously been there for several years, he decided he was going to be their friend as well as their boss.

He worked hard all that afternoon and until late in the evening. All the staff had gone home, but he was determined to make this venture work. Suddenly he realized it was too late to find anywhere to stay for the night, but he did not care. He had two rugs in his car, which he brought into the restaurant, and he rolled his jacket up to use as a pillow and bedded down in the Wimpy for the night, having decided that in the morning he would go out and buy some fresh clothes.

The following week, the owner, Mrs Montague-Patten, came down to find everything running smoothly. She was particularly delighted with the white coats of the staff and the cleanliness of the cafés, and over the moon when she realized the takings had doubled.

*

One day two young ladies walked into the Wimpy bar and asked for the manager. Nathan had placed a sign in the window saying, 'Waitresses required'. He gave them both a day's trial, and one of the girls, Suzanne, proved very efficient and hard-working. However, her friend was a bit lazy and at the end of the day Nathan offered Suzanne a job, but not her friend.

Suzanne got very angry and said she would not work for him unless he gave her friend a job too.

'That's my loss,' he said. 'I hope you change your mind, I really do.'

The next morning Suzanne realized she needed the money, as she only had a part-time job as a student pathologist, which didn't pay enough for her to survive on. She'd also taken quite a liking to the boss, although she couldn't yet put her finger on why. Nathan, meanwhile, was smitten. He thought, 'What have I done?' Suzanne had the most beautiful figure he'd ever seen, long, dark, film-star hair, a fantastic smile and lovely features, and he'd let her go. It simply made him want her more. He agonized most of the night.

As it turned out, he hadn't needed to lose any sleep. Bright and early the next morning, Suzanne appeared and said, 'So, am I working for you or not?'

'I told you that you had the job yesterday,' he said, desperately trying not to sound too keen.

Over the next few weeks, he invited her out several

times, but she always refused. When she finally gave in and they went for a quick drink together, they got on like a house on fire. A few days later it was the end of the season and time for Nathan to leave. He said his goodbyes to the staff and the manager of the pier and drove off along Bognor's seafront. They'd all come out to see him off and when he looked in his rearview mirror he saw all them heading back into the building. There was just one person left behind, watching him go. It was Suzanne.

He quickly did a U-turn, drove back to the front of the pier and pulled up next to her. They looked at each other. They both knew how they felt.

'I'm going back to Brighton to see my family,' Nathan said. 'Then, in the morning, I'm going to Spain. Do you want to come with me?'

Without a word, Suzanne opened the car door and took her place next to him. After going home to collect her belongings, they headed for Brighton. They didn't have to say much to each other. Their bond was sealed.

On their return from Spain, Johnnie and I were going to London, as the singer Johnny Mathis had requested a reading from me. 'Come up with us,' I suggested to Nathan and Sue. 'We'll make a day of it.' The tension in the car on the way up to London was high. Nathan had decided to tie in the trip with a visit to Sue's father. Because Sue was not yet twenty-one, they needed her father's consent in order to make their relationship 'legal' and get married.

We dropped them off at a restaurant near Piccadilly Circus and wished them luck. 'Don't worry, it'll be OK,' I comforted them.

They didn't need to feel anxious, as Sue's father liked Nathan immediately. Nathan said to me later, 'I could see from his attitude and the way he spoke that he knew I would look after his little girl.'

Two hours later, we went back and picked them up. Nathan was waving a piece of paper with the written consent from Sue's father. They jumped in the car happily, with shrieks of excitement. From there, we drove to St John's Wood, where Johnny Mathis was staying in a beautiful house. He too congratulated the happy couple and I gave him a private reading. He seemed very pleased with what I had to tell him and posed for a photo.

When the reading was finished, Johnny said, 'Can you do me a favour?' He pointed to a very good-looking young man. 'This is my PA. Would you tell him something clairvoyant, please?'

I protested. I really didn't work like that.

'Please,' the young man pleaded.

'I don't give readings in front of other people,' I said.

In the end they pestered me so much I gave in. 'OK,

you've asked for it, but you're not going to like it,' I said. 'You're going to leave Johnny, but you will return in about eighteen months.'

The young man's jaw dropped and Johnny started to laugh. 'Eva, how right you are,' he said. 'He got his call-up papers only this morning – for Vietnam!'

It was two weeks since Nathan had driven away from Bognor with Sue in the car beside him, and they were to be married. They had decided that they didn't want a big wedding and arranged for a register office do with just very close family. Nathan confided in Johnnie, 'I've booked a hotel in Jersey for Sue and me. We're flying over from Shoreham Airport in a small plane. Will you drive us out there?'

'Of course I will,' Johnnie replied.

It was dark by the time we set out after a soirée at Mummy's to toast the happy couple. When we arrived at the airport, a small aircraft was waiting to take them on their honeymoon. It was so romantic, seeing this little plane in the darkness, waiting to whisk them away to begin their married life. It reminded me of a scene from the film *Casablanca*.

They had a short honeymoon and four days later we picked them up at the same airport. Fortunately for Nathan, Sue enjoyed the outdoor life, and at the toss of a coin the pair would jump on Nathan's Harley and head for the woods, where they would listen to their music and cook on a stick fire. Nathan was, and still is, a chilli fiend. He loves curries, and will even slice up chillies to eat with his bacon and eggs in the morning. All of my family are 'foodies', and if we're not cooking it or eating it, we're talking about it or shopping for it.

Nathan and Sue once laughingly told us about one of their escapades on their honeymoon. One fine day, in winter, the couple jumped onto their bike, rode into the countryside and found a nice little pub. Inside were loads of bikers. 'We had a great time listening to the music, talking bikes,' Sue said. 'Nathan pitched our tent in a field near the pub. We lit a fire and sat around it, drinking red wine and eating and talking. The next morning, Nathan poked his head outside the tent and dragged me out to see. We were in the middle of a car boot sale! We had drunk a lot of wine, which is probably why we didn't wake up. Nathan bought some lovely little dishes from the sale anyway, ideal for his curries.'

Shortly after they were married, Nathan and Sue bought a bungalow in Peacehaven, in Sussex. It had belonged to Sid Fields, the brother of Gracie Fields, and two doors down was Gracie Fields' house. In the loft of Nathan and Sue's new bungalow, they found

Sid Fields' memorabilia in a wicker basket that was full of odds and ends.

'Mummy,' Nathan said, 'we've decided that when you retire we'll build you a granny flat on the side of the bungalow.'

'Retire, you silly boy? Romanies don't retire, we just fade away quietly.'

Nevertheless, at a later date, that granny flat was built.

ELEVEN

Prized Possessions

One of my favourite pastimes, and I'm pretty good at it, is spending money. When we moved into Ship Street Gardens, the furniture we had did not suit the property, and I was delighted. When Johnnie and I had first got married I bought all the modern stuff but now I hated it – I wanted some lovely old antique furniture like Mummy had always had. Our charming old cottage cried out for antiques, and I went out and bought a chaise longue for my waiting room as well as four lovely armchairs. White ruched drapes covered the windows, along with a gold velvet pelmet and matching curtains that could be drawn at night. I covered the armchairs and chaise longue in gold velvet too, and finished it off with a green and cream woollen rug with a fringed edge and lovely fresh green plants.

Behind the lounge, which I used as my waiting room, was a twelve-foot space which was the office where I had my typewriter and telephones, and beyond that was a little room which I used for my readings. Johnnie had decorated the upstairs beautifully. We loved our new home. The kitchen was average when we bought it, but by the time Johnnie had finished with it, it was spectacular.

I had fallen in love with a fabulous top-of-the-range cooker I had seen in the shops. 'Johnnie, I want that,' I said showing him the model, with its griddle and self-clean oven.

He examined it and said, 'It's very lovely, but I don't think it will go up the staircase.'

The kitchen was on the second floor and the cooker would have had to go up the staircase, past the banister rail that had been there for 300 years. This had not occurred to me. Johnnie took some measurements and we went home to measure the staircase. I was very disappointed when the verdict was in: it wouldn't fit.

Later that afternoon a friend of Johnnie's, Richard, turned up to say hello and I told him about my cooker. He just happened to be a carpenter and electrician.

'Let me have a look,' he said, disappearing up into the kitchen, and then examining and measuring the staircase.

Johnnie brought out the dimensions of the cooker. To our surprise, Richard said, 'No problem. I could get it up there with the help of one of my lads.'

'Really?' I said. 'When can you do it?'

'Now, if you like.'

Johnnie took him to the shop and bought my cooker, and on his return said, 'Jewel, you and I are going out because, on reflection, I don't think this job can be done and we don't want to embarrass old Richie. I've even made arrangements with the shop that I might have to return it.'

It was lunchtime and Johnnie and I decided we'd like an Indian meal, so we set off to our favourite restaurant, Nooris, in Ship Street. After a lovely lunch, we strolled home to see how Richard was getting on.

I dawdled to have a word with our neighbour, who was just coming out of her gate, while Johnnie went ahead to see what progress had been made. Within what seemed like seconds, he was back at my side, with a very angry look on his face. I swear I could see the steam coming out of his ears!

'We need to go for a walk,' Johnnie said. 'He's only gone and taken the 300-year-old staircase down! I've told him it had better be back up and solid by the time we return.'

We wandered around the Lanes for a bit until we couldn't stand it any longer. 'Come on,' Johnnie said, 'it's time to go see the damage.'

Thank God, Richard did know his job after all, and our lovely, ancient staircase was back in its proper place, solid as a rock!

*

That same afternoon, a young couple called Brian and Pat Dearson and their two adorable little girls, Annabelle and Louise, moved into the cottage directly opposite us. We bonded immediately. Both Brian and Pat were in business, a real pair of go-getters. Pat had recently sold a clothes shop in Burgess Hill, in Sussex, to be a full-time mother, while Brian had his fingers in many different businesses.

One afternoon, Pat was in my lounge when I received a call from the Press Association, telling me that I had a new column if I could get it to them by the following morning. I heard myself saying, 'Sure, no problem,' but as I put the phone down I wondered how on earth I was going to get it written, typed and sent to them in time as this was in the days when there were no such things as computers and emails. I told Pat my dilemma and she could see the concerned look on my face.

She smiled. 'No problem, pet. I can type it for you now, if you like. Brian has a breakfast meeting near Fleet Street tomorrow morning, so he can even drop it off for you.'

I set to writing the column immediately and handed it to Pat. I was amazed when she started typing and not at all surprised when she told me she used to work for the newspapers in Newcastle and had won a country-wide competition for the fastest copy typist in the land. She was flying along the typewriter!

At that time, my secretary was a lovely lady of seventy-two by the name of Jay, who had come to me after I had placed an advert in the *Evening Argus*. The five young women I had interviewed for the post were totally useless. They couldn't spell and they couldn't type. (Whatever did we do before we had spell check?!) I made a proposition to Pat. 'Would you like a job with me? You could do my typing while the girls are at school.'

She was delighted and accepted immediately.

I knew Jay had been wanting to take a step back from work and begin to ease into retirement, so I phoned her and suggested she could do additional typing work for me from home with the aid of my tape recorder, which I would often dictate into late at night. She agreed immediately and said, 'Eva, that suits me much better.' I understood it would be better for Jay to work when she felt like it and was overjoyed that I had not upset her but found a solution that suited everyone. We were three happy ladies!

While looking for furnishings for Ship Street Gardens, I had spotted in an antiques shop four cabriole-legged chairs, which we purchased and put into the waiting room along with the chaise longue. One afternoon, on a break from writing and typing, Pat and I went shopping for food together and on the way back, walking down Middle Street, I spotted two chairs in a shop just like the ones I already had.

'Oh, look,' I said to Pat. 'They're just like my chairs.'

Pat took a closer look. 'They're not like them,' she replied. 'They're identical.'

They were, right down to the fact that they were covered in olive-green velvet.

'Don't speak,' I whispered to Pat, as we went to ask about them. I had in mind that if they were identical, they were going to be a lot more valuable as a set of six as opposed to four.

Inside the shop, I innocently enquired of the shop-keeper how much he wanted for the two chairs.

'I could let you have them for £800,' he told me.

'That's a lot of money,' I said to him. 'What would a set of six like that cost me?'

'Oh, you won't find a set of six,' he informed me.

I could not resist the challenge. 'Well, sir, I'd like you to know that I've got the other four.'

His eyes widened and a look of disbelief came over his face. I wanted to be sure my chairs really were the same.

'Pat,' I said, 'would you mind going and getting one of the chairs for me? You're younger than I am!'

I only lived around the corner, and within five minutes Pat was back and had placed my chair down next to the others.

'I don't believe it,' the man said. 'The wood is exactly the same shade. When a set is split up, what often happens is the wood ends up different shades due to how much sunlight is allowed to fall on them. This hasn't happened to these at all.'

We all examined the chairs carefully. They could have lived in the same house for the last hundred years.

'Right, now,' the dealer said, rubbing his hands gleefully. 'How much do you want for your set of four?'

'They're not for sale,' I declared.

A look of disappointment crept over his face. 'Come on, Madam Petulengro, I know who you are. Let's put them into auction and we'll go halves on the profit.'

'My chairs are not for sale,' I repeated. 'But I'll do you a deal on the pair you've got for sale. I'll give you £600, because I'm not going to sell them on. They suit the house I live in.'

We couldn't come to an agreement, so Pat and I left, carrying the chair with us.

The next day, I headed off to Leicester on business. I was working for the *Leicester Mercury* newspaper at the time and had a meeting with the editor. We didn't want to travel at night, so decided to stay at the Grand Hotel in Granby Street and go to the Leicester market the next morning, which I loved, as I enjoyed dressmaking and could buy beautiful material at very good prices there. Also, there was a butcher's shop in the market square where you could buy beef and pork dripping, which I hadn't been able to find anywhere near home.

We got home at about three in the afternoon, and Pat let herself into her house while I walked across the lane and went into my waiting room. Johnnie was sat there, with a big beam on his face. Putting his hand in his pocket, he pulled out a wad of notes. 'Guess what? I've sold those old armchairs and made us a pretty penny!' he beamed.

My heart skipped a beat. 'How come?' I knew full well what had happened, but he looked so pleased with himself I didn't want to upset him. Hiding the fact that I actually wanted to scream, I said, 'How did you manage to do that?'

'A chap just walked in and made me an offer for them.'

He could see now from my face that I was not pleased. Johnnie was very naïve in the art of wheeling and dealing. 'He just walked in and made you an offer for them?'

'Yes,' he said.

'And just how much did he offer you?'

'He offered me £500 but I got him up to £800. After all, we only paid £20 each for them.'

'Come with me, Johnnie,' I said. I led him to the

antiques shop and as soon as I looked in the window, my heart sank. My chairs weren't there, and neither was his pair. He was definitely a fast mover, I thought to myself. The door was locked and a closed sign was on it. I knew there was nothing I could do: the chairs were gone. I didn't want Johnnie to feel bad about it, so I tried not to make a fuss, but I could have killed him.

That wasn't the only bad experience I had with an antiques shop owner over the years, though. I was walking through the Lanes one day, searching the windows of all of them, hoping I might come across some of my jewellery that had gone missing from home. I had come home recently to find that lots of my most precious items had been taken from my jewellery box, and although we had our suspicions about who might have taken it, we had no proof. To my absolute amazement, in the window of one of the shops, I saw what I thought was a charm bracelet of mine, a treasured family heirloom that Granny had given to Mummy on her wedding day and that Mummy had then passed on to me.

I went into the shop and asked the man behind the counter if I could have a look at it. Sure enough, it was mine. I recognized the dates on the sovereigns, which were all very old, and I remembered them because we'd had to get it insured. Stupidly, I told the man in the antiques shop, 'This is my bracelet and it was stolen from my home.'

'I'm sorry, madam, this is not my shop,' he said. 'You'll have to come in and see the boss and he won't be in until tomorrow.'

I went straight home, got on the phone to the police station and explained what had happened. The burglary had been reported, so there was a record of the incident. 'Well, I'm awfully sorry, madam, but we can't do a thing today,' the police officer on the other end of the line told me. 'Everybody's tied up and there is tight security in the town.'

'Why, what's happening?'

'Princess Margaret's in town and every available policeman and woman is needed for security.'

The next morning I was on the phone to the police station again, and I asked for an officer to come with me to the shop, to try to retrieve my bracelet. As I walked towards the shop window with the policeman, I was pleased to see my bracelet still on display. As we entered the shop, it was a different man behind the counter.

'Are you the boss of this shop?' I said.

'Yes,' he replied.

'Leave this to me,' the policeman said. 'This lady

believes that the bracelet in your window was stolen from her.'

The man went to the window, retrieved the bracelet and showed it to the policeman. 'It was sold to me about a month ago by a young man,' he said.

'Have you got any paperwork on it?' the policeman asked.

'Certainly,' the shop owner replied.

I was uneasy now, as the shop owner was too confident. I almost snatched the bracelet from the policeman's hand and examined it. I looked at the policeman in dismay.

'They've changed the sovereigns,' I said. 'Mine were much older than these. They're not the ones I saw when I came in yesterday.'

'Crafty bastards,' I thought. I felt like wrecking their shop.

The owner appeared from the back with some papers in his hand. 'Here you are,' he said, as he handed them over.

The policeman was not daft either. 'I'll take the paperwork, and I'll take the bracelet until we get this sorted out,' he said.

A phone call later that afternoon confirmed my suspicions. The young man who had sold the shop owner my bracelet had given a false address, and, realizing what had happened and knowing he would not get the money back that he had paid for my bracelet, the shop owner made sure that it couldn't be identified as mine. It was no good. The trail had gone cold and I never did get my bracelet back.

TWELVE

No Room at the Inn

My new friend, Pat Dearson, had now become my secretary. A recipe for disaster, you may think, to mix business with pleasure, but in actual fact, when we were working, we were both the ultimate professionals. She always called me Madam Petulengro and showed great respect in front of clients and business people. I loved her for her sense of humour, and we have remained great friends to this day.

It was time to visit Bristol again, but this time I hadn't done my homework, and when I phoned my usual hotel, they were fully booked. After trying several hotels I knew of, all to no avail, at last I found one that had a suite available. I was not happy, as I had not heard of it, but nonetheless it was a suite and a place to sleep, so we booked it. It was quite near to the railway station, which was one good thing, but when we arrived, to our dismay it wasn't what I would call a hotel. It was actually a run-down pub which had some *very* basic accommodation. When we were shown to our suite, our faces dropped. Pat walked into the bedroom and after a couple of minutes called to me, 'Eva, come here quick!' She had turned back the bedcovers and the mattress was crawling with fleas.

'We can't do anything about it right now,' I commented, trying to sound as calm as possible. 'But when we've finished work, we'll go and find a decent hotel to sleep in.'

We finished work that night at around eight and I whispered to Pat, 'Taxi, quick, let's go and find a real hotel.' We jumped into the taxi and I said to the driver, 'Do you know of a decent hotel that will have a room?'

'Oh, you'll have a tough time this week: there are three conferences on in the town and I know for a fact that most places are fully booked, as I've taken my customers to them all.'

'Well,' I said, 'take us out of the town then, wherever you think there might be a decent hotel.'

He raised an eyebrow. 'I wouldn't hold out much hope, my dears, but I'll try.'

We drove to around ten different hotels, and all were fully booked. Pat and I looked at each other. 'What are we going to do now?' I said, despondent.

'Well, we can't sleep in those beds, can we?'

I suddenly saw the funny side of our situation and

started to laugh. 'We're stranded with nowhere to lay our little heads.'

We always managed to keep a sense of humour, and even though our plight was a hard one, I'd been through worse and I knew others in the world were currently facing bigger woes, so all we could do was laugh. We were both beginning to feel tired, as we'd had a very long day.

'Mr Driver,' I said, begging now, 'how about you take us to a decent restaurant then, so we can at least get some food?' We tried three, but they were also fully booked and we could see now that this was beginning to turn into a farcical night. 'Drive us back to our hotel. There's only one thing for it,' I said, resolutely.

'What's that?' Pat said, eager to hear my plan.

'Well, they sell crisps in the bar, don't they? I'm sure they would go down well with a few drinks . . .'

By the time we'd eaten two bags of crisps each and downed three large gins, we were beginning to feel a little better about our situation. Neither of us dared mention the bed full of fleas waiting upstairs for us, and when we did venture up, Pat immediately pulled back the bedcovers.

'What are you doing?' I asked. 'Seeing if they've checked out?'

Gin taken into consideration, there was still no way we were getting into that bed. Then I noticed two armchairs and an idea struck me. I headed off to see the landlady, before returning a few minutes later with a clothes brush in hand. 'This should do it!' I said enthusiastically as I started vigorously brushing the armchairs.

Pat stood watching me, shaking with laughter. The brush, due to my aggressive usage, had turned on its side, so that I was now brushing the armchair with the hard side. 'Get out of here! Get out of here!' I yelled at the fleas. I'm sure the people in the next-door rooms would have thought we were doing some sort of an exorcism, if it were not for the laughter in between the shouting. We took some clothes out of our bags and began draping them over the armchairs.

'I don't know about you,' I said, 'but it's going to take another gin and tonic to get me to sleep tonight.'

'I was just going to say the same thing,' she replied.

Pat went and got the drinks, and as we were sipping them, we could hear noises coming from the room next door. Bang. Thud. It sounded as if someone was falling over, and then we heard some sort of scuttling noise. We put the TV on as loud as we could and sat having our drinks. It had been a very long night. Gingerly, we lowered ourselves onto the armchairs and, luckily for the fleas, we fell straight to sleep.

*

The next morning, I woke up aching in all my joints from having rested my weary body in such an uncomfortable spot. As we were leaving the hotel to go and find some real food before my first clients arrived, we bumped into the landlady.

'Did you sleep well, ladies?' she said. Pat and I could not help ourselves. We just burst out laughing, unable to answer her question. Pat did manage a question in return though.

'Excuse me,' she said, 'but who's in the room next door to ours?'

The landlady gave her a curious look. 'The room next to yours? No one.'

'But we heard so many noises coming from there. Do you think it's ghosts then?' Pat said, her eyes widening.

'Oh no, don't be so silly. That'll be the rats.'

Ravenous, we headed straight to the station for breakfast and as we wolfed down our food, I looked at Pat and asked, 'Do you think it can get any worse?'

She laughed. 'I wouldn't be surprised if it did.'

I felt the same. 'As soon as you've shown the first client in, Pat, I want you to get on the phone and call round all the hotels to see if any vacancies have come up. Check and double-check, and give them our number and tell them to ask for you when something comes up,' I instructed.

But nothing did come up and in the end we slept on those chairs for three nights. Pat made daily trips out to buy us food, which we mostly ate outside of the hotel – we could not stomach eating in the room. The day of our departure came and I asked Pat to phone the station to find out the time of the last train to London, where Johnnie and Brian would be waiting to pick us up. The last train left at seven thirty that night.

'Well, we'll be at the station for seven,' I said, 'just to make sure we've got plenty of time.'

We could not get away from those armchairs and the hotel quick enough. I don't think either of us had ever been so desperate to get home to our own comfortable beds. We stuffed the clothes we'd used as our bedcovers into some bin bags we'd bought, so that if anything was on them it wouldn't infest our suitcases, and vowed to send them straight to the cleaners when we got home. At the station, thinking we had half an hour to wait, we walked onto the platform and spoke to the guard.

'We've come to get the last train to London. What time is it due?'

He pointed up the line to a train that had just departed. 'That there is the last train. It's just left.'

We both gasped in horror. 'But my friend here phoned up and asked, and was told the last train was at seven thirty,' I said. When he shrugged his shoulders and looked at me as if to say 'It's not my problem,' I saw red. 'Who's in charge?' I demanded.

By this time his face had changed as he could sense my anger, so he was more than willing to palm me off on his boss. 'You want to talk to him in there,' he said, pointing to a door leading off the platform.

Without knocking, I unceremoniously opened the door and a startled middle-aged man looked up from his newspaper.

'Stop that train at the next station,' I demanded.

'What did you say, girly?' he said.

'Don't. Call. Me. Girly. Somebody told us, when we called today, that the last train to London left at seven thirty.'

'I was on duty today and a lady did enquire on the phone for the *first* train going to London, and I told her it was seven thirty,' he said.

'She asked you for the *last* train,' I told him. 'Now stop that train!' With this, I whipped out the press card I kept in my purse and poked it under his nose. 'You either get me a fast car and stop the train at the next station or you'll find yourself all over the national press tomorrow, I promise you. If you concentrated on your job more and the racing results a little less, neither one of us would be in this pickle. Now let's see some action.' I was barking at him like a sergeant major.

I must have hit a nerve because he immediately picked up the phone to contact the next station and then called for a car to pick us up. He really was holding up the train for us! Meanwhile, out on the platform, Pat, knowing what I was like by then, was stood by the porter, pointing to the roof of the office. They could hear me ranting from outside. Pat turned to the porter and said, 'Watch that roof – it's going to come off in a minute.'

Within five minutes, a black car pulled up to the entrance of the station and the manager helped load our bags into the boot. We got in and instructed the driver to get us to the next station as quickly as he could. When we arrived, we found a guard looking for us. As we hurried to the platform where the train was waiting, he said, 'Petulengro?'

'Yes, yes,' I cried.

'We've been waiting for you.'

'Thank you,' I replied as he began helping us with our bags. Once on board, we sat down on clean seats, our first clean seats in days. I went to the bar and returned with a bottle of champagne, every drop of which we savoured as we sped onwards to London, knowing we would be in our own beds that night. We let out a sigh of relief and then immediately broke into hysterics.

'Johnnie and Brian are not going to believe what's happened,' Pat said.

'Johnnie will,' I replied. 'He's used to me!'

The men were waiting for us in London, where we had arranged for the four of us to go out for a late meal, but we were too tired and, much to their disappointment, we asked them to take us straight back to Brighton instead. We were both asleep in the car before we'd left London and, once we got back, my bed had never felt so good.

There really is no place like home!

'The fleas in the bedroom can't be your only tale to tell,' Johnnie said the next morning, and of course it wasn't. I always enjoyed going to see my clients, but one client who will forever stand out in my mind – I shall call her Jane – had a problem with her husband. The problem was that they were no longer having sex. They had given up after trying everything from dirty magazines to sex toys, and eventually had even sought advice from the doctor. She came to see me, I felt, as a last resort.

I said to her, 'Do either of you drink?'

'Oh no,' she replied.

'Well, I suggest that when you have your dinner tonight, you have a bottle of wine with it.'

This was to get them both to stop thinking about the sex and relax a little and, hopefully, with the help of a little alcoholic lubrication, allow nature to take its course!

'Oh, but we don't have dinner at night. We only have a snack or a few biscuits.'

This stopped me in my tracks for a minute. 'Well, have the wine with your biscuits,' I replied.

Thinking this over doubtfully, she nodded and left with a very bemused look on her face. Before I could turn around to take my seat again, there was a knock on the door. It was 'Jane'.

With her head to one side, she peeked around the door and asked, 'Red or white?'

Gobsmacked, I pronounced in my most confident voice, 'Get one of each!'

I received a letter a few days later. It had worked. I didn't hear from her again though. I just hope I didn't turn them into alcoholics!

THIRTEEN

Mystery and Mischief

One afternoon, I was working away behind my desk in my office at Ship Street Gardens when a couple of people walked in. A very smart young lady with long black hair, wearing a dark business suit and a white shirt, was followed by a uniformed chauffeur, complete with peaked cap.

'Madam Petulengro?' the girl enquired.

'That's me,' I smiled. 'How can I help you?'

'We've come to ask if you would come to give a reading to an important lady?'

'Can't she come here?' I asked.

'I'm afraid not. She's very keen to have a reading though, and you come highly recommended.'

'Well, who is she?' I was keen to know the identity of my mystery client. 'And where does she live?'

'It's on the outskirts of Brighton,' the girl continued, 'and we can pick you up and bring you home again.'

I was intrigued by now. She had spoken very

respectfully to me and so I agreed and made arrangements that they would pick me up the following evening at seven. After they had left, I went over to Pat's house across the lane and enquired if she'd like to accompany me.

Pat and Brian were involved in many different businesses and were always entertaining people, so I wasn't in the least bit surprised when she said 'I'm sorry, but I can't because we've got people coming for dinner tomorrow night.'

The following evening, about twenty to seven, Brian came to my door. 'Everyone's just about to arrive for our dinner and although I've got plenty of booze, I forgot to buy vodka for Pat. Have you got any you could lend me?'

'Hang on,' I said, and ran upstairs, where I found a new bottle of vodka.

Brian, Johnnie and I were always playing jokes on each other. It was what kept us smiling. So, just as I picked up the bottle, a naughty idea came into my head. I poured the vodka into a big green water jug and filled the bottle up with water from the tap. Keeping a straight face, I went downstairs and handed the bottle to Brian.

'Hope the evening goes well for you,' I said. 'That's not chilled, you'd best put it in the fridge straightaway.' Away he went, with a bottle of water that he and Pat would think was vodka.

'Johnnie,' I said on my departure, 'while I'm gone, Pat or Brian should come over shortly asking for vodka, as I filled up the bottle they've borrowed with water for a laugh.'

Johnnie grinned, wondering, as I did, how long it would take them to come back for the real drink. Childish maybe, but amusing nonetheless.

Discreetly dressed, I was driven out of Brighton in a sleek limousine. We turned into a very long driveway through some gates. I could see trees, deer grazing and peacocks strutting about on the lawns. I was overawed by the beauty of the place. I was also starting to become quite intrigued by the thought of who lived in such a beautiful home.

'We have to take you in the back way,' the chauffeur informed me.

The car drove along a gravel driveway and stopped in front of the main house – a beautiful white three-storey mansion that the driver told me was called Buxted Park and dated back to the early 1700s. The driver opened the car door for me and I was met by Maria, the lady who had come to my office to request the reading, who then ushered me inside the breathtaking building.

We went through several corridors and, as we walked along one, there was a maze of bedrooms and running in and out and along the corridor were six or seven children, all immaculately dressed in satin pyjamas of various colours. The children were absolutely beautiful, with big eyes and long eyelashes.

At the end of the corridor, we turned left into a very large and luxurious lounge. On the walls were paintings and photos, and I was overwhelmed by the quality of the furniture. The carpets were the colour of fine golden sand and made me think of a desert. Three ladies wearing yashmaks and flowing robes in various colours entered the room and talked among themselves in a language I couldn't understand or identify. Maria exchanged a few words with one of the ladies and then turned to me and said, 'I am the interpreter, as these ladies do not speak English.'

I was not happy with this at all. I didn't like working through interpreters and had I known this at the outset, I would not have agreed to come, but since I was there, I decided to make the best of it. Another of my rules was that I very rarely read in front of an audience as I'd had some bad experiences, one of which was when a man and a woman turned up for an appointment along with a television crew.

'What we'd like you to do,' the TV people had said, 'is to give a reading on camera.'

I felt uncomfortable about the whole thing, but they had put me on the spot so I agreed. I read the gentleman's hand first and told him I could see that he was involved in publishing and writing, to which he replied, 'No.'

'I don't want to argue with you,' I said, 'but your hands and my sixth sense tell me that you have had your works published.'

'Well, I have in the past,' he replied.

Anyone who'd ever been to me for a reading knew that I didn't stand for nonsense. 'That's all I've got to tell you,' I said. I was very impatient with him.

I then turned to the young woman who spread out her hands. 'According to your hands,' I said, 'you've been married four times.'

'No, I've never been married,' she replied. My anger was building.

'OK, I'll put it another way – you've lived with four different men as man and wife.'

To this, she replied, 'Yes, I have.'

By then, I'd had enough. I realized I was being used. 'They're going to try and use this against me,' I thought. I said, 'Pack up your equipment and leave.'

It was to be aired, I discovered, on television the following week. 'I don't want this to go out until I've seen the film,' I said. They assured me a tape of the interview would be sent to me, but of course it never turned up and, with trepidation, Johnnie and I sat and watched the programme when it aired. It was a setup. They'd edited the footage, so that when I told the man about the writing, all they showed was him saying, 'No, I'm not a writer.' They didn't put in the bit where I'd asked him if he had had work published and he'd said he had. With the girl, they showed me saying, 'You've been married four times,' but cut out the bit where I said she had lived with four men, which she agreed was correct. There was only ever one intention – to make it appear that I was a fraud.

Who had set this up? I had a rough idea. It was someone whose advances I had spurned years earlier. I'd always known he held a grudge and had been waiting for this day for a long time. He'd tried to set me up once before, with three ladies whom he had paid to have readings and had told to report back, but they had been so happy with their readings that he had got nothing from them.

I made a vow then that I would never be set up again, which was one of the reasons I loathed the idea of an audience. But mainly I disliked the idea as it interfered with my work.

I explained to Maria, the interpreter, that the circumstances were not ideal and it was going to be very difficult for me to give a reading because I would be picking up vibes from everyone in the room.

Maria said, 'Madam would like to ask you some questions, if that's OK.'

I glanced in the direction of the lady of the house.

I guessed she was in her late thirties and she was strikingly beautiful, with long, shiny black hair, an oval-shaped face, olive complexion and huge brown eyes, framed by sweeping lashes. But there was a shadow of worry on her face. Something was troubling this woman.

'OK,' I said. 'What would she like to ask me?'

She translated my question for the lady, who walked over to me, got hold of my elbow and steered me towards a very big photograph mounted on the wall. It was a picture of a young man, who must have been aged roughly nineteen at the time the picture was taken.

Maria said, 'Madam would like to know if you feel anything about this person.' Madam was standing very close to me, and I looked at her. Where the vibes came from – from her or the picture – I wasn't sure. 'That young man has chest problems,' I said.

'Yes, yes,' responded Maria. I asked Maria to tell Madam that I would like to look at her palms and was guided to a small table, where two chairs were arranged. I sat on one side and Madam sat opposite me and held out her beautifully manicured hands. We have a rule in clairvoyance that we never touch a client's hands, but I could not help myself, I was so fascinated by the elaborate artwork etched in henna on her skin. I then did the usual thing and interpreted what the hands told me. Each time I paused, Maria passed on the information to the woman, who was by now very relaxed and very happy with what I had seen and told her.

The house, the people in it and the atmosphere were all quite alien to me, and I was very relieved when it was over. The chauffeur led me out of the room and along the passageway where I had seen the beautiful children. Maria joined us in the car and passed me a white envelope. I assumed it would be my fee because no money had been mentioned at all. I slipped it into my purse, overcoming the desire to see what they had given me. As we drove back down the long driveway, Maria said, 'Madam has invited you and your family for dinner.'

I didn't want to go, but at the same time was flattered. Amazed that I was turning down the invitation, the chauffeur interrupted. 'Don't be so silly,' he said. 'If this family invites guests for dinner, the guest never leaves without a gift of £5,000. They are very wealthy people.'

They both tried to persuade me, but I was often invited to parties just to do readings for the other guests. Been there, done that, and didn't want to do it again!

On my return home, I'd forgotten completely about the prank I'd played on Brian, but was reminded when Johnnie said, to my amazement, 'No one came for the vodka.' Surely they would have sussed by now? I could not have imagined Pat would get through a dinner party without a drink. I nipped out of our front door and back across the lane and rang Pat and Brian's door-bell. To my astonishment, Pat answered the door with a flushed face and eyes which were brightly sparkling. She definitely looked tipsy!

'Have you finished your vodka, Pat?' I asked inno-cently.

'No, there's plenty left, would you like one?' she replied.

'What did you drink it with?' I enquired.

'Tonic water.'

'No, you've been drinking tonic water with *water*,' I said triumphantly, holding up the green jug.

'Away man,' Pat said in her Newcastle accent. 'No way.'

'Pat, you're as pissed as a fart, have you been drinking anything else?'

She laughed, obviously convinced I was winding her up.

'I'll leave you to it,' I said, and walked back to my cottage, giggling all the way.

When I locked the door behind me, I noticed my bag on a table in the hallway and remembered the envelope Maria had given me. Curious now, I pulled it out of my purse and took out the wad of notes from inside. I had to count it three or four times as I couldn't believe my eyes – she had paid me £5,000 for a ten-minute reading! What an evening it had been!

FOURTEEN

Dirty Business

Pat, Brian, Johnnie and I had decided to go out for a meal one evening. Babysitters organized, off we set, and spent three hours in the Nang King Chinese restaurant talking about our children and thoroughly enjoying ourselves. The four of us walked home together through the Lanes and instead of ringing the doorbell, which might have woken the children up, the men fished in their pockets, looking for their keys, when all of a sudden Pat exclaimed, 'Oh my God.'

She was pointing at our doorstep, which stood a little way back from the lane. Sitting on the step was a very large turd, and not something a dog had done either. Someone had obviously dropped their trousers and done their business at our front door! Johnnie quietly let himself in and came back very quickly with carrier bags and cleaned the mess up, while Brian was curled up, laughing his head off. He obviously thought it was hilarious!

As does everyone with children, we had a very early start the next morning, and Johnnie went outside to collect the milk for everyone's breakfast. He called out to me: 'Quick, you've got to come and see this.'

I rushed outside, wondering what I was going to find this time, to see that on the wall next to my front door was a toilet roll on a holder and next to it a sign that said, 'Please help yourself'. There was also a nail with a hand towel hanging from it. We could not help but laugh, as Brian and Pat had the same sense of humour as us and were obviously behind it all. Under his breath, I heard Johnnie promise, 'I'm gonna get them back for this one,' and I knew he would!

Johnnie came up with a good idea to pay Brian back. We saw the family go out about seven o'clock in the evening, and Johnnie put his head out the window and said, 'Where are you all going?'

'We're going out for dinner,' Brian said.

'Have a good time,' Johnnie replied. Walking into the lounge with a big grin on his face, he announced, 'Right, action stations – where's your needlework box?'

I thought I was being funny when I said, 'What, you want a needle and thread to stitch him up then?'

'You could say so,' Johnnie said mischievously. Going out of the room, he returned with a box and from it he pulled a see-through button. He also produced a reel of fishing line and handed them both to me. There I stood, with a button in one hand and the fishing line in the other. Johnnie fetched his ladder from the little yard at the back of the house and carried it, along with the button and fishing line, through the lounge and out the front door, propping up the ladder outside Brian and Pat's bedroom window. He deftly threaded the button onto the end of the line and tied it into a secure knot. Then, using a small pin, he secured the line that held the button to the top of the window. At this point, I still didn't have a clue what was going on in my husband's head. Johnnie then put the ladder next to our top window and threw the reel of fishing line into the bedroom.

As I followed him upstairs, all became crystal clear.

'Look at this, Jules,' he said. He opened the window and pulled the line taut, which was invisible from the street, and demonstrated how he was going to annoy Brian and probably Pat too. With the window wide open, he tugged the line with the button secured at the other end and, as he pulled it backwards and forwards, we could hear it tapping on their window. We could not wait for them to come home and go to bed that night. When they did return, we watched and waited for the downstairs lights to go out and knew they'd gone upstairs to bed.

'We'll give them half an hour to get settled,' Johnnie said with a mischievous grin. Half an hour seemed more like an hour, but when the time came, he announced, 'Right, leave the downstairs light on, turn the bedroom light off, but whatever you do, don't let anybody see you peering through the window.'

I had to put my hand over my mouth to stifle my giggles. Johnnie began pulling the fishing line backwards and forwards and it began tap-tap-tapping on their bedroom window. It took several minutes before Brian's face appeared at the window. He must have thought it was a seagull or something. Johnnie stopped tapping and watched as Brian opened his window and looked left and right for the source of the noise. After looking up and down the lane for a couple of minutes, Brian disappeared from view and the window closed.

'We'll give it a couple of minutes,' Johnnie said, enjoying himself. 'Let him get nicely settled in bed again.'

We went through the routine again, then we too went to bed.

The next morning, Johnnie pretended to be doing something to our window box outside as he waited for Brian to emerge. 'Morning, Bri,' Johnnie said, as Brian came out of his door.

'Morning,' Brian said with a yawn. 'Did you hear any funny noises last night?'

'What kind of noises?' Johnnie enquired.

'A bit like a bird pecking the window.'

Johnnie looked at him. 'You need to take more water

with it, Brian,' he said, and went inside and closed the door, stifling his giggles.

After returning from work that evening, Brian came and knocked on our door, holding my see-through button in his hand. He must have been thinking about it all day. He must also have seen something in Johnnie's naughty schoolboy look that morning that made him very suspicious. We all had a good laugh about it and Johnnie and Brian both promised to call a truce, which I doubted would ever happen. They both had exactly the same sense of humour, and I could already see their brains ticking over, thinking about what they could do next.

FIFTEEN

A Royal Snub

I was invited backstage to give a reading to the singer Tony Bennett, who was performing at the Dome in Brighton. Joy, oh joy! I loved the man's voice, and especially the song 'I Left My Heart in San Francisco', one of his top tunes, and here I was backstage with him.

On such visits, Eddie, Nathan or Johnnie always came along to take the photos, depending on who was available, and that evening Johnnie was with me, sitting silently at the back of the room. But there were tons of other people milling all around us, from managers and publicists to hair stylists and make-up artists, and I wondered how on earth I was ever going to be able to give a reading. But luckily for me they were also making Tony feel quite uncomfortable, so once I had been introduced to him, he whispered in my ear very quietly, 'Eva, can you get rid of the other people in the room?'

I must admit, I was taken aback, as he knew them all already whereas I didn't have a clue who any of them were. I thought to myself, 'Why doesn't he just ask them to leave? Why get me to do it?' However, I quickly sent everyone on their way, telling them I didn't give readings with an audience. I felt genuinely sorry for Tony, who was so shy. I won't reveal what we talked about but I can say, however, that his hands revealed he had great artistic gifts aside from his voice.

'Have you ever tried painting?' I asked him.

He smiled. 'Does that really show in my hand?'

'Well, it's not written across your forehead, is it?' I replied. I frequently came out with silly remarks like this when I was giving a reading, as my brain was rushing ahead of what I was saying, and immediately I regretted being so curt. I felt embarrassed but, to my relief, he started to laugh.

'Well, it sure is true, Eva. It's one of my hobbies and I find it very relaxing.'

Reading done, I had a photograph taken with Mr Songbird, and his publicist requested that Johnnie went behind Tony on stage, to photograph him with the English audience. Johnnie was only too happy to oblige and he sent the pictures over to America for him. When we inspected the photographs more closely, we found at least fifteen people in the audience that we knew, and they were thrilled when we presented them with big photos of themselves watching Tony. This included my brother Eddie with a girl we didn't know! Some things never change . . .

As I had been introduced to more and more famous people over the years, I had begun to realize that they are just normal people and that most of them have the same hang-ups as the rest of us. But although they most often don't like to live their lives under the media spotlight and crave some privacy, most would hate not to be recognized by us mere mortals when they walk down the street!

Around the same time as I gave Tony Bennett his reading, a friend of mine by the name of Miles, who was also a regular at Winnie's pub, the Cricketers, owned a coffee bar called the Lorelei in the Lanes. A man walked in one day and although his face was familiar, Miles could not place him and said, 'I'm sorry, sir, we're closing now.'

The following day, Miles received a note from a friend who owned an antiques shop next door. Apparently, Princess Margaret and her husband had been in his shop buying antiques and he had recommended the Lorelei to the couple. In the note, the owner of the antiques shop said, 'Oh, so you don't serve royalty?'

The man he had turned away, who looked so familiar, was Lord Snowdon!

I often see Miles to this day. He is a fabulous person with a great sense of humour, a man who lights up a room and enables everyone in it to bask in his inner glow of happiness and well-being. He's just never been very good with putting names to faces!

I almost had my own brush with royalty shortly after through a gentleman called Bill who had been coming to see me to seek my advice. He had the idea to start a lobster farm in England. It was an area I knew nothing whatsoever about. I also found out, after talking to him for a while, that he was buying up land in Portugal, where he told me lots of the locals had small plots of land, just large enough to build a house on. He was buying this from them for peanuts, hardly anything at all.

'Do you mind if I just run some of my ideas past you?' he asked me. 'To see what reaction I get from you?'

'Be my guest,' I said.

He became a regular visitor, coming to see me about once a month, and each time he would bring a box of about a dozen live lobsters. I hadn't much room in my small fridge and freezer, so I could not cook them all. On the seafront was a restaurant that was part of a chain called Wheelers. Johnnie and I would dine there occasionally and the manager would make a big fuss of us. I knew Bill would be coming the following day with another dozen lobsters for me and asked the manager if he would like to have them.

'I believe they're bred in Canada,' I told him. 'A friend of mine has been bombarding me with them for the last six months.'

The manager said, 'How about we do a deal, Eva? You and Johnnie can eat here once a week for free, including drinks, in exchange for the lobsters.'

It was a done deal and we shook on it.

A couple of weeks later, about ten thirty in the evening, Johnnie and I were watching television when there was a knock at the door. Johnnie invited the caller in. It was the manager from Wheelers. Thinking he wanted lobsters, I said, 'The cupboard is bare, darling, I'm not expecting any more for ten days.'

'It's not lobsters I'm after,' he said.

'Sit down then. What can I do for you?' I indicated a chair.

'I have a party of people in and somehow or other your name was mentioned and they've asked me to see if I can get you to come round to give them readings.'

'Well, what time did they arrive at your restaurant?'

'Eight o'clock,' he said.

'And what drinks are they on?' I asked.

'An assortment,' he laughed.

'So they'll be a little bit merry then?' I enquired.

'You could say that,' he replied with a smile.

'Well, darling, I'm not a side show or a cabaret for people who have been drinking. If they're serious about a reading, give them my card and tell them to come and see me during the day.'

A look of dismay spread over his face. 'All right, Eva, I'll tell you the truth. It's Princess Margaret and her friends.'

That threw me for a minute, but I stuck to my guns. 'That makes it worse,' I said. 'Here I am in my dressing gown, relaxing. It means I've got to get dressed and do my face and hair, and it's nearly eleven o'clock. Please give her my apologies, but tell her I'm otherwise engaged.'

With that, we showed him out and settled back down in our pyjamas and dressing gowns to continue watching our movie.

'Royalty or not, I'm not missing a good film,' I told Johnnie.

SIXTEEN

A New Arrival

It was May 1968, and I had ten days before the predicted due date of my third baby. I was supposed to be going to my mother's flat in West Street, where I would be seeing some clients, but when I woke up, Johnnie was staring at me with a look of shock on his face.

'What's the matter?' I said.

'Look in the mirror,' he replied.

My face was completely contorted. My mouth was lopsided, my left eye was wide open and I could not blink, no matter how hard I tried. Johnnie, without a word to me, phoned the doctor and told her to meet us at my mother's flat.

When we arrived and rang the bell, Mummy opened the door, took one look at me and said, 'That's not very nice.'

She too had a contorted face, from an abscess, and thought I was taking the mickey out of her. Before we could close the door, Doctor Roe appeared. We all went into the lounge and the doctor examined my face.

'I'm sorry, Eva,' she said. 'You're stuck with this for a while. It's called Bell's palsy. We're not really sure what causes it, but some say that it can be brought on by sitting in a draught.'

Immediately, Johnnie said, 'Well, we did have a long drive the other day, with the car window open.'

Dear Doctor Roe was being kind because there was no cure for Bell's palsy, which had paralysed the muscles down one side of my face, but she obviously didn't want to upset me in my pregnant state.

My third birth was at the same maternity hospital in Buckingham Road where I'd had my first two sons. When I arrived, the matron said, 'Eva, this is becoming a habit, isn't it?'

I certainly had a feeling of déjà vu.

But unlike the previous two times, everything went without a hitch, and I gave birth to another beautiful boy, who Johnnie named Carl Gregory. Johnnie arrived with Warren and Bradley in matching new outfits, and they gazed at their new brother, their faces filled with curiosity as they touched his tiny hands.

'How little he is, Mummy,' they said, almost in unison.

'Can he sleep with me?' Brad said.

'No, me,' Warren chimed in.

'We'll see,' I said. 'Perhaps when he's a bit bigger.'

Doctor Roe then came round and explained to me the truth of my condition, and said that it was unlikely to improve.

'Good job I didn't marry you for your looks,' Johnnie chimed in.

I looked at him and saw immediately from his eyes that what had happened to me made not the slightest difference to the love he felt for me, and I fell in love with him even more. 'Nor I you,' I replied with my lopsided smile.

Over the years, the effect of Bell's palsy has brought us a great deal of laughter. For instance, wherever I went, men would wink at me, simply because they thought that I was winking at them, as my left eye could no longer blink. I would have to move the eyelid manually if I needed to clear or close my eye.

On one occasion, there was a crowd of us going to the Goodwood races and facing me on the coach was a table of men playing cards. When we got off the bus at Goodwood, the man who had been sitting opposite me came and shook my hand.

'I know who you are, Eva,' he said. 'And thank you ever so much for your help.'

'Why are you thanking me?' I asked.

'Well, I know you're a clairvoyant and every time

I looked at you, wondering whether to bet on my hand, you gave me a wink and I took this to be a sign that I should go for it. I've won £250!'

SEVENTEEN

Two Peas in a Pod

Life was blissful. Johnnie and I had never been happier and my three boys – Warren, five, Bradley, four, and Gregory, three – were all perfect in their own ways. And, yes, all of my boys had become known by their second names rather than the names we had given them. I don't know why we didn't just use their middle names as their first names to begin with!

They had all inherited their father's wicked sense of humour, and were gradually starting to show their creative sides. Bradley loved to sing and was very musical, while Warren and Gregory would spend hours sitting with Johnnie as he taught them to draw and paint.

It was 1971 and family attitudes were still very traditional, but I had always been so lucky with Johnnie, who believed we were a partnership and should share all the jobs that needed doing. He would help to get the boys up in the morning, bath them and get them ready for bed at night. And when I was away for work he would do everything himself, although not always quite to my standards! There were many occasions when I walked in the door and found a tin of Smash in the kitchen as he couldn't be bothered to peel potatoes!

With everything going so well with my work too, life really was wonderful. And to top it all off, I was pregnant with our fourth child. Recently I hadn't been able to shake the feeling that something was missing, but it didn't take me long to realize what that was – I wanted a little girl. I longed for that female bond that had always existed between me and my mother, and I knew how much the boys would love a baby sister to look after. Not to mention Johnnie who was desperate for a little girl.

I was a week overdue when the contractions started. Johnnie stayed at home with the children while I went to the Sussex County Hospital. When I got to the ward, I was shown to a room and told the baby wouldn't arrive for another four or five hours. 'What rubbish!' I thought. Within half an hour, I knew the baby was on its way and called for help. No one came.

There was an emergency bell on the wall above the bed, which I only just managed to reach. Whoever had installed it had not thought about how hard it would be for a pregnant woman to stretch so far. I almost had to stand up to get to it. Suddenly, in ran several midwives in response to the bell, which was lucky as my baby's head had already appeared. I didn't even have to push – the baby just about swam out and was immediately whisked away to a corner of the room, where everyone crowded round. After what seemed like an eternity, to my relief, I heard the baby cry. A smiling midwife brought my little bundle over to me.

'Well done, Mrs Tullett. You've given birth to a beautiful little daughter.'

At last I had my little girl – I was thrilled. I couldn't wait to tell Johnnie and the boys. I looked into her big inquisitive eyes and knew then and there that we would be like two peas in a pod, forever close, just like I had always been with my own mother. I gave her a kiss and said hello to my new best friend.

I called for a phone to tell Johnnie he had his girl.

'I don't believe it,' he said joyously. 'I'll be there in ten minutes.' Within seven minutes, Johnnie and the three boys ran into my hospital room. 'Where is she?' Johnnie asked eagerly. This was in the days when babies were kept in a room together away from the mothers, so when a nurse followed Johnnie into the room I asked her if she would be kind enough to get my daughter and bring her to me.

After about fifteen minutes of waiting, Johnnie said, 'I'm glad that's not our child in the hall. Everyone is stopping to touch it and look at it.'

As he said these words, our eyes met and Johnnie jumped up and ran into the hall. I followed on his heels and there was our baby lying gurgling in a cot. I whisked her up and took her into the ward, while Johnnie and the boys just gazed at her in amazement. Although I had declared that I wanted six children, I knew that Claire Victoria would be the last. My family was now complete.

Bradley said, 'Can we take her home?'

'Oh, yes, right now,' I said. I didn't even wait to sign myself out. Handing our precious bundle to Johnnie, I said, 'Home, James, and don't spare the horses.'

The boys helped carry my stuff out and I left the hospital in my nightdress. Once home, the boys came up to the baby carrying parcels, all prettily wrapped.

'You open them for her, boys. She isn't big enough yet to do it for herself,' I told them.

Warren said, 'I'm the oldest, am I the boss of her?'

Years later, she would always say to Warren, 'You're not the boss of me.'

I wonder, had she heard him?

Eddie and Mummy were waiting for us at home, desperate to meet the recent addition to the family, and Eddie's latest girlfriend was sitting next to him. Our family had nicknamed his latest flame Clarence, after the cross-eyed lion in *Daktari*, a popular children's television programme at the time, because this young woman, although beautiful, was also cross-eyed. She refused to wear spectacles and yet couldn't see the hand that was in front of her face. We all sat down, admiring our beautiful new baby, when Clarence said something that surprised us all.

'Come on then, Eva,' she said, 'let's have a look at this new baby, Go and get it.'

We were speechless and looked at each other in wonderment. Eddie jumped to his feet. 'Come on, you silly cow, that baby's been sitting in front of you on Eva's knee while we've been talking about her. Time we got you out of here,' he said with a laugh. From the fact that she stayed with Eddie for a while after he said that to her, I can only assume she was deaf as well as cross-eyed!

Although the boys were now at school, my workload at this time was very heavy. I was doing daily, weekly and monthly horoscopes for the newspapers and periodicals, as well as producing my horoscope guide, which I did completely unaided. I was also giving personal readings, and I realized something had to give. After Claire was born, I held her in my arms, looked at her and thought, 'I'm going to spend more time with this little girl.'

One morning, the phone rang and it was the printer

asking for the copy for my next horoscope guide, which was due out quite soon. I heard my voice say, 'Oh, I'm giving it up. I'm not going to be publishing my own horoscope guides anymore.'

It had always been a worry, and a lot of pressure, knowing that I had to write so much copy on time. To meet the deadlines, most nights I was at my desk working until ten o'clock.

Mummy greeted this news with two simple words. 'Thank God,' she said. 'Johnnie's been so worried about how hard you work, but we didn't want to influence you in any way. Not that we could have!'

When we sat down and talked about how much money the guides were bringing in, Johnnie said, 'Forget about the money. I think it's a good idea to have a break from the guides. Give yourself a year or two and then if you do decide to start them up again, I insist you get staff to help you. It's too much for one person, with all the other things you do.'

We agreed on this and I embarked on a more relaxed lifestyle with my sons and my daughter. At weekends, we would take off in the car, and Johnnie would always plan exciting places to take us. I'd never seen Arundel Castle, and as we walked around it, we all decided we didn't want to live in a castle, as it was too cold and bare. As we travelled round the country, we learned about England's past. I was getting the education I'd missed out on earlier in my life, and I was enthralled by it. I always had preferred experiencing something to just hearing or reading about it.

'How would you like to see the Crown Jewels?' Johnnie asked one morning.

I don't know who was more excited, the children or me, although when we got to the Tower of London, I have to admit, I was quite disappointed. After queuing for almost an hour, we were pushed past the jewels and were not allowed to stand and look at them, which was what I'd imagined. We did, however, have a good old look around London. I'd dressed Warren, Bradley and Gregory identically, as I always did, and because they were so close in age people assumed they were triplets. Johnnie had Claire in his arms as usual, and we jollied around London like real tourists, visiting Harrods to buy our little girl some pretty dresses. This reminded me of my cousin Daisy, as when I was expecting Warren she warned me that once you have a child you don't look at anything for yourself any longer and just want to buy things for your children. We continued our sightseeing, ending up, of course, at the famous Hamleys toy shop on Regent Street, where the children all chose a toy each. Having time off with my family was just what I had needed.

Other weekends, we'd go to Littlehampton and take the children around the amusements, which took me

back to when I was young and worked in the amusement parks. How strange it was to be a gorger now,
instead of a Romany trader punting on the stalls. As I
looked around, a young man called out from a dart
stall: 'Try your luck on the darts!'

I could not resist, because when I was fifteen and
we were living in Rhyl, in North Wales, I'd run a darts
stall myself. When it was quiet on the stall I would
practise throwing, but the darts were much lighter
than normal darts as they were made from cork
instead of wood and metal, so had I bought myself a
proper set and practised so much that I could beat
most of the other stallholders. This came in handy
later, when I started going out with Johnnie. The Shire
was a friendly little pub where some of his friends
played in the darts team, and they persuaded us to
join too. The first time Johnnie saw me play he was
so impressed. He would call out, 'Double top, Jewel,'
or whatever was needed, and wait for me to notch
up exactly the right score.

In Littlehampton, it wasn't until I got the darts in
my hand that I realized they'd been made deliberately
light, which made it difficult for anyone to aim properly. I managed to win a little plastic duck, though,
which we gave to Claire. Then I went on to the hoopla
stall and showed my boys how to cheat. You had to
throw the hoop over a plinth, which was cut so that

it slanted. If you threw the hoop at the top of the plinth, it was too wide to go over, so the trick was to aim to hit something behind the plinth – usually a stuffed animal or toy – and then the hoop would bounce onto the sharp bit of the plinth and wiggle its way down. Three bow-and-arrow sets and a stuffed penguin later, the stallholder gave me a wink.

'Got enough, love, move along now,' he said firmly. He'd obviously been watching my technique, and was more used to dusting his prizes than giving them away.

We walked past the waltzer, and it reminded me of a similar ride, the Twist, that was my favourite as a child, with its several arms, each with three or four cars that would spin in opposite directions. We would often go on it just before the fair was opened to the public and we would squeal with delight as it spun us round and round, the excitement numbing us to the bruises we developed on our hips as we slid from side to side on the seats. After the rides had been shut down for the evening and everything covered over with tarpaulins, us children would often climb underneath the plastic sheeting and put our hands down behind the seat cushions on the rides to collect any coins that had fallen out of people's pockets!

They were wonderful times, but my childhood days seemed so far behind me now. We wandered back to the car and at that moment, with my children round me, clutching their ice creams and candy floss, I knew my life was good. On many occasions the children and I would head off on days out with my neighbour Pat and her children, particularly during the summer when we would often go to the paddling pool on Brighton seafront or for picnics. One day I decided to take my big iron frying pan and my kettle hook, which had been a gift from my cousin Honour and her husband Eric, down to the beach. Before I left home, I chopped up some onions, or 'onons' as the family called them, and packed them up with some of my home-made sausages and some buns, to make hot dogs. I piled them all into Claire's pushchair, along with some wood, and off we set for our cookout.

When we got there, I noticed lots of bits of drift-wood and got Claire and Pat's daughters, Annabelle and Louise, to gather some wood for our fire. Pat and I pushed the kettle prop deep into the pebbles next to the fire, which was already underway, and laid my sausages in the pan. They began to sizzle almost immediately and after a while I turned them over. They were beautifully brown on one side and I intended to do the same to the other side. I'd made the sausages into the same shape as hamburgers and toasted the inside of the buns before I'd left home. When the sausages were cooked, I placed them on a metal dish which I'd heated over the fire. By now there was enough fat from the sausages in the pan to do the onions. Pork fat and onions are a wonderful combination. As I stirred the onions, Pat and I were chatting and the girls were filling their buckets with pebbles. We looked up and saw a policeman heading in our direction.

'Oh dear, we're in trouble,' I said, as he approached.

To my surprise he said, 'Is that you, Eva?'

'He's definitely going to lock me up,' I thought.

'Hello, kids,' he said pleasantly to the children.

I now recognized him, but could not work out exactly where I knew him from.

'I can smell your cooking from the seafront,' he said, 'and it smells bloody lovely.' Nodding his head towards the food, he said, 'I don't suppose you've got one of them going spare, have you?'

I made him a very large hot dog with all the trimmings, wrapping it in a piece of kitchen roll so as not to mess up his uniform, and handed it to him.

'Enjoy yourselves then, and thank you for the hot dog,' he said, and off he strolled.

It then occurred to me where I knew him from. He'd come to see me a year previously, about his penchant for dressing up in women's clothes! Hot diggity dog!

EIGHTEEN

A Whirlwind Romance

The first visit I had from the singer Kathy Kirby was in late 1969. She was about to kick her partner Bert Ambrose – who was more than forty years her senior – out of the flat they shared. Ambrose had been hugely influential in her career. She sang with his band and had many hit records with him. Kathy, a glamorous blonde bombshell, drew comparisons with Marilyn Monroe and was best known for her cover of the Doris Day hit 'Secret Love'. In 1965 she had represented the UK in the Eurovision Song Contest, but her most recent few songs had failed to chart. Ambrose was by then in his seventies and I advised her to wait, as I felt he would not be in this world much longer. Sixteen months was the date that came into my head, and I told her so.

'Because you're so very sensitive, I think you would blame yourself if he died after you'd kicked him out,' I said.

On a night out with Mummy and Daddy, just before Mummy decided enough was enough and sent Daddy packing.

Me and the love of my life, Johnnie, only a few weeks after our wedding.

Johnnie loved our cookouts as they gave him a glimpse of true Romany life. My cousin Daisy is on the left and Honour is on the right.

My consulting rooms on the ground floor of our house in Ship Street Gardens.

YOUR 1964 HOROSCOPE GUIDE BY **EVA PETULENGRO**

THE EVENING ARGUS ROMANY CLAIRVOYANTE

2/6

FEATURING
GODFREY WINN
DAME FLORA ROBSON
ALAN MELVILLE
TERENCE MORGAN
ELIZABETH ALLAN

...DS FROM THE SALE OF THIS PUBLICATION TO THE EVENING ARGUS APPEAL FOR CHILDREN AND OLD FOLK

An early issue of my horoscope guide. I had no idea it would be so successful.

Carrying out a reading for a client in Ship Street Gardens.

Johnnie with Warren, the eldest of our beautiful children.

At home with Warren and his little brother Bradley. Gregory would follow soon after – there was only a thirteen-month gap between the births of each of my boys!

Mummy in her dukkering (palm-reading) place on Brighton's Palace Pier.

Russell (right) with Eddie. He was the only one who could lift Eddie's spirits after his relationship with Nicky ended.

Eddie and Nicky. They could have been so happy together, but their lives pulled them in different directions.

My family was complete when my little girl arrived. Shortly after giving birth to Claire, I decided to stop writing my horoscope guide.

The boys were over the moon to have a little sister to fuss over!

With Kathy Kirby (to my left) and my good friend Winnie (opposite me).

Johnnie decorated my shop on Middle Street exactly like the inside of my granny's vardo (caravan). It looked very different from the sex shop it had been before we took it over!

On holiday in Cornwall. Nathan and Sue are on the right of the picture, and either side of me are John and Anna, who ran the Old Smithy where we stayed.

I always dressed the boys identically, so people often thought they were triplets!

Hunting for hedgehogs. Daisy's husband Sonny Boy is in the middle and Honour's husband Eric is leading the way.

At my cousin Pamela's wedding. We always loved an excuse to get the whole family together and to dress in our finest! Mummy is on the far left, next to Shunty and then Aunt Adeline. Daisy is in the grey dress (fifth from left) and to her left are Aunt Vera and Aunt Lena. I'm on the far right, next to my cousin Adeline.

The Vicarage, before we renovated it. We fell in love with it instantly and went on to spend many happy years there.

Claire with Lord Boothby, his watered-down whisky by his side. He and his wife Wanda became close family friends and Bob would capture the children's imaginations for hours with fascinating stories from his life.

'Eva,' she said, 'I have felt the very same thing myself. I'm going to take your advice.'

Exactly sixteen months later, Ambrose passed over. After his death, Kathy became a regular client of mine and would come to see me every time she had a major decision to make. She told me that she wanted to be my friend. 'Eva, I feel so comfortable in your company, and you make me laugh. Can we not be friends?'

'I'm sorry, Kathy, but I've never mixed business with pleasure. I try not to advise my friends on their problems, so you can either be my client or my friend.'

'Then I'll be your friend, Eva.'

A little while after this meeting, I was in London with my brother Eddie and I called Johnnie to tell him which train we would be getting on.

'Call Kathy, Jules, she's in an awful state. She needs to see you.'

I phoned the number Johnnie gave me and Kathy gave me an address and asked me to meet her there. It was a nightclub in central London, a very classy place. The taxi Eddie and I were in drew up at the same time as another cab, from which Kathy and her mother emerged. We entered the club together and from the way the manager greeted Kathy, it was easy to see they were old friends. As soon as we went inside, I searched for a phone booth and called Johnnie to tell him where we were in case any emergency arose. Then

I settled down to hear Kathy's latest woes. Of course, it was all about a man! However, the moment she set eyes on Eddie, she stopped telling me about her latest heartache and started fawning over him. He was loving every minute, relishing the attention being lavished on him. All of a sudden, a journalist friend of mine, Fred Pye, who used to work for the *Evening Argus* in Brighton, walked into the club and asked for me by name. The manager brought him to our table.

'I phoned you at home and Johnnie told me where you were,' he said, talking to me but looking the whole time at Kathy. Kathy's mother seemed to hate him on sight, but it was the opposite for Kathy, who turned all her attention on Fred, letting Eddie off the hook.

Kathy insisted we all return to her flat, which was in a mews in London, facing the 21 Club. The flat was marvellous, with a mirror all along the lounge wall and a barre where she practised ballet and went through her exercises.

'Eddie,' Kathy said, 'please go over to the 21 Club and ask for three bottles of champagne. Just tell them to put them on my bill.' Eddie did so, and we talked and drank champagne, watching romance blossom between Fred and Kathy all the while. I had rung Johnnie earlier to tell him what was happening, and just as well, as we did not leave the flat until the next morning.

A few days later, at about seven thirty in the evening, there was a knock on the front door at Ship Street Gardens. Johnnie opened up to find Fred and Kathy on the doorstep. Kathy looked very glamorous in a red fox fur jacket with a lovely black cocktail dress underneath and pouting, glossy red lips. Johnnie ushered them into our lounge.

Kathy said, 'Eva, we wanted you to be the first to know. We're going to get married!' I must say, I was really taken aback.

'But you've only known each other a few days. It's too soon,' I advised them in a motherly fashion.

'We both know this is the right thing,' Fred declared. 'We want your blessing.'

I looked at them and could see from their faces that whatever I said, they would go ahead with their plans anyway.

'Don't expect me to give you my blessing. I think you should wait for a little while,' I said.

'OK, Eva, I'll take your advice, but we're going to start living together anyway,' Kathy said.

It was clear they were besotted with each other, but I felt they did not yet know who it was they were besotted with, for they barely knew one other.

A few days earlier, Johnnie and I had inspected a windmill which was for sale in Brighton, more out of curiosity than anything else. It was beautiful, but not right for our family, as it wasn't suitable for the children. When Kathy declared that she'd like to live in Brighton, the windmill came to my mind.

'Well, there's always the windmill that's for sale,' I said, half jokingly.

'But Fred has always wanted to live in a windmill!' Kathy screamed.

'Really? How odd,' I said.

'Can you arrange for us to see it tomorrow?' Fred asked.

'I'll see what I can do. I'll ring them in the morning.' And with that, the loved-up couple went on their way, like two excited teenagers.

The next morning I phoned the agent and explained the situation. He was very excited that he would be meeting the great Kathy Kirby, and I arranged a time for them to meet at the windmill. Fred called shortly after, and I gave him the details.

'We'll ring you as soon as we've had a look at it,' he said.

Instead of phoning, a few hours later, they turned up at my door, and Kathy announced, 'We're moving in next week, Eva. He's going to allow us to rent it until the sale goes through.'

They certainly didn't let the grass grow under their feet, but as I looked at Fred, I sensed that there was something very much amiss with him. While Kathy went to the bathroom, Fred confessed that he was very worried, as this woman he had fallen so deeply in love with was drinking a bottle of vodka a day.

'Then it's up to you to help her, Fred,' I told him. 'I can't help her. If you two are truly in love, then she'll allow you to get her some help.'

He looked me squarely in the eyes and said, 'That's why you didn't want us to get married, isn't it?'

'Make a bargain with yourself,' I advised. 'If you can cure her of this addiction – not the easiest thing in the world to do, as she's got to want to do it too – but if you *can* wean her off it, then marry her. It will take time,' I warned him.

The following week, they did indeed move into the windmill. Kathy was doing a lot of work in London, as was Fred, so I didn't hear much from them until a couple of months later, at half past one in the morning, when the phone rang. It was Kathy.

'I need a drink, Eva. Fred won't go and get me any. Can you get me some?'

I scolded her like a naughty child. 'I'm a mother of four and you've rung me at this hour. Don't you think that's rather selfish of you? We've discussed your addiction and I told you that if you want a life with this man, you're going to have to be very strong, or you're going to lose him.' With that, I said a curt goodnight and placed the receiver back in its cradle.

I didn't hear anything for another six weeks, then we began receiving bills from hotels and health farms which I had certainly not ever visited, all addressed to Eva Petulengro. After making a few phone calls, it became clear that the bills had been run up by Kathy. What a cheek! Unsurprisingly, I didn't hear from her for many years after that.

NINETEEN

Instincts

I believe everyone has clairvoyant instincts. Usually people don't make use of them, however. I've heard many people say, 'I had a feeling that was going to happen,' or 'I wish I'd followed my instincts.' I've always followed my instincts, as do all my family.

Johnnie's brother was getting married in Nottingham, and the plan was that we would go to Littlehampton to pick up Johnnie's two sisters, Bubbles and Jean. We now had a wonderful nanny called Rosie. She was twenty-two and had blonde hair cut in a fashionable bob. Her ambition was to be a teacher, and she definitely seemed cut out to work with youngsters. She'd only been with us a short time, but immediately became one of the family, and the children adored her. As we set off, Johnnie walked in front of me, carrying our suitcase with our wedding gear in it, but as soon as I put one foot out of the door, I froze. I was looking at the big spiked railings that encased the front window.

I knew I should have followed Johnnie, but I had a feeling that stopped me in my tracks.

I called out, 'I can't go.' Johnnie didn't even enquire why, but started walking back towards me. I said, 'I need you to go without me.'

He knew me well enough by now to know there would be a good reason why I wasn't going to accompany him. I went back inside the house and the phone started to ring. I knew immediately that it was going to be bad news. It was Rosie's mother.

'Eva,' she said, sounding desperate. 'Thank God you're there. Rosie's dad has fallen off a ladder and impaled himself on a spiked railing.'

It suddenly clicked into place why I'd had that feeling when I'd seen the railings. 'Where are you?' I asked.

'I'm at the hospital.'

'Which one?'

'Sussex County.' Her voice began to break down with emotion.

'Right, I'm going to put Rosie in a taxi right now and send her up to you.'

I replaced the receiver and immediately phoned for a taxi, and heard myself ask for a large vehicle. In that split second, as I dialled the number, I had decided to accompany her and take the children with me, as I felt that both Rosie and her mother would need some support and comfort. Circumstances such as these confirm to me that one should always follow one's instincts, no matter how bizarre they may seem at the time.

Rosie's father did survive, by the way. He was a very lucky man.

But the incident deeply affected Rosie and her mother, as they were a very close-knit family. Once her father was on the mend, Rosie looked into my eyes and said, 'Eva, I know you'll understand when I tell you that I can't come back to work for a while.' I assured her that the right place for her was with her mum and dad.

It was then that I met Linda, who became our next nanny. She was in her twenties, slim, with dark curly hair and had a jolly, good-natured disposition. A former nursery nurse, she was a guardian angel to the children and my saviour. She saved me from going off my head when I found myself with so much to do. Linda could turn her hand to anything, and the bond between her and Claire was immediate. Our baby girl was only eighteen months old, so naturally we wanted to make sure we had someone we felt was capable, and Linda had all the right qualities. She very quickly became a surrogate member of our family and even today we still keep in touch.

*

The reason people came to see me, Mummy or my aunties was to ask us to use our clairvoyant instincts to help them with a problem or to see what lay around the corner for them, but often all they needed was some plain old common-sense advice. I remember the story of one man in particular who came to see Mummy when she was working on the pier. He seemed quite on edge as he walked into her dukkering booth, but what immediately caught Mummy's attention was the brown paper bag he was clutching tightly to his chest. When she asked him how she could help him, he said he had been growing increasingly concerned about his new wife who was incredibly jealous of his first wife, who had died several years earlier. He was in a quandary as she had said she would leave him unless he disposed of his late wife's ashes. When Mummy asked him where he kept them, he replied that they were in fact in the very paper bag he was holding on to for dear life! After recovering her composure, Mummy advised him to go to a favourite park or place his late wife enjoyed visiting and to scatter the ashes there. The man returned soon after and couldn't thank Mummy enough. She had only told him what anyone else would have, yet he firmly believed that it was her clairvoyant instincts that had saved his marriage!

There were many things people attributed to our 'powers' over the years. One particularly hot, sunny day when Auntie Vera was giving readings to raise money for a church fete, she was sitting in her caravan waiting for the next person to come through the door. A young woman walked in and, as was the done thing, slipped her £5 note under Aunt Vera's crystal ball before they began. The sun was blazing through the window, shining directly onto the bank note, and as the reading went on the crystal ball began to act as a magnifying glass on the money and the £5 note caught fire. There was a perfectly rational scientific reason for it, but that didn't stop the woman from running out of the caravan waving her arms wildly in the air as she shouted, 'She's a witch! She's a witch!'

TWENTY

The Two Duchesses

Our house in Ship Street Gardens took on an air of regal glamour when the Duke and Duchess of Leinster moved in next door to us. The duchess was opening up a dress shop, and she'd often pop into my waiting room for a chat and a gossip when I wasn't busy. She was a very entertaining lady. One day she popped in to say, 'Eva, dear, are you doing anything tomorrow?'

'Why?' I enquired.

'I'm having a grand opening,' she said excitedly. 'I'd like you and a friend to come.'

I accepted and the next day I dressed carefully, choosing a fitted black cocktail dress and my highest pair of black patent heels. When I got to her shop, I found myself at a very swish affair, with waiters walking around with champagne and trays of canapés. Sir Laurence Olivier and his wife Joan Plowright were there, as was the actress Dora Bryan and many other familiar faces. I thoroughly enjoyed myself and didn't turn down the champagne, knowing I only had to stagger next door to get home!

The duchess popped in the next day and said, 'Eva, I've got some lovely dress lengths. One in particular made me think of you. It's pink and grey tweed, and I want to make you a coat dress out of it.'

She had a tailoress on the premises and I had to have three fittings. It was the most beautiful outfit, designed and made especially for me. When it was finally ready, I was very happy indeed. However, when I asked for the bill, the duchess insisted it was a gift. I don't like taking liberties and refused any further offers to make outfits for me, although I loved the coat dress and wore it at every opportunity!

The duchess told me she was having her autobiography written by Michael Thornton, whom I had met at her opening, and he became a frequent visitor to her shop. I got to know him during his visits, and on one of them he told me he had a friend in London who had heard about me and that she needed some urgent advice. I explained to him that I didn't usually do home visits.

'But she'll pay all expenses and any fee you'd care to name,' he argued. He confided to me that his friend was, in fact, the Duchess of Argyll, a society beauty with a notorious reputation.

In 1963 scandal had raged around the duchess's divorce from the Duke of Argyll, after Polaroid snaps emerged of her frolicking naked with a man whose head had not been captured by the camera. Speculation was rife over the identity of the so-called 'headless man', who was rumoured to be a senior figure in the government, cabinet minister Duncan Sandys. At the time of the Argyll divorce, other pictures were discovered in the duchess's boudoir, of a second mystery man. Many years later, it was claimed that he was the actor Douglas Fairbanks Jr.

Reluctantly, I agreed to go and see her at her home. A few weeks earlier, I had been booked to go to a celebrity party to give readings, where I had met the singer Marion Ryan, who had scribbled her address and phone number in my address book. She lived in a square in London close to the American embassy, and on the day of my appointment with the Duchess of Argyll, I went up to town on the train, jumped into a taxi and hurriedly looked in my book for the address. In my haste, I gave the taxi driver Marion Ryan's address, which happened to be in the same square as the duchess's home.

I jumped out of the taxi, ran to the door and pressed the buzzer. Over the intercom came a man's voice, with an American accent. 'Who is it?'

'It's Eva Petulengro,' I explained. 'I have an appointment with the Duchess of Argyll.'

The voice chuckled back at me. 'Honey, Frank Sinatra

is staying here. You want the other side of the square, near the embassy.' The chuckles carried on.

'How bizarre,' I thought to myself. Was Sinatra really staying there or was this just some madman sending me on a wild goose chase? And why the laughter? Anyway, I ran like hell, really late for my meeting now, and out of breath. Finding what I prayed was the right address, I got the correct response when I rang the bell.

'Come in, Eva,' the Duchess of Argyll said. Not such a good response followed her initial welcome, as her eyebrows rose in disapproval. She was like a cross between a high-class whore and the wicked witch who gave Snow White the poisoned apple. 'You're late!' she snapped.

I thought I'd better explain what had happened. 'I went to the wrong address, I'm afraid. I went to Marion Ryan's house, and apparently Frank Sinatra was there!' This didn't help matters much and she said, coldly, 'Never mind that, I'll take you to my study.'

She relaxed after that though, and I carried out a very private reading.

Before I left to make the journey home, I used her bathroom. On a glass shelf next to the washbasin was every brand of perfume imaginable. I suppose this was so that guests could top up whatever they were wearing.

When I got home and explained to Johnnie about my day, he broke into a very long and very loud laugh.

Then he got up and picked up the daily newspaper from that morning. He placed it in front of me and pointed to an article that told of an incident earlier in the week, when Frank Sinatra had pushed the Duchess of Argyll out of a bar and she had landed on the pavement. No wonder she was angry with me: she must have thought I was taking the mickey out of her! Still, it didn't stop her from using me as her advisor.

A couple of weeks later, Vivien, the Duchess of Leinster, asked me if I would give a reading the following evening to a couple of her friends. 'They'll only be in Brighton for a couple of nights, Eva,' she pleaded. 'They'll be returning to America after that.'

I could not refuse, especially after the gorgeous coat dress she had so graciously made for me. Only an hour after I had agreed, the Duchess of Argyll telephoned.

'Eva, I need you here at seven tomorrow evening,' she said.

'Oh, I'm so sorry, I already have a booking tomorrow night. I've arranged to see some American friends of the Duchess of Leinster—' I began to say.

She cut me short and thundered down the phone, 'Well, cancel them!'

'But I—'

'Eva, I *must* see you. It is absolutely imperative you come to my home tomorrow evening.'

She was so insistent that I told her I would call her

back. I picked up the phone to Vivien and told her of my predicament.

'I really don't know what to do,' I said. 'She just will not take no for an answer. Whatever it is must be very urgent indeed.'

Vivien was very good about it. 'The Americans were only curious and so of course you should go and see the duchess.'

An hour later, Vivien came knocking on my door to say that her biographer, Michael Thornton, had called her to ask if I had been telling the truth when I told the Duchess of Argyll I was booked to see the Americans. It was all very cloak and dagger.

When I arrived the following evening, I was shown into the duchess's lounge and the scene that greeted me was one I really did not appreciate. She was wearing a see-through negligee – and I *mean* see-through – and on the coffee table was an ice bucket with a bottle of champagne and two glasses.

'Come on in, Eva,' she said, smiling sexily at me. I turned on my heels, slamming the door behind me. I couldn't get out of there quick enough – I didn't need my sixth sense to tell me what she had in mind. It was a shameless seduction scene! Although I was many things to my clients – a counsellor one day, a best friend the next – there were some things I would never be.

TWENTY-ONE

Dressed to Impress

A couple of friends of mine used to collect clothes and other bits and pieces for a charity shop. They popped in to see me one day and said, 'Have you got your stuff sorted out, Eva? We'll take it with us to the charity shop for you.'

'I haven't had a chance yet,' I replied.

'Oh, we can't get out again until Tuesday.'

It was a Saturday, a busy day for me with clients. 'I tell you what,' I said, 'bring your stuff into the back and I'll sort mine out tonight and get Johnnie to drop them all off on Monday.'

'Fine,' they said. They went out to the car, brought back a black bin bag of ladies' clothes they had collected and I put it behind my desk.

That evening I was expecting Eddie and his friend Brian Saunders to come round for dinner as it was Brian's birthday. Brian was a fairly quiet chap, an estate agent who dabbled in antiques, and he and Eddie often went on the hunt for good stuff together. Eddie had asked me to make him his favourite, a steak and kidney pudding, which took five hours to cook and was already halfway through the process. By the time they arrived, at about seven in the evening, they had obviously been out to celebrate and wanted to have a good lining in their stomachs in order to carry on for the evening.

I was very fond of Brian, as were all my family. The last time I'd seen him was after an accountant I'd had for quite a long time had suddenly disappeared. No one knew where he was. He was missing for several years. A few months after he'd gone, I was summoned to court for non-payment of his accountancy bills. When I arrived, Brian was sitting there. 'What are you in for?' he asked.

'Non-payment of bills,' I said. 'What are you in for?'

'Parking fines, as usual,' he said.

At the time, Brian didn't care where he parked his car, as long as he could show clients his properties. So much so, in fact, that he earned himself a place in *The Guinness Book of Records* for receiving the highest number of parking tickets in England! I went up first, and stood in the dock facing a judge, who looked at me over his glasses and then addressed the courtroom.

'I'm really sick of these cases,' he declared. 'This is number twenty-three this morning for non-payment of bills.'

I had produced receipted copies of my bills, all stamped 'paid', but nevertheless, as I stood there, I felt as if I had committed murder. It was a really terrifying experience, even though I knew I'd done nothing wrong. After looking at my documents, the judge threw them on his desk and looked at me.

'You can go, Mrs Tullett. These people have wasted your time as well as mine. Everyone who has appeared today has paid their bills, apart from one. I had forty such cases yesterday, and it's a total waste of the taxpayers' money and the court's time.'

It came out later that someone had taken over the accountant's practice and re-billed every person on his books, and it was explained to me that a lot of big companies just paid bills as they came in, without really checking if they were correct. Years later, my old accountant reappeared in Brighton and told me he had been held prisoner in a flat in Paris and forced to continue doing his accountancy work, for which he'd received no payment. He said he'd finally been allowed to come home when his captors lost all their clients, much to his relief. It all sounded a bit strange to me and I've always wondered what the rest of this story was but, I have to admit, sometimes ignorance is bliss. My appearance in court was a big waste of time, but at least I had had Brian to keep me company in the waiting room!

On the evening of Brian's birthday dinner, after devouring two bottles of red wine with their steak and kidney pudding, Brian and Eddie were ready for a good time. Eddie had gone to the toilet behind my dukkering room at the back and as he came out, he knocked over the bag my friends had brought in earlier in the day. He bent over, looked through the contents and produced a lady's dress. 'Oh, this is nice,' he said, and took off his polo-neck jumper and slipped the dress over his head with a drunken giggle.

'Oh, Eddie, that really suits you,' Johnnie and Brian said, laughing.

'All you need now is some make-up,' I said.

'Go on then,' Eddie said.

I sat him in a chair and applied eyeliner, eyeshadow and bright-red lipstick. I had been told that my Bell's palsy had been caused by a draught in my ear, so I did not like going to the hairdresser's and sitting under a hairdryer as, according to the doctors, this could cause further facial paralysis. As a result, I often wore a wig, so I placed that on Eddie's head once his make-up was complete.

We all laughed. 'You could pass for a woman, you know,' I said, looking him up and down.

'I tell you what,' Johnnie said, 'I'll give you five pounds if you stand in the lane outside the house for five minutes looking like that.'

With that, Eddie rolled up his trousers over his knees. I rushed over to him and said, 'You've forgotten something, darling,' and sprayed my Chanel No. 5 behind his ears.

'I knew there was something missing,' he chuckled.

As he went merrily out the front door, Johnnie quickly turned the lock and said, 'Let's leave him out there.'

Brian immediately piped up. 'You obviously don't know him as well as I do then. He'll do anything for a laugh.'

'Come on, boys, open the door now, he's had enough,' I said, beginning to feel sorry for my tipsy little brother.

Johnnie relented and opened the door. 'Was funny though,' he said, but when he checked the lane, Eddie was nowhere in sight.

'I know where he's gone,' Brian said. 'Are you coming, Johnnie?'

Johnnie grabbed his jacket. 'Look after him,' I shouted after them.

Johnnie returned after two hours, and I was waiting anxiously for his news. 'Come on then, tell me what happened,' I urged.

'Well,' Johnnie began, 'we went straight to the Druid's Head pub and, as we walked in, Eddie was standing there, pint in his hand, like something out of a pantomime, and when he saw me and Brian, he said in his manly voice, "Give these two guys a pint, please." Eddie then looked at Brian and said, "There's a couple of fit birds there, look, Brian."'

According to Johnnie, Eddie moved straight over to the girls and started chatting them up, leaning on the bar in his dress, men's shoes and wig, with his hairy legs on show – all the while smelling like a lady of the night's boudoir.

Johnnie said, 'I couldn't believe it. After about five minutes of talking to these girls, he called Brian over to come and join him. He ordered champagne for them all, while I watched in awe, not quite believing my eyes. The landlord looked at me and said, "Do you believe this, Johnnie?" I told him I'd believe anything with Eddie. The girls were actually interested in him!'

To say Eddie was charming when it came to the opposite sex would be a massive understatement. I had often heard my brother say, on greeting a good-looking woman, 'My God, you're ugly.' Of course, he would only say it to the most beautiful women, knowing full well they knew they were most definitely not ugly. He knew it was a wonderful chat-up line. When the woman was not so beautiful, he would say, 'Excuse me, could you turn your head slightly to the left?' Then he would look her straight in the eyes and say, 'When the light hits you on that side of your face, you look absolutely stunning.' These flattering lines were usually a winner with the girls.

To this day, we don't know what happened after hours in the Druid's Head, as Johnnie left the girls talking and laughing with Eddie in his charity-shop dress and wig. All I do know is that I never did get the dress back!

TWENTY-TWO

The Sex Shop

As the children grew, Ship Street Gardens started to feel too cramped for us all, bearing in mind that I conducted my business there too, and we realized we needed a bigger house. It was a strange thought, I'm sure you'll agree, coming from a woman who was raised in a 22-foot caravan with three other children and our parents. However, I was living a mostly gorger life now and wanted the luxuries that came with it. My children needed a garden. As it was, we were only a short walk from the beach, and there were several parks in Brighton where they could run wild, but I still longed for our own garden, where we could have our stick fires and grow herbs, and which the children and I could make our own.

Mummy was totally in love with Ship Street Gardens. She had been on her own in a flat in West Street, which was far too big for one person, and although we spent an awful lot of time together, she felt lost rattling about in all that space. I suggested to her that if and when I found my ideal home, she should take over my current premises. She ran her business from West Street and could easily transfer it to the Gardens.

At the top of the lane above Ship Street was a street called Middle Street, which ran from the seafront down to the famous Brighton Lanes. There was a school on Middle Street and, further up, of all things, a sex shop!

For a long time, I'd thought about getting into the herbal business, as, along with palmistry and astrology, this was what my family had been skilled in for many generations. There was nothing we did not know about herbs. The sex shop on Middle Street was up for sale and it would make ideal premises as I expanded my business. As I generally did, I dived in nose first, with Johnnie's blessing and help.

On the day we got the keys, I hired a typist-come-secretary whose name was Eleanor. The three of us trooped over to the shop to have a look around. There were piles of naughty magazines and empty boxes that had held sex toys.

'We're going to have to clean this up before I start remodelling it,' Johnnie said. He opened up a little cup-board under the stairs and retrieved something from the back of it. 'Look what I've found hiding under the stairs.' He grinned, holding up a big piece of black rubber.

'What is it?' I asked curiously.

'It's a blow-up doll,' exclaimed Johnnie. 'A man doll!'

Both Eleanor and I shrieked with laughter. 'Put it in the bin,' I said.

'Oh no, please, can I have it?' Eleanor asked. 'I'll take it home for my boyfriend for a laugh.'

Without further ado, Johnnie screwed it up, placed an elastic band around it and Eleanor shoved it into her bag.

'Johnnie,' I said, 'I've seen some paint in Woolworths called Romany Red. Let's go and have a look at it.'

'OK,' he replied.

This was all getting exciting, and off the three of us trooped up to Western Road. I led them to the paint department and as soon as he saw what I had in mind, Johnnie said, 'Perfect. It's a lovely shade.'

I couldn't help thinking, 'Who is he kidding?' After all, he was colour blind! Anyway, in this instance, he was right, so he ordered what he felt he needed and we headed towards the door. All of a sudden an announcement came over the Tannoy: 'Ladies and gentlemen, we're conducting a search as you leave the premises, so please have your bags ready for inspection.'

Woolworths was well known for shoplifters, as everything was laid out in a way that must have been a great temptation for the light-fingered. Eleanor's face was turning about the same colour as the Romany Red paint. She did not know what to do with herself, knowing she had the blow-up doll in her bag. Johnnie and I were very amused and we couldn't wait to see if the guard at the door discovered her 'secret'. Not a word was said. Even though he did look in Eleanor's bag, he simply gave it a glance and moved her on.

When we returned to our new premises, Johnnie turned to me and said, 'Now, I want you to leave the shop to me to decorate, Jules, and I don't want you to come anywhere near until it's finished.'

'Why?' I began to protest.

'Mind your own Romany business. Go and look in your crystal ball if you want the answers.' He did give in and feed me a few details of what he had planned. There was a second floor above the shop. 'That will be your waiting room,' he began. 'I'm going to put a partition at the back to make a cosy little dukkering place for your readings. I have some other ideas for the shop, but it's going to be a surprise, which you will love, and I don't want you to see it, OK?' I gave in. I wondered what on earth he could be up to. Whatever it was, I knew it would be wonderful. He was so clever and imaginative.

The day arrived when Johnnie was ready to show me my brand-new business premises. I had kept to my word and stayed away, although it had been agony to do so.

'I haven't put anything in the window yet; that's your job,' he said. He unlocked the front door and ushered me in first. I could not believe my eyes. It was just like stepping into Granny's vardo. He had somehow created a sloping arc on the ceiling, exactly like those of the old wagons, and had stayed true to the originals, even to the extent of putting gold leaf on the fancy pieces of wood which he had designed and cut out. On the wall, he had placed lamps that were replicas of the old-fashioned oil lamps. Our friend Winnie Sexton had recently had some remodelling done in her public house, and behind the bar had been some antique shelves which resembled the mantelpiece in Granny's vardo and which I had frequently mentioned when we'd gone in for a drink. She had given them to Johnnie and he'd fixed them on the walls! Absolutely ideal for little bottles of herbal tablets and tarot cards and so on. He had also bought plants and put them in all the right places.

'I'm leaving the furniture for you to choose,' he said. I raced upstairs to see my new waiting room and mentally made a note of what type of chairs I would have, with a table in the middle and newspapers and books to help pass the time when my clients were waiting to see me.

By now I had ordered my herbal remedies to be made, and Johnnie set to work designing the labels and, in long-hand, wrote out the wording to be printed on them. The logo was a Romany caravan.

Once we had completed the labels, they were to be sent to the factory, which already produced many other brands of herbal remedies, and they would stick them onto my bottles and deliver them to me. It was all so exciting. Johnnie had taken great care to get all the spellings absolutely correct, and he gave them to Eleanor to type. I had a range of about ten different remedies, everything from feverfew for headaches and moss compound for chesty coughs, to valerian for insomnia and peppermint for tummy aches.

When Eleanor handed the typed wording for the labels to Johnnie, he checked it and found at least forty misspelled words.

'What did you do with the original I gave you to copy from?' he asked Eleanor.

'I didn't think I'd need to keep it,' she said.

It took Johnnie hours to prepare the list again, with the correct spellings. He handed it to her and sternly said, 'Get it right this time, please, we've got a lot to do.'

However, when she returned the copy to Johnnie again, there were still mistakes.

'I'm sorry, Eleanor,' I said, 'I can't rely on you. I know you're doing your best, but it's not good enough. I've got to let you go.'

Eleanor left quietly and never said a word. I felt bad as I liked her as a person, but I knew I'd been more than fair – after all, we had taken her on as a typist and she couldn't spell, even when it was all correctly written down for her to copy! I gave her an extra month's wages to soften the blow, but, to my amazement, a week later, I received a letter from a solicitor to say she was taking me to the small claims court for unfair dismissal.

'If she wants to play hardball, fine. I'll go to court,' I said to Johnnie.

When I arrived at the court, it comprised a man at a desk and two chairs opposite one another. Eleanor sat in one and I sat in the other. I took an instant dislike to the man dealing with the case. I could see that he was not fair-minded. Both Eleanor and I gave our sides of the story, after which he looked at me and said, 'You will pay her compensation for unfair dismissal.'

I said, 'Sir, I've explained how she cannot spell, and that she caused my husband a lot of work in correcting her spelling, and then she *still* got it wrong. How can dismissing her be unfair?'

He looked me straight in the eyes and said, 'Madam, I do not agree with the kind of work you do and are known for.'

I scraped my chair back and held his gaze. 'And,

sir,' I said, '*I* don't like dealing with unknowledgeable arseholes.'

With that, I swept out, slamming the door behind me.

On the way home, I started laughing to myself. 'What an ignorant man,' I thought. 'I'm not going to let him upset me.' I started thinking about all the other people who had insulted me, and how over the years people had said, 'I don't believe in what you do.'

My standard reply was invariably, 'Have you ever had a reading? No? Then how can you comment on something you know nothing whatsoever about?' I would leave them with that unanswerable question. I had no time for ignorant people.

TWENTY-THREE

Head Over Heels

There are many ways to describe a man like Eddie. Good-looking, charismatic, charming, debonair and witty are but a few. My brother was all of these things, and he knew it. Similar to a young Peter O'Toole, he had the same quizzical eyes that were not afraid to look into yours, and expressive eyebrows. Although he was very outgoing and sociable, he chose his friends and didn't let them choose him. He knew how to dress and how to carry himself, which he'd learned from Mummy and Nathan. His taste in shoes was exquisite. Our mother would often say, 'One good suit is better than a wardrobe full of cheap stuff,' and Eddie was of the same mindset. He loved the travelling life and the outdoors and the way we lived when we were on the move. Being settled down did not suit him, so he bought himself a caravanette. Sometimes he would park outside my house or Mummy's house, or wherever the fancy took him. He much preferred the traditional Romany life; he felt claustrophobic stuck inside four walls.

In the summer of 1973, at the age of twenty-four, he fell, quite literally, in love. What I mean is, he fell off his barstool! He had never been interested in gorger girls. As far as we knew, he'd had a fling or two, but never anything serious. Until he met Nicky. She was just eighteen, looked like a young Goldie Hawn and never had a negative word to say about anyone. I don't think two minutes ever passed without her laughing at least once. Her father, Leslie, was an ex-Spitfire pilot who owned his own light aircraft, a Piper Cherokee. Flying was his main passion, next to his family, of course. He had a beautiful wife, Josephine, his daughter Nicola, always called Nicky, and a son, Malcolm. Nicky had the same spirit as her father, and Leslie encouraged her love for flying and exploring different places. Her main job was working for an advertising design consultancy, but to pay for her flying lessons, she took a job at the Druid's Head, one of the trendiest pubs in town at the time, attracting lots of young professionals.

The first time they met, Eddie arrived at the Druid's Head to join some friends for a drink. The minute Nicky spotted him, she began to feel nervous and flustered and felt in awe of this elegant, sophisticated stranger. Later, she told me that as she gazed at him, she felt almost invisible and struggled with the strangest feeling of uncertainty that was welling up inside her. She deliberately placed herself at the other end of the bar, away from Eddie's crowd. But Greg, the landlord, a man with film-star good looks and a cool and calm demeanour, kept telling her to go back and deal with the customers clamouring for service. She was so nervous that, in her haste, she slipped on some beer slops and fell, sliding ungracefully across the floor of the bar, attracting the very attention she was trying so hard to avoid. Getting up unsteadily and without taking her eyes off the floor, she tried to ignore the claps and cheers from the customers, in particular Eddie, who had a sparkle of amusement in his eyes but showed no signs of mockery. She forced herself to resume her duties, trying not to look his way and wishing the floor would open up and swallow her.

For several weeks, both were in the pub at the same time in the evenings, Eddie with his friends and Nicky working. There were no further embarrassing incidents, although she was in constant trepidation at the thought of having to serve him. Then, one Wednesday evening after closing time, she was clearing up and Eddie, who was sitting in his usual spot at the bar, had stayed behind to talk to Greg. At one point Nicky turned round and saw that he had suddenly disappeared. 'Where's he gone?' she thought to herself. 'I didn't see him go.' It was time for her to leave, so she made her way to the door. Suddenly she heard a noise behind her and quickly turned back, alarmed. There, on the floor and on his hands and knees, was Eddie, crawling towards her. She realized he must have fallen off the barstool in his drunken state! Eddie reckoned that rather than trying to get back up, he was much safer where he was. He looked up at her, with a deadpan expression, and uttered what were to become immortal words. 'Would you like to have a drink with me sometime, young lady?' Eddie would normally never have allowed himself to become so much the worse for wear, but on that particular night he had been so desperate to spend as much time as possible near Nicky that he had spent the whole evening at the bar, buying more and more drinks as an excuse to talk to her! But he remained on the floor and made no apology for his unconventional proposition.

Nicky stared down at him, wondering if the whole episode was just a dream, as an amused Greg walked over and addressed her. 'Well,' he said sternly, 'do you want to go out with him or not? Answer the man.'

Bewildered, she just gulped, 'Yes,' and disappeared outside to her waiting taxi.

Nicky had no recollection of the taxi journey home, all she could remember was the vision of Eddie looking up at her from the floor with his puppy-dog eyes. According to her parents, she was speechless for the whole of the following day.

Just as she had convinced herself that it had been a crazy dream or that he was just having a laugh or a cruel game with her, the phone interrupted her thoughts with its shrill ring. To her disbelief, it was Eddie.

'Greg gave me your number,' he began. 'I'm phoning to make our date. Let's do it tonight, gal.'

He took total control of the conversation and within one hour, she was in the lounge bar of the Old Ship Hotel, on Brighton seafront, ready to meet him.

From that day, they were inseparable and went on to live a Romany-style life for four years. Eddie encouraged her to leave her secure and steady job to travel the country in his beloved caravanette, which he had kitted out luxuriously with light oak panelling, a Persian carpet and a top-of-the-range mini bar. Before they could embark upon their life together, however, Nicky and Eddie first had to go through the Romany marriage ceremony.

The ceremony can only be conducted by a Romany elder, and in Eddie and Nicky's case it was my mother who did the honours. Unlike standard wedding vows, there are no scripted words; it is up to the elder to choose words that they feel are appropriate for the couple and that represent their relationship. Mummy talked about the deep love they had for one another, and the inspiring way they accepted, and adored, each and every thing about each other. Her words were very emotional and I found myself welling up at them.

Once the words had been spoken, it was time for the mingling of their blood, but the romance of the moment was lost when Eddie leaned over and said to Nicky, loud enough for us all to hear, 'Don't worry, darling. Just a little prick,' at which we all fell about in hysterics!

Mummy took Eddie's finger and used a pin to draw some blood, then did the same to Nicky, before placing their bleeding fingers together and then binding their wrists with a silk neckerchief to signify that they had now become one. She then broke a twig and gave half to each of them, and did the same with a piece of bread that she handed to them to eat. 'You will share everything in your lives,' Mummy said, looking at each of them in turn, 'and your love for one another will be unending. You have my blessing.' We all began to clap and cheer, and then the celebrations began in earnest.

The next day Nicky and Eddie set off to visit the prettiest villages and towns they could find and rested in the countryside. They were deeply in love and it was all so romantic. It would be impossible to imagine a happier couple than they were at that time.

Eddie was extremely practical as well as artistic and entertaining. He knew his caravanette vehicle inside and out and could repair any other vehicle single-handedly. He was proud and fiercely independent. To finance their lifestyle, he would craft model vardos to sell. He was also very knowledgeable about antiques. He could spot something of great value in a shop, and he'd buy it and sell it on to make a profit. He was often seen in the auction houses, where he was well known and respected. Nicky would read the many books on antiques to him, to help him increase his knowledge, as Eddie could not read and write well, due to his lack of schooling. Although Nathan and us girls were self-taught, when he was younger Eddie had his attention on the more practical crafts, rather than wasting valuable time learning to read and write. He was nicknamed 'the Romany Rye', as he was always impeccably dressed. Nicky's father, Les, and he were kindred spirits. They recognized the gentleman in each other immediately.

Nicky wanted to travel further afield, so they made a long trip to France and Spain, choosing spots such as under the Eiffel Tower in Paris and on the cliffs near Bilbao to park up and explore. However, Eddie's independence was threatened by his lack of knowledge of foreign languages, and he never felt comfortable away from the UK. They returned to spend time roaming in England, with frequent visits to Brighton, where they could both catch up with their loved ones.

It was on one of these visits that they took me to London in their caravanette. I had been asked to attend a big celebrity bash at the Dorchester Hotel on Park Lane. Johnnie didn't like these affairs and suggested that Eddie and Nicky accompany me instead of him. They happily agreed to the idea of a party, with celebrities thrown in to boot. Once there, Eddie parked the caravanette on Shaftesbury Avenue, outside the Cambridge Theatre of all places, and from there, we took a taxi to the Dorchester. It was a fabulous do and we were seated at a table alongside Dickie Davies, the sports commentator, Barry Sheene, the motorcycle champion, and many other well-known faces. Sitting at the next table was Farrah Fawcett Major, who must have recognized me because she sent a waiter over to ask me to read her palm. We were all chatting away when, all of a sudden, Eddie felt a hand on his shoulder. He turned to find Cary Grant, the legendary film star, whom we all adored, looking down at him. 'You're sitting in my seat, old chap,' he said.

Eddie twisted round with a look of shock and disbelief at the sight of his idol behind him. 'You touched me,' he said, awestruck. 'Wait until I tell my mother.'

The evening went with a swing, and when you're enjoying yourself time flies, doesn't it? We were in high spirits and getting peckish. I decided to take Eddie and Nicky to a restaurant in Mayfair called Tiddy Dols, where Johnnie had taken me several times. Once there, we had a nice, juicy steak each and a good bottle of wine between us. But as we got closer to the end of the meal, I began to worry about sleeping in the cara-vanette, parked in the middle of Theatreland.

'What am I supposed to do if I want to have a pee in the middle of the night? You couldn't get further away from a field if you tried,' I complained.

Eddie laughed. 'You'll just have to wet yourself, won't you?' he said in his usual nonchalant, jokey way.

Next to the cash desk in the restaurant was a plastic bin, which was being used to put the old coat-check tickets in. I called the waiter over.

'I want to buy that plastic bin from you,' I said.

Thinking I was joking, the waiter laughed at my request.

'I'm serious,' I continued with urgency. 'If you can't help me, can you bring the manager, please?'

Without further ado, the manager arrived. 'How can I help you, madam?'

I repeated my request. He said, 'They're only ten shillings; you can get one tomorrow, they sell them two doors down.'

'But I need it tonight,' I continued.

He looked at me quizzically, as if I was quite mad. 'May I ask what you need it for?' I explained that we were sleeping in a caravanette and I was worried what I would do if I needed a pee in the night. With this, he started to laugh.

'Hang on a minute. I've got a solution for you.' He withdrew and, a few minutes later, returned with a large ice-cream container with a lid on it and a handle to carry it with. 'Will that do?' he enquired, still laughing.

'Perfectly,' I replied, 'and on account of that, we'll have another bottle of that wine!'

When we returned to the caravanette, Eddie pulled out the bed in the front of the vehicle and I busied myself making up my bed on the long seat at the back. Nicky was sitting down with the ice-cream container on her knee and a bottle of red nail varnish in her hands. When I'd finished making my bed, I turned round to see her holding up the ice-cream bucket, on which she had painted with the nail polish: 'The Tiddy Dols Tiddly Bin'.

TWENTY-FOUR

The 'Other Woman'

One day in October 1973, Mummy and I were sitting in her palmistry place on the Palace Pier when the manager came walking past. I remember Mummy wagging her finger at him and saying, 'I want a word with you.'

'What is it, Laura?' he said smiling.

'I don't feel safe here. I want to go on the forecourt of the pier.'

He laughed at her and shook his head. 'Not possible, my dear.'

She tried to argue with him, but to no avail. He walked off, shaking his head, thinking his resident clairvoyant was nuts.

Less than a week later, a barge drifted into the Palace Pier during the night and caused a million pounds' worth of damage to the theatre, our palmistry place and many of the other attractions. Within a week, the manager had settled us into our new palmistry place on the forecourt of the pier, all the while looking at us as if we were two witches.

'He used to always come and say hello and now he avoids me like the plague,' complained Mummy.

'No wonder, you've frightened the life out of the poor man,' I laughed.

Of course, we learned as children to listen to my mother's feelings, and to trust our own when it came to our own lives as well as those of our clients.

Seeing a client is rather like watching clips of a film or reading a few chapters of a book. I see glimpses of their lives, as long as the client is with me. Regular clients will consult me over any problems or decisions they have to make, and so when I don't hear from them for a while, I know that all is well. In a way, my clients are like my children, who only need me when they have problems, and it's a big relief to me when I know that their problems no longer exist.

One man came to see me after his wife had died and said he was going to kill himself. I asked if he had children.

'Yes, but now my wife's gone, I've got nothing to live for.'

His wife had been one of my mother's clients. I slapped him hard across the face. 'I'm sorry,' I said, 'but that wasn't me: that was your wife.'

He looked stunned, but gave me some pearls that had belonged to his wife and said that she had wanted my mother to have them. The next day I got a call from one of his sons.

'I don't know what you've done to our dad, but he's a different person today,' he said.

The following week, a big bunch of flowers came from the father, with a message to say that all was well.

As quite a lot of men visit me to talk about their business and financial problems, as well as their emotional lives, I was accused several times over the years of being 'the other woman'. One lovely client who I had been seeing on a weekly basis came along one week and announced that he wouldn't be coming back to see me again. 'I'm sorry, Eva,' he said, 'but my wife looked in my diary, saw your name and assumed you were my fancy woman! I'm afraid I can't risk coming to see you anymore.' We had a good laugh about it all; I was only in my twenties at the time, while he was about seventy-five, so I think he was quite flattered that his wife thought he still had it in him! Another time a woman came marching into my consulting room waving an umbrella angrily at me.

'My husband came to see you yesterday and you told him to sell our bungalow,' she ranted. 'I came home from work last night and he'd gone and put our house on the market!' It has always been a policy of mine never to tell clients specifically what they should do – I only interpret thoughts and feelings and leave the rest up to them – so I knew that wasn't true.

'I'm very sorry, madam,' I replied in my most diplomatic tone, 'but I only told him that I could see signs of a change of residence in the future and that I could tell he was unhappy. He loves you very much but he obviously isn't happy there.' Her face seemed to soften then as she realized that she already knew that. As she left, I could sense that she would come round to her husband's way of thinking; she just needed to get used to the idea. I've always liked to think that clients pay heed to my advice, but I'm not sure many have ever done so as enthusiastically as that lady's husband!

Although I would never told clients what to do, there have been times when I have wished I could. I remember one lady who would visit me from time to time whose husband was forever in and out of prison. He was a burglar, she told me with regret. I could always tell when he'd been home because her poor face would be black and blue and swollen. She loved him desperately, and just as long as he didn't leave her, she was quite happy to welcome him home, even though she knew she'd be in for another beating. I have learned that some women are like this and that as long as they can keep their man, they don't care what torture they go through, but how I longed to tell her to get as far away from him as possible. All I was able to do was gently advise her and hope that she reached the same conclusion on her own. As far as I know, she never did, though.

A very affluent and beautiful lady in her seventies visited me one day and wanted my help, advice and guidance on a problem she had with her son. 'I don't want a reading,' she said. 'I just want your advice, Eva.'

I settled back to listen to what she had to say.

'I have a very handsome and clever son, my only child. I had him late and he means the world to me. He's very successful in his career as an architect and I've recently found out he's gay, or thinks he is. He's confessed to me that he has a boyfriend who's Italian and has begged me to meet him. Of course, I wouldn't dream of it.'

I listened to her story without interrupting. 'Does your son appear to be happy with this young man?'

'Yes, but it's not natural, is it?'

I smiled. 'Not in your circles, perhaps, but people are born different. In fact, my dear, I have many clients and friends who are gay, and I find them to be just as normal as we are.'

I suggested she got to know her son's partner, to find out what he saw in him.

'But I want grandchildren,' she wailed.

'Perhaps your son does not want children. Perhaps he would like a life without. Give your son the respect he deserves. See how you feel once you've got to know his partner. You must give them, and yourself, a chance, dear.'

Three weeks later, without an appointment, the lady turned up at my office. 'I'm in Brighton for the day and had to come and tell you the news,' she said. 'I took your advice and asked my son to invite his friend round for a cup of tea. I was very pleasantly surprised. He was well turned out and very polite, and after twenty minutes he had me laughing.'

They had all gone to dinner that evening and she had found her son's partner charming. His parents had not spoken to him for three years, as they disapproved of his lifestyle.

'He is taking us on a cruise to Italy to meet his family, and I hope we will be able to bring them round to my way of thinking.'

Another satisfied client! I hoped they would be able to persuade the boy's family to see things their way, for their own peace of mind and happiness.

A young woman who made a lasting impression on me walked in for her appointment holding her hand over her mouth. She had beautiful, thick, curly red hair. She also had very low self-esteem. Once she sat down, she dropped her hand from her mouth and I saw she had very bad teeth. The two at the front crossed over and the rest were uneven. She wore no make-up and her clothes were plain, chosen so as not to draw attention to herself. She was twenty-one, but looked sixteen and had never had a boyfriend. It turned out she was very wealthy.

'It's obvious to me that you know your teeth are not in good condition,' I said, 'and I'm sure you spend most of your time hiding them. You can afford it, so go and find yourself a good dentist.' Her beautiful hair was fastened up in an elastic band. 'While you're about it, find a good hairdresser too.'

I thought no more about her until nine months later, when a very striking young woman walked into my office. She had a dazzling smile, was perfectly made-up and it took me a couple of minutes to realize this was the girl with wonky teeth and no self-esteem. In front of me stood a very confident and assured woman who had remodelled herself. On her left hand she wore an engagement ring.

'You look fantastic, darling,' I said.

'Eva, thanks to you, I feel magnificent. I took your advice and made myself over. I'm now engaged to my boss, whom I've adored for years, but who never seemed to notice me until I got my new teeth and hairstyle. The hairdresser put me in touch with a make-up artist who showed me how to put it on properly.'

I glowed with pride. The duckling had turned into a swan.

A few months later, a widowed lady called Jane, who had married a man much older than her, came to see me. After three or four visits we became friends. She lived in a house in the middle of the country and was afraid of burglars.

'Eva, I have some 1920s Cartier jewellery my father bought for my mother. She never wore any of it and confessed to me they really were not her kind of thing. I don't know quite what to do – I think I ought to sell them, as I'm so nervous having them in the house. What do you think? Do you know anyone I could trust in the Lanes who would buy the jewellery?'

'I know one or two,' I said.

She went home to get the jewellery, and returned with a carrier bag. When she tipped out the contents, there were six Cartier boxes containing diamonds, emeralds, rubies and sapphires.

'I've never seen such beautiful jewellery in my life!' I exclaimed. The boxes were in perfect condition too. I rang Cartier in London and explained the situation, and they said to bring the jewels in to be looked at. 'Any idea what they might be worth?'

'Priceless,' the lady on the other end of the line said.

I replaced the receiver and said, 'How do you fancy a trip to London tomorrow? I'll take you to Cartier. This is so exciting.'

'Yes, please, Eva. I'd hate to do this on my own. I'll even give you a commission of 20 per cent on whatever I get for them.'

I was really excited now. The word 'priceless' kept going through my head.

The following day, Jane arrived at lunchtime with a bunch of roses. 'These are for you, Eva.' I could not see the carrier bag. 'I've decided that the jewels should stay in my family. I don't need the money, so I've given them to my son, whose daughter is getting married. They'll make a lovely wedding present.'

I thought that was a lovely thing to do. It would give them just the sort of start in life that all young couples could do with, even though it was a shame I had to say goodbye to that 20 per cent commission!

One of my liveliest clients was a very beautiful dark-haired girl, with dark-brown eyes that looked almost black and lovely long curly lashes. The first time we met, it took me about seven or eight minutes to realize that she was a 'lady of the night'. There was, however, nothing common about her. She looked like a top model and only went out with the very best. She'd been visiting me for two or three years when she gave birth to a little boy who was the spitting image of her. As all her clients were very wealthy, she confided in me that she got support from her son's father.

'Well, actually, there are four "fathers", or at least

they think they are, and they all help me to maintain the lifestyle to which I've become accustomed,' she said.

I thought immediately of the film *Buona Sera, Mrs Campbell*, with Gina Lollobrigida, and told her so.

'That's what gave me the idea,' she said with a giggle. I really have met a dazzling array of people over the years in my role as a clairvoyant.

However, I've also met some people who have very strange ideas about what it means to be a clairvoyant.

My brother Nathan called one evening. He and his wife, Sue, had a few people round for drinks and one of the guests was keen for me to be there.

'I've got a friend who wants to meet you,' Nathan said. 'I'm going to have a little party. Get your arse over here.'

We were all standing around chatting, as you do, about this, that and the other, when the man who wanted to meet me asked me to prove my ability to him. This was something I normally refused to do. However, that night I decided to have a laugh and with a wink at Nathan I said to the man, 'I can make you invisible, if you like.'

'Go on then,' he replied.

I took the party into the kitchen and told the man to lie on the floor and close his eyes. Looking around for props, I saw a pile of clean tea towels. I draped two of them across his face. Looking around again, I saw a loaf of bread, which I placed on his forehead, and asked him, 'Are you comfortable?'

'Yes,' he answered, 'and I'm very relaxed.'

'Good,' I replied. I motioned to the others to get out of the kitchen very quietly, holding my finger up to my lips. They all filed out without a noise. I then asked him to count back from a hundred in his head. With this, I extinguished the light and crept out, closing the door very quietly behind me.

We were all giggling in the front room (quietly of course!) and replenishing our drinks, wondering how long it would take before he joined us. It was three-quarters of an hour before he came into the lounge. He must have had forty winks. He firmly believed I had made him invisible.

TWENTY-FIVE

A Terrible Accident

'It's beautiful,' I said, gazing in awe at the large kitchen, everything white and shiny.

'And look at the garden, Eva,' Johnnie laughed, pulling me towards the windows. It was small, but neatly planted, with a lawn and pretty shrubs. Our own garden, where the children could play and I could grow herbs.

It was 1975, and we'd found a semi-detached house in Wish Road, in Hove, with three bedrooms to accommodate our growing family. It was opposite a glorious green park. As soon as I saw the park, I thought I'd buy the children bicycles. Happily, our friends Pat and Brian had bought a house within walking distance so we already had neighbours we were friends with. It was a perfect family home, somewhere a young family could grow with for many years to come.

Wish Road did not need to have any work done to it: it was in immaculate order. The lady who had lived there before us had passed away and because it was being sold by the executor of her will, they had wanted to move it along quickly so, of course, we obliged. Eddie, Nathan and Johnnie had their hands full, moving all of our stuff out of Ship Street Gardens and into the house, while all Mummy's belongings and furniture had to be moved from West Street into Ship Street Gardens. The downstairs of Ship Street Gardens was to be turned into a big apartment for Eddie and Nicky to use when they weren't travelling round in the caravanette. They had a separate entrance downstairs, meaning they would have their independence, but as Mummy was nervous of living by herself, it put her mind at rest to know they were just downstairs. It seemed the perfect solution all round.

It was quite a hectic time, and a very happy time too. The boys were all happy at school and I had our nanny, Linda Lump, as we'd nicknamed her, to look after Claire while we were all busy. In order to cope with my workload, Johnnie had built me an office in the back of the garage of the house, complete with strip lighting. He built me a big desk, large enough for me to sit on one side and a secretary on the other. Filing cabinets lined the back wall and there were shelves for books. It had everything I needed to get my work done in peace and quiet, away from the noise of the television and the children playing. It was like a cosy little bomb shelter. When I had appointments, I would go down to my shop on Middle Street to see my clients.

One evening, about three or four weeks after we moved in, Johnnie and I were sitting in the kitchen after we'd put the children to bed. I caught him looking at me with a certain expression on his face, and I immediately knew what he was thinking. I always did; I could read him like a book.

I looked at him and said, 'Johnnie, I know it's not us – it's too modern – but we got it at the right price, £19,000. These houses are going for £25,000, so we got a good deal. Now, let's start house-hunting – we need a bigger garden.'

But although we knew we wouldn't stay there, our time in Wish Road was still happy. We'd had to move the children from their schools in Brighton to one in Hove, and another reason we had bought the house was that you only had to go across one main road and then it was a very short walk to their new school. I insisted that Johnnie would walk Gregory there each day, because Greg was very impulsive and never stopped to think. I wasn't worried about Warren and Bradley, as they were quite streetwise and very well primed when it came to crossing roads.

I'll never forget the day I was working in my office with Pat, dictating as she was typing, when suddenly the doorbell started ringing like mad. I knew instantly that something was very wrong. Johnnie came bounding in from the kitchen and we arrived at the front door all together, including Pat. When we opened the door, there stood a neighbour, with tears in her eyes.

'Eva, I'm so sorry to be the one to tell you this.' I instinctively knew what she was going to say and started running up the road with no shoes on. I heard her shouting behind me, 'Gregory's been run over.'

As I ran up the road, I shouted over my shoulder, 'Didn't you take him to school, Johnnie?'

'I thought he'd be OK,' he said, looking frantic. 'He's been begging me for days to let him walk up with the other boys.'

As I reached the top of the road, on my left was a pile-up of three Minis and, as I ran over, I could see my little boy lying at the side of the road with blood pouring from his head.

'No!' I heard myself scream. I cradled his head in my lap, as all around I heard people shouting.

'Don't touch him, don't move him!'

A voice shouted, 'Look out, here comes the ambulance.'

Our lives were destroyed, I thought to myself, as I held my little boy. I was too numb to cry. Pat arrived at my side, holding a blanket, a packet of cigarettes and a lighter and my shoes. She said, 'What do you want me to do?'

'Nothing,' I said. 'I'll go with him in the ambulance. Just do what you think is best, but don't tell my mother yet.'

She nodded, and they lifted Gregory into the ambulance and we set off. I started to panic when the driver swerved to the left and went up a side road, heading away from the hospital.

'You're going the wrong way,' I said, confused.

The ambulance pulled up outside a house and the crew started to get out.

'What are you doing?' I screamed.

'We've got a cardiac arrest here. Your boy's OK – we've checked him. We'll be back soon.'

'But he's unconscious,' I begged.

'He's OK,' the ambulance man insisted again. With that, he ran in the house.

It all seemed so unreal, sitting there alone with my unconscious child, and not a thing I could do about it. It did actually occur to me for a fleeting moment to jump in the driver's seat and drive to the hospital myself, and if I had seen the keys in the ignition I certainly would have tried. I held Gregory's hand and checked his pulse, to see if his heart was still beating. After what seemed like an eternity, the two ambulance men returned and drove us to the hospital.

I was speechless the whole way there. How could they do that?

When we arrived at the hospital, Gregory was rushed into the operating theatre. I tried to follow, but they wouldn't let me in. I was pacing up and down, and after what seemed like a lifetime, the doctor came out to see me.

'Mrs Tullett,' he said, 'your boy is a very lucky young man. Your husband informed me that Gregory was running across the road when a car hit him. He bounced off the windscreen and was then flung in front of the vehicle. Two other cars collided with the car that hit him – and he hasn't broken a single bone in his body! I can honestly say that his situation is quite miraculous. He has a nasty cut on his head, but it's not serious. He must have been protected by the angels.'

That was Gregory's first lucky escape.

A few weeks later, Johnnie decided to go and pick up my letter headings from the printer and Gregory asked if he could go with him. Johnnie pulled up outside the print shop in our Daimler Sovereign and instructed Gregory not to touch anything.

'I'll be two minutes,' Johnnie said and dashed inside.

He'd already phoned ahead to say he was picking up the paperwork, so he was in the shop less than two minutes and emerged just in time to see Gregory sitting in the driver's seat, having pulled the brake off, pretending to drive, and the car slipping down the road into yet another Mini, which it hit right in the backside. Open-mouthed, Johnnie ran to check that Gregory was OK. He was, and they drove home in the very dented Daimler.

'I've done it again, Jules,' Johnnie said as he walked into the kitchen hand in hand with Gregory. 'I left him in the car for less than two minutes. He took the brake off and destroyed another Mini.'

My jaw dropped and I looked from Johnnie to Gregory, lost for words. Then Johnnie scratched his head and turned to Gregory. 'Just tell us this, son, what is it that you've got against Minis?'

We had to stop ourselves from laughing, while at the same time vowing that we would be keeping a much closer eye on Gregory in future, especially where Minis, or any car for that matter, were concerned.

It's never possible to completely avoid scrapes where children are concerned. The lovely park opposite the house was where the children would ride their bicycles. I had bought a bike for each of them, including a three-wheeler for Claire. One day she was happily cycling along when the trike hit an obstacle and she was thrown forward and cut her bottom lip wide open on the handlebars. Leaving Linda in charge of the boys, Johnnie and I rushed her up to Brighton Hospital, where we sat and waited for three solid hours, only to be told by a nurse that there were no doctors available to attend to her. My two-year-old bleeding baby had to be taken home without any medical attention whatsoever. She has the scar to this day.

While we were living a suburban life in Hove, my relatives on my mother's side were all getting on with their lives and had settled down in Blackpool. One by one, like I had, they were moving into houses and they had their own families now, so we didn't see as much of them as we used to.

My Aunt Vera had a palmistry place on Blackpool Promenade, in front of which was a forecourt where her son, Johnnie, my cousin, ran a hot dog stall. Johnnie's nickname was Loagy, and when I asked him where it had come from, he told me a story about a horrible little man who had worked at the same fairground as my family many years before. Although most Romanies kept themselves to themselves and didn't mingle with non-Romany travellers, we always had a great respect for those travellers who worked at the fairgrounds as they had an incredible work ethic, often working fourteen- or sixteen-hour days, seven days a week, throughout the entire summer season. However, there was one short, stocky man named Loagy, who always left his darts stall unattended, instead spending his days jumping onto empty seats on rides and helping himself to candy floss when stall owners weren't looking! Poor Johnnie. I don't know what he must have done as a child to inherit such a nickname!

One day a police car pulled up in front of Johnnie's stall. Aunt Vera had several people waiting for readings and Johnnie had a queue of people waiting for hot dogs.

The policeman got out of his car and made straight for Johnnie. 'I've got some bad news for you,' he said. 'Your mother's house has been burgled.'

The police officer and our family knew each other, as my relatives were famous characters around the town and were on first-name terms with most of the locals. Johnnie immediately pulled the policeman to one side. 'For God's sake, don't tell me mother yet,' he pleaded. 'I don't want to frighten her.'

Johnnie walked over to his mother's palmistry booth. 'Mother,' he said, 'something's happened to one of my stalls up the road. You'll have to keep your eyes on my hot dogs and onions or they'll burn. I won't be long.' He then turned to the clients waiting for his mother and said, 'Sorry, ladies, I won't be long, hot dogs on the house while you're waiting.' And off he went, following the policeman.

On hearing this, Aunt Vera, who had never served a hot dog in her life, picked up the apron he had thrown down and looked at the hungry crowd. With a nod she said, 'You next, love?'

Her waiting clients had begun to join the back of the hot dog queue, not wanting to lose their place. Aunt Vera washed her hands in the enamel bowl that stood on the small table behind the stall, picked up a roll, sliced it down the middle, laid it on a serviette, placed a sausage from the hot plate into the roll and stirred the onions round in the pan next to the dogs. This was easier than Johnnie had made it look, she thought, a bit smugly.

She looked at her first customer and uttered a line which was to become famous for years to come: 'Do you want any onons?' It was what Romany women called onions.

The man at the front of the queue stared back at her blankly. 'Pardon?' he said, unsure of what he had just heard.

'Onons,' she said again confidently.

The man blinked twice and quickly looked to the woman behind him for help, who just shrugged her shoulders. Aunt Vera looked at them both as if they were stark raving mad, pulled her shoulders back, and with a voice as loud as she could muster said to the whole crowd, 'Now, if any of you want any bloody onons, you'd better make your minds up before you get to the front of the queue!'

She gave a defiant look to the bemused man and piled not just one but two giant helpings of 'onons' onto his hot dog, and then waved him to the side, shouting, 'Next!'

The crowd started to roar with laughter as they realized what she had meant, then all of a sudden Aunt Vera clicked and began to laugh too, nodding her head and giggling. 'I meant *onions,* didn't I?!'

Meanwhile, at Aunt Vera's house, Johnnie and the policeman arrived at a scene which was horrifying. All of his mother's beautiful silverware and her Crown Derby pots and ornaments were gone. He raced upstairs, where he knew his mother kept her jewellery and her safe. With slight relief, he noticed the safe was still there, but was horrified when he saw that there was no jewellery in the tray on her dressing table. He was always warning her about putting her beloved belongings in the safe, and now his worst fears were being played out before his eyes.

'How did they get in?' he said to the policeman as he struggled to suppress the deep anger which was slowly but surely beginning to bubble away inside. As was the way with us Romanies, rather than putting money in the bank, Aunt Vera had invested hers in beautiful china, gold and diamonds, and Johnnie knew he had to go and tell her that everything she had to show for her life's work had been taken.

'They broke a window at the back,' the policeman said. 'We're doing what we can, Johnnie. The neighbours are all being asked if they saw anyone hanging about.'

Understandably Aunt Vera was completely devastated when Johnnie told her what had happened, and unfortunately the thieves were never caught and none of Aunt Vera's prized possessions returned to their rightful owner.

Aunt Vera's daughter Daisy had married Sonny Boy over a decade earlier – and it was through Sonny Boy that her sister Honour came to know her future husband, Eric Boswell. Most Romany people who end up marrying know each other from when they are small children, but Eric and Honour did not meet until they were adults and both attended a Romany wedding in Blackpool. Eric was good friends with Sonny Boy, and had been since a young age, so he used Sonny Boy as an excuse to visit Blackpool, so he could see Honour. If there was a funeral or a wedding, or if it was Christmas, Eric was sure to turn up. Honour and Daisy would meet with Eric and Sonny Boy and go out for meals because Romany people don't go out as couples on their own unless they are married, or at least they didn't in those days.

Eric eventually popped the question and Honour said yes, and, in the family tradition, they decided to elope. Three times they set a date and had everything arranged, but on the first two occasions Honour lost her nerve. The third time, in early December, Eric picked her up near her home to make sure she couldn't get cold feet and change her mind, and off they went to get married at the local register office.

Time went by and, as it got near to Christmas, Honour was still afraid to tell her parents she had a husband. Eric was handsome, he had a wonderful voice, he earned a good living trading horses, but he could not persuade Honour to own up that she was a married woman until the New Year. This was because Honour did not want to spoil the Christmas festivities by stealing the limelight and having the Romany ceremony which would have had to follow. She knew she could not go and live with him until this marriage ceremony had been performed, as well as the one they had been through together. On New Year's Eve, they finally dropped their bombshell, and, as in my case, Honour needn't have been worried at all as Aunt Vera was as over the moon as Mummy had been when mine and Johnnie's elopement had been announced. Eric had been hanging round for quite some time by this point anyway so it wouldn't have taken Sherlock Holmes to work out that a wedding was on the cards!

So on New Year's Eve, Aunt Vera carried out the Romany ceremony and gave the newlyweds her blessing, before they jumped in Eric's car, with its brand-new trailer behind it, and took off to begin their new life together.

Honour and Eric spent their winters with family in Blackpool and the rest of the year travelling round, but due to Eric's work as a horse trader they always made sure to visit Appleby, in Cumbria, which was (and is still) well known for its horse fair, where all the Romany men, and other horse traders, would gather to buy and sell horses. There was a piece of ground just outside a village called Sedbergh, near Appleby, close to a big woodland called the Brackens, and for hundreds of years it was a place where travelling people would stop before going on to Appleby, to give the horses a rest and make them presentable for the fair.

Each year, Eric and Honour would do just that on their way to Appleby, but one year, about a decade after they had got married, they and their children – Kay, the eldest, Eva, who was nicknamed 'Muzzer' as she could never pronounce 'mother' properly, and Baby Honour – had a rather strange experience there. Travelling people had always believed this place to be haunted, and Eric and Honour were about to find out why.

Eric and Honour had a stallion named Jack, the only male horse they owned, and they had eight black and white fillies, along with their string of foals tethered on chains. One evening, on checking the animals,

Eric came in to report to Honour that the horses were all bucking, jumping and screaming. It was quite late and there was nothing he could do to calm his animals, although he tried every method he knew. He couldn't understand what the matter was with them.

Early the next morning, all the animals had broken free of their chains and disappeared. Eric and Honour's daughter, Kay, who would have been seven or eight at the time, had a great way with horses and, with a determined look, turned to her father and said, 'I'm going to look for them, Daddy. We'll get them back.'

They set off to look for their animals, her father going one way and Kay another. Roughly three miles down the lane, Kay found Jack, the fillies and the foals. Knowing the fillies would follow Jack and the foals would follow their mothers, she jumped onto Jack's back, without a saddle, and rode him back to the Brackens, with the rest of the animals following behind. Once they were safely back, Honour declared, 'That's the last time we pull in here. This ground obviously has something which frightens the horses.'

Once they reached Appleby, they recounted their story to the travellers, who all claimed to have had similar experiences. 'Well, that was definitely our last time there,' Eric declared. 'Ghosts aren't company I want to be keeping.'

Two days into their trip to Appleby, Eric turned to

Honour and said, 'We're going to buy a nanny goat. I've just been hearing how good the milk is for the children.'

Honour looked at her husband and knew that he was a man of his word and that they would shortly be proud owners of a nanny goat. And sure enough, a few days later Eric had acquired a goat and the next morning proudly stated that Nanny's milk was on the table. It didn't go down too well with the children, though – it tasted horrible. They weren't used to anything but cow's milk, but how could they tell Eric, who was so sure he was giving the best to his family? Honour tried to raise the point that it did not taste quite the same, but Eric was adamant.

'It's like gold dust,' he declared.

She didn't want to upset her husband, so early the next morning, she crept out of bed and grabbed the jug with the goat's milk from the belly box, their larder at the back of the vardo. She knew there was a farm nearby and quickly and quietly walked up there and acquired some cow's milk from the farmer. An hour later, safely back in the vardo and preparing breakfast for her family, she watched as Eric picked up the jug of cow's milk and poured it into a glass. He raised it to his lips, took a sip and with a proud look said, 'See, you need to trust me, gal, I've never tasted better milk!'

Honour smiled, but the beauty of the story was that Eric had secretly been pulling the same trick on her!

'I couldn't drink the goat's milk,' he later admitted to her, 'so I've been getting buckets of cow's milk from the farmer.'

It wasn't long before Eric had sold the goat on to a farmer who already had a few goats on his land, and the children were able to rest easy that they would always get cow's milk for their breakfast from now on!

TWENTY-SIX

A Crop of Shirts

I had to go to Manchester on business and Eddie and Nicky volunteered to drive me up in their caravanette. Linda Lump, our nanny, was going to be at home during the day to look after the children. Johnnie, meanwhile, had a long list of errands to run. We were all very busy little people.

It was planned that on the evening before I went away, Johnnie and I would take the children for an early dinner at our favourite Chinese restaurant, the Nang King. He'd been in meetings with our accountant, and when it got to six o'clock and he was supposed to be back at home to pick us up, he was nowhere to be seen. The children watched out the window for him, but still no Johnnie.

By seven o'clock, I couldn't wait any longer and phoned a taxi to take the children and me to the restaurant. There we found Johnnie with our accountant, our solicitor and two other friends. They were all obviously very merry and were enjoying glasses of wine, which Johnnie never usually drank. His tipple was only ever lager, and he never touched spirits. 'What sort of state is he going to be in?' I wondered. I sat the children at the other end of the restaurant, as I didn't want them to see the state of all the men, especially their father, whom they had never seen inebriated. After one of the quickest meals we'd ever had, I phoned another taxi and took them home and bathed them. I was fuming. It was the first time Johnnie had ever let me down. I hadn't even spoken to him in the restaurant, for fear I would lose it in front of our children and our solicitor and accountant.

After I'd put the children to bed, my blood was really up, as he still hadn't returned home. 'Right,' I thought to myself, 'payback time.' I grabbed a spade from the garage, went into the garden and started to dig a hole, a really big hole. I took my anger out on the soil. I then went up to our bedroom and gathered up all of Johnnie's shirts. Taking them back out into the garden, I dropped them one by one into the hole, counting as I went. By the time I'd counted up to seventy-two, I gleefully threw the last of the shirts into the hole and covered them with soil, doing a war dance on top of them.

But then I started to feel really guilty. He hadn't really done anything so very wrong. A simple phone call from him would have put things right. I felt wicked, but I also felt that justice had been served. After all, I could have cut the shirts up or burnt them, but I'd only buried them. Johnnie got through two shirts a day, one in the morning and a clean one just before dinner. 'Not tomorrow,' I thought to myself with an evil chuckle. I put a note on the bedroom door – 'Do not disturb' – and when he returned, he did not dare enter.

I woke up bright and early the next morning and got the children ready for school. Eddie arrived with his caravanette and I left everything in Linda's capable hands, with Johnnie snoring away on the sofa in the background, in a very deep sleep indeed.

Eddie, Nicky and I set off and I related what I had done to Johnnie for letting me down. They howled with laughter.

'He will see the funny side of it,' I told them. 'Imagine when he opens the wardrobe door and instead of a neat row of ironed shirts on hangers, he sees nothing.'

We laughed all the way to Manchester. I had not told Linda what I had done, for I knew she would have dug his shirts up for him.

When we arrived at the hotel, there were several messages from Johnnie. I called to check on the children and a laughing Johnnie answered the phone.

'OK, you witch, where are they? I've phoned your

mother, I've phoned your friends and I've phoned Pat. Where have you hidden them?'

I refused to answer.

Later that evening, Johnnie rang me at the hotel again. 'Linda was in the kitchen ironing the boys' shirts. It was raining, and she called for me to come quickly. I did and saw your hidden treasure immediately. The sleeve of one of my shirts was sticking out of the ground where the rain had disturbed the earth. Poor Linda thought there was a dead body buried in the garden! Pity it didn't rain earlier in the day as I could have saved the money I spent on six new shirts.'

He was taking my escapade in very good heart, and we both began to see the funny side.

When I returned home the following evening, Johnnie had drawn me a cartoon of our garden. It had little bushes with miniature shirts growing on them and the caption underneath read, 'Your planting has been very successful!'

It wasn't the only time some unaccustomed booze was to cause us problems. Not long after this incident, Petulengros from all over the country were phoning each other as my cousin Pamela, Aunt Lena's daughter, was about to get married. 'Are you going to Pam's wedding? What are you wearing?' Everyone wanted to know. It became a family joke that we would always say to one another, 'I'm wearing my purple mink, what about you?' In those days, we all wore mink and fox fur and so on, and I had a fabulous furrier called Mr Dudkin. With a wedding approaching, I walked into his shop and decided that if he had anything I liked, I would treat myself for the Big Day.

He slid open one of his large cabinets saying, 'I've just done a big show in London and these are what I had made for it.'

I couldn't believe my eyes when I saw a purple mink jacket next to a yellow one and a green one.

'You wouldn't be interested in those,' Mr Dudkin said.

'Oh, wouldn't I?' I replied, slipping off the coat I was wearing and putting on the purple jacket. It was perfect: not bright purple, more brownish with a purple tinge.

That evening I noticed, from our calendar in the kitchen, that the day before the wedding Johnnie and I were booked to go to France on a day trip with a group of friends.

'We need to cancel the trip, Johnnie,' I said.

'Why?' he asked.

'Because we have to leave very early for the wedding. If we have a late night, how are we going to feel the next day?'

I argued my point, but to no avail. We had both been looking forward to the French trip, but my clairvoyant senses told me it was a silly idea to go the day before such a big event. What should I do? Argue with him or go along with it? I knew what the answer should be but, against my instincts and common sense, I agreed to go anyway.

On the morning of the French trip, around twenty of us boarded the ferry and set off. We had ordered a massive seafood lunch at the other end, and our plan was to eat and then hit the shops and have a leisurely look around.

I particularly liked French children's clothes and usually bought my children new outfits on those trips. We did two or three trips a year and, of course, stocked up on our duty-free.

By the time we arrived at the restaurant, we were all starving. The waiters filled the table with large bowls of steaming little brown shrimps, plentiful in Lincolnshire, but not at all easy to find in Brighton. The shrimp was followed by lobsters and crabs and assorted salads and fruits, washed down with lovely French wines. Now fed and watered, we sat back and relaxed with our friends Pat and Brian, Prince and Sammy, and Allan.

Brian called to the waiter, 'Brandy all round, please.' My heart sank. Although Johnnie never drank spirits,

I realized this was going to be a booze-up. I knew I couldn't be a spoilsport, but I also dreaded him having a hangover for the wedding the next day.

Later that evening, when we all went to board the ferry, Johnnie was nowhere to be seen, and there was no sign either of another couple who had accompanied us, Mr and Mrs Fitzherbert. I was quite angry at this. As we set off back to Brighton, I wondered what had happened to my husband, and as I looked in my bag, I saw with a sick feeling that Johnnie's passport was staring back at me. I explained to the man in charge on the ferry what had happened and he assured me he'd have my husband on the next boat out – if, that was, he was at the dock in time. He verified the passport I had and went off to make the necessary communications. How I wish we'd had mobile phones then! The journey felt like a nightmare and, yet again, I wished I'd listened to my instincts.

Later that evening, long after I'd got home, Johnnie arrived at our front door, with Mr and Mrs Fitzherbert in tow. He was very shame-faced, but I didn't have a go at him, as I realized it was my fault I hadn't given him the passport. I don't know whether he thought I was going to cut his head off or what, but he must have felt bad, as he'd clearly brought Mr and Mrs Fitzherbert along as back-up, in case my reception was a frosty one. He looked relieved when he saw that I was not angry, but I soon wiped the smile off his face when I said, 'That's OK, darling, next time we go anywhere, I'm going to put you on a lead.'

But we could never stay angry with each other for long and so after I glared at him for a few seconds with my arms crossed, I began to feel the corners of my mouth turning up, and then he winked at me. That was it then; we were both in fits of laughter.

The next day the convoy of cars hit the road for the wedding. We had all arranged to meet at a large, luxurious hotel, where we were booked in for two nights. Together again. Mummy, Aunt Vera, Aunt Adeline, Aunt Lena – the mother of the bride – and Shunty, all huddled into a corner, catching up on all the latest gossip, with raucous laughter erupting every time one of them said something they shouldn't. The conversations were far too good for any of us to have an early night.

Inevitably, the story of the cat that killed itself came up. My mother was one of the bravest women I knew, and yet she was terrified of cats. When she saw a cat she would freeze and say, 'Go away, go away.'

As a child, this made me think that cats could harm me. In my teens, Mummy told me why she felt this way. Apparently, when she was fifteen, someone had given the Smith girls, as they were called, a kitten, which they all adored. They even allowed it into their vardo, which is not something Romanies would usually do. One afternoon Mummy was alone with the cat, which was now grown, when, for some unknown reason, it suddenly went berserk and was jumping all over the place.

'It was banging its head on the wooden walls of the vardo, hissing and angry and almost demented,' Mummy recalled with a shudder.

She had stood looking at the cat, appalled, not knowing what to do. 'I wanted to run from the vardo, but I was frozen to the spot, couldn't move a muscle.'

The cat was crashing against the walls of the vardo with such force that it eventually fell to the floor, dead. Mummy went to the vardo next door, where her brothers were. She told them what had happened and they went to investigate. Nathan, her eldest brother, felt sorry for his sister and came in with a smile on his face, while the other boys disposed of the cat's body.

'Laura,' he said, 'I think it was trying to tell us that it doesn't like living with the Romanies.'

My brother Nathan chipped in with another story about Mummy. She was on the forecourt of her palmistry place on the front of Brighton's Palace Pier one hot Sunday afternoon. It was a Bank Holiday weekend, so there were swarms of people all over the seafront.

There was a queue of people waiting for readings

and Mummy was in with a lady who was a regular. All of a sudden, the curtain at the door was swept to one side and a shaven head poked through, that of a young yob, who started shouting. Mummy could tell immediately from his eyes that he was high on something.

'Rubbish, rubbish,' he was screaming at the top of his voice, and turning his head from one side of her room to the other. Mummy was immediately on her feet, and when he saw this, he started backing away to join his two friends, who stood outside laughing.

'Don't mess with me, boys, or you will really regret it. Now go away and play,' she said calmly, exactly the right thing to say to young men to make them feel inferior. With that, she took her seat again with dignity, knowing that the people outside were watching her. She continued with her reading. Five minutes later, the same boy's head poked back through the top of the curtain. He must have been sitting on someone's shoulders. At the same time, another boy's head peered through the bottom of the curtain. She ignored them, knowing full well they were going to do it again. Sure enough, the heads disappeared and she whispered to the client, 'Don't be alarmed, I'm going to deal with them.'

She picked up the broom she used for sweeping litter from the front of her place and as soon as the head popped through the curtain again, she was ready.

She lunged forward with the broom, knocking him off the shoulders of his friend. People outside, of course, could see what was happening, and she could hear the boy shouting, 'Ooh, ow!' She opened the curtain to see the boy she had attacked on the floor, blood running from his nose, rubbing the back of his head, which he had obviously hit when he had fallen. He was crying like a baby.

Mummy turned round to head back into her booth and calmly said over her shoulder, 'You reap what you sow, boys.' For good measure, she gave a hearty laugh, at which the crowd started clapping and shouting, 'Well done, Laura – you showed them.'

Needless to say, she did not see them again!

Now that Nathan had an audience, he kept coming out with his tales. 'Back in the sixties, while at my photographic stall on the forecourt of the Palace Pier in Brighton, I was talking to this great guy called Chris who was working for me,' he said. 'He was showing me his new camera with pride, as it was the latest thing – fully automatic, electric rewind and so on. He asked me to take a photograph of him on the stall, which I did. At this point, one of the Red Arrows was flying overhead and hit the aluminium mast of a yacht that was anchored between the two piers. Terrifyingly, the plane came straight towards us, flying upside down.

'I was clicking away with his camera on automatic

when the pilot pressed the eject button and, to my amazement, the seat shot out downwards, turned and shot up into the air. "What a photo!" I thought, still clicking away. The pilot finished up in the sea, and we all helped to pull him out. More magic photos! This was the first time Chris had used the camera and – guess what? You've got it. He hadn't loaded the film properly!'

It was nearly dinner time, and we'd all arranged to eat together in the hotel restaurant. I sat with Honour, Daisy, Aunt Cissie's daughter Adeline, and Aunt Lena's daughters Dixie, Lavinia and Vera, the sisters of the bride, around a big table. None of them could believe their eyes when I turned up in a purple mink coat. The bride and groom were moving from one table to another, to do the rounds and greet their guests. The bride, my cousin Pamela, was a very curvy redhead, who had fabulous legs and was once approached by a famous lingerie company who wanted to use her legs in an advert, but of course she refused. With naturally curly red hair and huge sparkling eyes, she was a real head-turner.

The ceremony was to take place in a lovely little church in Gorleston, near Great Yarmouth. Pam looked beautiful in her wedding dress, and about half an hour before the ceremony, Clarence, the groom, a tall, imposing chap, pulled me to one side and told me, 'One thing that would make this whole day complete would be to have our photograph in the local paper, Eva. As you work for the papers, do you think you could help us get it in?'

'It's a bit short notice, Clarence, but I'll do what I can. Get me to a phone, quickly.' Luckily, I was able to get hold of the picture editor of the local paper that ran my horoscopes.

'You have an opportunity to take a photograph of something that's never been photographed before,' I said impressively.

'Just what would that be?' he asked sceptically.

'Well, firstly, it's a Romany wedding, *and* the bride and groom will be jumping over a broomstick.'

To my amazement, he was interested and agreed. I quickly sent Clarence off on a mission to borrow a broomstick. I did lie, I admit it now. Jumping over a broom is not part of our ceremony – never has been and never will be – but they got their wish to have their picture in the local paper.

Meanwhile, just as Pamela and Clarence were embarking on their life together as happy newlyweds, Eddie and Nicky, who had always seemed like the perfect couple, were drifting further and further apart.

One of the things that had first drawn Eddie and

Nicky to one another was their shared love of travelling, exploring and discovering new and exciting places. But when they had travelled abroad and Eddie had realized that his inability to communicate with people who spoke languages other than English made him feel out of control and unsafe, he confined his desire to travelling Great Britain. Nicky, however, had a wanderlust that she just couldn't suppress.

Nicky desperately wanted to travel further afield and she so badly wanted to make her journey with Eddie. She couldn't recognize his need to stay where he felt safe and in control. She thought that if she went, he would follow her, but it wasn't to be. Eddie was very much his own man. He, in turn, couldn't understand that she had a desperate need to fulfil her desire to see the world, as her father had done, and a tragic, never-to-be-healed split occurred between them. It had nothing to do with their love for each other, which remained strong. It was just two obstinate people, each refusing to give in.

Time went by, and eventually Nicky decided that she had to go and do this thing that meant so much to her. She left Eddie and went to stay with her grand-parents, spending the next two days crying over photographs of her and Eddie, reminiscing and making her own plans.

Nicky spent the following two years travelling the

world, learning and experiencing everything she had ever dreamed of. But Eddie didn't follow her, and they would both regret their decision for the rest of their lives. Their stubbornness would always keep them apart – two people who could have been one of the happiest couples I'd ever known.

Eddie never got over her, but has always been there for her through thick and thin, as have we all. She was to remain an important member of the family, who was never seen as an outsider but instead as one of us. She always will be.

TWENTY-SEVEN

Daisies and Buttercups

'Oh, I do love travelling,' I said to Johnnie.

We were driving down narrow lanes in Cornwall, and I dreamily watched the trees through the window, all different shades of green and brown. The sun shining down through them was very therapeutic. Occasionally I saw a small animal, such as a rabbit or a squirrel, and it always fascinated me how they would run and then stop, in an attempt to blend in with the scenery. We passed fields with horses chewing away at the grass, oblivious to the outside world, swishing their tails to get rid of the flies.

'Mummy, I want to go to wee,' Warren began.

'So do I, so do I,' followed Bradley.

'So do I,' echoed Gregory.

'There are no toilets on this road, boys,' Johnnie said.

I laughed. 'Don't be silly. They can go at the side of the road.'

Johnnie was horrified at the suggestion. He might have become a Romany in many ways over the years, but some traveller ways he would never adopt!

'We are going to Cornwall on holiday,' I'd told the children the night before. 'Back to where we went last year.'

They had all become very excited at the thought of the good times we'd had before, with Nathan and Sue, their two girls, Georgie and Lisa, and their two boys, Douglas and Eddie. But this year we had told the rest of our close Romany family our plans, and they'd all decided they too wanted to come with us. After we'd described the acres of fields that were perfect for coursing and a posh hotel called the Old Smithy, behind which were around fifteen to twenty chalets, they simply couldn't resist. We booked six of the chalets, as six families were going.

We had decided to leave very early in the morning, to avoid the traffic, and hoped to arrive around six in the evening, at the same sort of time as the others. Sonny Boy, my cousin Daisy's husband, and Eric Boswell, my cousin Honour's husband, had told us that they were bringing their coursing dogs with them. They each had a trailer attached to their car for their dogs.

It was a long journey, and by the time we arrived at the Old Smithy it was almost quarter to seven. The landlord was a charming man called John Mailier, with his German wife Anna, and once we'd all arrived and he'd fed us huge platefuls of his delicious beef Wellington, anyone would have thought we were old family friends. They made us feel so welcome.

The children, who were sat around a big table that held lemonade, orange juice, snacks and loads of paper and coloured pencils that John and Anna had set up for them, were all beginning to look quite tired. 'Good,' I thought. 'They won't be waking me early in the morning.' Fat chance! They were up before Johnnie, who was about to go coursing for the first time in his life. He had told our boys they could go too, so they had every reason to want to wake up earlier than I'd planned. Dressed in Wellington boots and warm sweaters I had knitted for them, navy blue with a white stripe across the neck and the back, the boys looked like triplets. Why not? There were only thirteen months between each one of them.

After they left, I dressed Claire. There was a knocking on our door. It was Honour's three girls, Kay, Muzzer and Baby Honour.

'Auntie Eva,' Kay said, 'we're going to look for flowers. Can we take Claire with us and look after her for you?'

I wasn't worried because the field the chalets were in had a high fence all the way round it, so Claire wouldn't be able to wander off or get lost. After about five minutes, Claire came running back into the chalet, clutching a handful of wild flowers. 'These are for you, Mummy,' she bellowed enthusiastically. She quickly ran outside again to join her cousins. Watching from the doorway, for a few seconds I was a child again myself. In a flash, I could see myself in a field with Honour and Daisy, playing buttercups. You would pick a buttercup and hold it underneath one of the other girls' chins. If the sun was in the right position, it would shine on the flower and make a yellow glow under the chin, and we would shout, 'You love butter!' If the sun was in the wrong position, and there was no shadow on the chin, we would shout, 'You don't like butter!' We would roll in the grass and laugh with each other. With this thought in my mind, I could not resist. I ran outside to join the children and showed them how to make daisy chains.

Later that afternoon, the men returned, with the older children in tow. My boys were so excited.

'We saw rabbits and the dogs were chasing them,' Warren screamed, full of excitement.

Again, this made me remember my own experiences at their age, and I felt sorry for my children, as what was so normal and natural for me at their age was such a rare adventure for them. Their childhood was taking place in the middle of Brighton, where there were no fields, wild rabbits or hares.

'And we saw squirrels,' Bradley told me, wide-eyed.

'There were some cows in the field going *moo*, Mummy,' Gregory informed me.

I smiled at my three boys. It was good to see the colour in their cheeks and the excitement of the unknown shining in their eyes.

Mummy had got Eddie to run her down to the village, and when she returned, she informed me that she had bought some chickens for the cookout that evening. It was getting on for six o'clock by now, and the menfolk had been to the woods to gather dead wood for the fire. With nothing else to do, us women sat around the fire the men had lit for us, gossiping and watching our children play together. It felt as if life could not get any better. The weather was perfect, as were our moods.

One of Daisy's children came running over. It was Julie.

'I've stung my leg, Mummy, it hurts,' she moaned.

Daisy said, 'I did warn you to watch out for stinging nettles. Now run off and find some dock leaves that I can put on it.'

I exchanged knowing looks with Daisy and Honour, remembering the many times we'd had to go looking for dock leaves for exactly the same reason when we were children.

John, the landlord, appeared, together with his

barman, pushing a large trolley laden with a big plastic dustbin which was filled with ice and cold lager and lemonade. He also produced a folding table.

'This is your kitchen, Laura,' he said to Mummy. 'And here are my best kitchen knives,' he went on, carefully handing her a box.

Mummy produced her four chickens. She dramatically poked the sharpened sticks up their backsides and proceeded to throw salt, pepper and herbs all over them. They had only been cooking a few minutes when she pronounced them done. Everyone protested, saying they couldn't possibly be cooked, but Mummy went ahead anyway, ripping the birds apart with two forks and passing them round. The meat was perfectly done, although no one could work out how she'd managed it.

Apparently, our landlord had informed the locals that the lounge bar was out of bounds, as he had reserved it for the Romany families, realizing that we liked to talk among ourselves and needed our own space. This, however, did not go down well with some of the locals. We could understand why. They did, after all, support the bar all year round, and it was no surprise they felt as if their noses had been put out of joint.

After having been in the public bar for about an hour, two of the locals, fortified with a little Dutch courage, pushed into the lounge bar and started to use unnecessarily strong language. They shouted at the land-lord, 'All of these gypos are thieves and cheats. What are you doing giving them preference over us?'

Eric and Sonny Boy stood up and moved towards the two locals, with Eddie and Nathan close behind. Eric looked at the landlord and with a cock of his head asked, 'Is it OK if we put these two idiots outside?'

'Yes, please,' John replied, as he stepped out from behind the bar.

It took no time for them to manhandle the two abusive men outside. No one from the public bar, thank goodness, tried to intervene. They could see that these two had had a skinful and were looking to cause trouble. A little while later, the local bobby strolled into the bar.

'I hear the Romanies have been causing some trouble,' he said. With this, he grinned. He was a friend of John's who often called in for a 'quick one' at the end of his shift, and he had popped over to make sure everything was OK, so he was only winding us up! John had wanted to make sure that things did not get out of hand, as they so often easily could, where tempers and alcohol were concerned.

Some of us women were creasing (gossiping) in one of the chalets about what titbits we had heard. When the men came in, Daisy stood up. 'Don't tell me which locals were the troublemakers, Sonny,' she said. 'I'll bet it was the two propping up the end of the bar when we came in – am I right?'

The men were not surprised at Daisy's instincts, which were, of course, correct, as they experienced this almost every day with their women.

'We knew they were no good, didn't we?' She looked at the other women. 'But we're not going to let it spoil the handsome time we're having.'

Mummy suddenly came in and asked, 'Has anybody been in my chalet? Eddie's gold cufflinks and my gold chain are not where we left them.'

We all looked at each other and were silent until Nathan spoke. 'Listen, I suggest we don't mention it to anyone. We all know each other well enough to know we haven't moved or stolen them. We can catch the monkeys out for ourselves if we lay a trap.'

We all knew from experience that you don't leave valuables in a hotel room or anywhere that might prove too much for those who might be tempted to take them. We almost always carried them with us. What had happened in Mummy's chalet was a timely reminder. The men spent the rest of the evening plotting how to trap the culprit or culprits. Eddie laughingly named it 'the Agatha Christie Project' and nicknamed himself Clouseau, after the bumbling French inspector from the Pink Panther films. John the landlord had also been brought into the sting, as he wanted to know as much as we did who was responsible for taking our belongings and causing such friction between the Romanies and gorger folk.

The next day he contacted the two men who had already tried to cause trouble and explained that they were welcome to come into the bar.

'Everyone had been drinking,' he explained, 'but you're welcome to come back into the bar anytime.'

'This is fun,' laughed Sonny Boy.

Everyone nodded in agreement, and amid laughter, they all headed to the pub. When they walked in, Eric, Sonny Boy and Johnnie went up to the pair we had christened 'the chorers', which was Romany for thief. They put out their hands.

'No hard feelings, mate,' Sonny Boy said. 'I think we'd all had one over the eight last night, don't you?'

Nervously, the chorers nodded in agreement. They couldn't believe their luck. The men spent the next half-hour telling jokes and being very matey with the locals, particularly the chorers.

'No more drinks now, as we're driving,' Eric said. 'We're all off to a friend's, at Clovelly. Won't be back till the morning. See you tomorrow night.' They gave a nod to the gorgers.

Little did anyone other than the landlord and landlady suspect that all of the Romany women and children had been smuggled upstairs into the guest rooms, with strict instructions to keep the noise level low and stay out of sight. Meanwhile, the men took off and went to hide their cars. They decided to lie in wait quietly, two men to a chalet, no lights, in case anyone decided to chance their luck and break in.

It was too easy. Within half an hour, the door to the room where Eddie and Nathan were waiting opened. Two figures crept into the main bedroom. Nathan jumped up and turned on the light and the startled chorers took in the sight before them, of Eddie lying on the bed with his hands behind his head and a big smile of welcome upon his face.

'We've been waiting for you, boys,' he said. He didn't move and neither did Nathan – the startled chorers could not have moved if they had tried. They looked like rabbits caught in the headlights of a car. All of a sudden, the other eight men flew into the chalet, with John the land- lord close behind them. They came to a halt, glad to see that there was no violence occurring. Everyone was rooted to the spot until Nathan's voice broke the silence.

'OK, I'm going to give you some options,' he announced. 'The first is that you take us to where my mother's chain and my brother's cufflinks are. The second option is that I'll take you to the police station and they'll search your homes and bang you up.'

The crowd of men watched as the two chorers began to visibly shake.

'The third option,' Nathan went on, 'is that we're going to give you the hiding of your lives.' Checking his watch, he said threateningly, 'You've got one minute to pick your option.'

'Please don't hurt me,' begged the first chorer, while the second one gave a big gulp, pulled his shoulders back and announced, 'We didn't touch nothing.'

Eddie said, 'Don't forget, my friends, that all our women are clairvoyant and they knew you were no good even before you took anything.' Turning to the other men in the room, he suggested, 'Let's just give them a good hiding anyway.'

This broke the second chorer's nerve immediately, as he realized these Romanies meant business. 'OK, OK,' he said, defeated, 'they're in the boot of my car.'

The men frogmarched both of them to the car and the landlord demanded the keys and opened up the boot. The contents were more than they had bargained for.

'I don't bloody believe this,' shouted Nathan. 'They're my golf clubs. They were in the boot of my car! And look – there's my camera bag.'

As a professional photographer, Nathan had worked hard for cameras that were the best money could buy. Mummy's jewellery was there, along with other unidentifiable jewellery. Nathan was breathing heavily. 'Get the gavengros [police].'

John interrupted him. 'They're already in the pub. The law can deal from here in.' He shook his head with disdain at the culprits and muttered, 'I should have guessed it was you two all along.' He turned to the others. 'Why did you go to such lengths if it was only a hunch?'

'Well, you've been so good to us, and we could tell a bad 'un a mile off. We just didn't want them to do the same to you when we were gone, so rather than warn you without any real proof, we decided we'd better give you some,' Nathan explained.

'Actually,' John said, 'things have been going missing for several weeks now, which is why I've gone out of my way to keep you all separate. I was too embarrassed to tell you the reason why, but now you've saved me the trouble, and caught two toerags in the process. Drinks on the house, boys. What'll you be having?'

The rest of the holiday went peacefully and happily, and soon we were all driving out of the car park, waving goodbye to our friends in Cornwall. I said to Johnnie, 'Why can't we just have a nice holiday? My life is always an adventure.' I sighed. 'I don't think I'd enjoy a normal life though, do you?'

He winked at me and replied, 'And I don't think I'd love you so much if you were normal. You make my life an adventure!'

TWENTY-EIGHT

April Fools

It was August 1976, and Winnie Sexton from the Cricketers phoned me up.

'Eva, it's me. There's a lovely couple, Brian and Jenny Richardson, who had a pub in London. They're good friends of mine, and they've now taken a pub in Brighton called the Iron Duke. They open tomorrow. Will you and Johnnie come with me for the opening?'

'We'd love to, Winnie,' I said. If they were friends of hers, then they had to be nice people. 'We'll pick you up.'

We arranged a time and said our goodbyes. The following night, we picked up Winnie and went on to the Iron Duke, where I was introduced to Jenny. We bonded immediately. She had two daughters, Jane and newborn Lisa. We'd been talking in the pub for about half an hour when I decided to go out and buy a bunch of flowers for my new friend. I bought two bunches of beautiful yellow roses and then I spotted an antiques shop and went in.

'Do you have any vases for sale?' I enquired. The shopkeeper did, and I thought a vase would be a wonderful bonus to go with the roses. After I had paid, I asked the shopkeeper if he would put some water in it. He obliged, and I arranged the two bunches of roses in the vase. Glancing round the shop, I also spotted a lovely side table. It was very ornate, and I instantly fell in love with it. The man told me it was £60. I had to have it and, after some bargaining, I managed to get him down to £35. Little did I know that, years later, it would be identified as a piece from the Palace of Versailles.

After presenting Jenny with her vase and roses, I asked Johnnie to go and pick up the new table I had bought for us, as the antiques shop was just up the road from the Iron Duke. He did, and after managing to get it into our car, we headed home, pleased with our purchase and the new friends we had made.

Jenny and I became firm friends, and she turned out to be a superb cook. The Iron Duke became first port of call for Johnnie and me when we went out to eat, keen as we were to sample Jenny's dishes of the day or evening. She was the only cook I knew to serve lobster curry. It was delicious!

A few months later, Winnie's friend from the

brewery offered to take a coachload of people to France, to be guests at Moët & Chandon, in the famous champagne region, for lunch. As we climbed aboard the bus, along with Brian and Jenny, the man from the brewery shouted, 'Have you all got your passports?' We nodded. Alas, when we arrived at the airport, the man from the brewery, so busy remembering to tell everyone else to bring their passports, had forgotten his! Somehow, after a series of phone calls, he was allowed to board the plane. We landed, boarded another coach and headed for the winery. We were treated to a most wonderful meal, accompanied, of course, by glasses of Moët & Chandon. We were then led to a steep flight of stairs, to go below and see how they made the champagne. I grabbed Jenny's arm before we headed downstairs and took her to one side.

'Jenny, do you really want to know how it's made?'

'Not really,' she giggled.

'Hold on a minute, let the others go down.'

We waited until everyone else had gone downstairs, with me pretending to look for something in my handbag. We were like two naughty little schoolgirls. We found our way out of the building and headed towards the gates, where a guard was on duty. 'Just popping out to the shops,' I said to him.

He let us out and we walked across the way, where we stumbled upon a little French bar where live music was being played. Without saying anything to each other, we drifted straight in and went up to the bar.

'It's got to be champagne,' I said to Jenny.

She nodded. 'This is better than dragging round some old cellars,' she giggled.

I excused myself to go to the ladies' and was shocked to find that instead of a traditional toilet, there was just a hole in the floor. *Mon Dieu!* I hadn't been in there more than a minute when someone started hammering on the door and hollering in French at me. I had no idea what the woman was saying, but whoever she was, it was obvious she was inebriated and, by the sound of her, wanted me to come out so she could come in.

As I came out of the toilet, there was a man in a grubby beige mac, who looked most unkempt. He appeared to be telling off the woman who had been hollering at me. As I went back into the bar to Jenny, he followed me.

'Come on, Jenny, let's get out of here,' I said, nodding my head towards the man on my tail. He then began speaking perfect English.

'It's all right, ladies, she's just the local prostitute,' he said. 'She's had too much to drink.'

'We're going anyway,' I said to him firmly.

'I am Gerard, the local commandant,' he said. 'I'm in charge of all the police here.'

'I don't care who you are, we're off.' As we made our way out of the bar, I saw Johnnie and Brian coming towards us. 'Thank God,' I said to Jenny. The man in the grubby mac was still following us. We ran towards our husbands, who were grinning like monkeys back at us.

'We didn't fancy it either,' Brian said. 'And we guessed where you two might be.' The man now joined our group and introduced himself to our husbands. 'That bar is no place for you people,' he said. 'Come with me and I'll take you to a nice place.'

'OK,' Johnnie said.

Indeed he did take us to a nice bar, and he turned out to be a nice chap. 'I think it was the grubby coat that gave me a bad first impression,' I whispered to Jenny.

After our drink, we left and returned to the brewery to meet the others, where the guard at the gate stood to attention and saluted our scruffy friend. He was indeed the local commandant!

Two days later, I was booked to go to Guernsey, to give readings at the Old Government House Hotel, known locally as the OGH. Pat was accompanying me. As usual, we missed a particular regular guest at the hotel. Every time we went there we either just missed him or he was coming the following week, but we would hear some wonderful tales about him from the porters. His name was Oliver Reed.

As we walked through the lobby, the manager approached us and said, 'You've done it again, he left yesterday. When you've settled in come and see me and I'll tell you the latest!'

We couldn't wait. 'Tell us now,' we pleaded. 'We've got an hour before our first client.' We all went into the lounge and sat down.

'Well, three days ago,' the manager began, 'Oliver didn't like the programme that was on TV in his suite, so he threw the television out of the window and it landed in the swimming pool! Two days ago, he was entertaining two ladies in the dining room, and they were all completely sozzled. At the next table, two lady residents were tutting at the noise and raucous goings-on. Oliver was out of his skull with alcohol and he stood up, unzipped his trousers and put his, ahem, *tool* on the table. This was quickly reported and so we had to throw him out. I told him that this time he had gone too far.

'The next night, about seven o'clock, he called us up and apologized profusely. He didn't sound drunk and pleaded to be allowed to come back. I told him that if he promised to behave, he would be welcome. Half an hour later, he arrived in a taxi and I was quickly alerted to go to the front door. When I got there, Oliver was back all right, but stark naked. The taxi driver was staring as if he knew what was going to happen. I said, "Get back in that taxi and don't come back again." Luckily for our residents, he did.

'He was here to make a television series about the war, about when the Germans invaded Guernsey, and a lot of the local boys had been in the bar when Oliver was there. They had been advertising for local people to dress up as German soldiers, and Oliver decided to join them. They all trooped along for auditions and most of the boys were taken on. Three were rejected, and one of those was Oliver! The star could play the lead in a film, but he didn't make the cast of extras! He's quite a character, ladies, I tell you.'

We added another pub to our list of Brighton favourites when John Mailier and his wife Anna, the couple who ran the Old Smithy in Cornwall, moved to our home town. They had desperately wanted to move to Brighton for a while and knew that the area manager from the Watneys brewery was a personal friend of Johnnie's, so they called him up and implored him to see if a decent public house could be found. Could he help them? He did! After a few months, with all negotiations sorted out between the brewery and the Mailiers, they became the proud tenants of the Battle of Waterloo in Kemp Town. It was in a small lane which was mostly occupied by little workshops for cars. The occupiers of these units would use John and Anna's public house regularly, and they all quickly became good friends.

On our first visit to the Battle of Waterloo, we were laughing and talking about our holiday and how our men trapped the chorers, when John Mailier came out with a stunner.

'Your mother is a real laugh,' he said. 'I'll never forget the day she came in with four frozen chickens and asked me to lay them in some hot water in order for them to defrost for that evening.'

At this, my ears pricked up. 'Well, you did a good job, John,' I volunteered. 'It only took them ten minutes to cook.'

He looked at me. 'Didn't she tell you I'd put them in the microwave oven for her?' he exclaimed.

None of my family had ever had a microwave, and we didn't even understand what they were. 'How does that go, John?' I enquired.

'Well,' he began, 'you can defrost a chicken in no time. In fact, I didn't just defrost them, I cooked them for her as well, in my big industrial micro oven.'

This had never occurred to me or any of my family, for we all assumed the chickens were raw and we thought Mummy had performed a miracle by cooking them in no time. In fact, all she'd had to do was brown the skins! She'd kept this secret from us for a long time. I could never have kept something like that to myself all that time. I remembered how she'd prepared the birds by throwing on herbs, lemon juice and salt and pepper and then stuck them round the fire to brown. My cousins and the menfolk all thought she had lost her marbles as she tossed herbs and spices about with such confidence.

John explained how microwaves worked, and the following day Johnnie and I went out and bought two. One for us and the other we took to Mummy's home.

'There you go, Mummy,' I said. 'Just in case you want to defrost any chickens!'

We would visit the Battle of Waterloo about once a fortnight, taking the children with us. Anna did a very nice Sunday lunch and had a lovely little girl called Sara Jane for Claire to play with. On one trip, at the end of March, Johnnie decided to play an April Fool's joke not only on John but also the other occupants and tenants he had become friendly with in the lane. With the aid of a photocopier, he had mocked up a letter heading from Brighton Council and had typed roughly the following: 'This road will be tarmacked commencing 6 April and we require all vehicles which are parked in the lane to be removed. The road will be closed for approximately one week and any vehicles or furniture left in the lane will be confiscated and destroyed.'

He posted one to all the residents he knew in the lane, including John, and waited for the fireworks. At eleven thirty in the morning on 1 April we walked into the pub, where ten angry men stood voicing their disapproval of the way this had been done. There was not a car in sight in the lane.

I whispered to Johnnie, 'I think you've gone too far, darling.'

As we approached the bar, John pulled out his letter and gave it to Johnnie to read. 'What do you think of that then?' he said angrily.

Johnnie pretended to scrutinize the letter, pulled out his pen and marked the first letter on each line then turned it round to John and announced, 'I think you've missed something.'

The capital letters at the start of each line spelled out APRIL FOOLS.

'Youuuuuuu!' shouted John. He stood up and addressed the crowd. 'Relax, men, it's all down to Johnnie, look.' He turned the piece of paper and pointed out each letter and announced, 'April Fools!'

The angry men didn't know whether to deck Johnnie or laugh and buy him a pint, but with the realization that their businesses were safe, they decided on the latter, thank God.

TWENTY-NINE

The Old Vicarage

'Stop the car, Johnnie,' I said.

We were driving along Ditching Road in Brighton when I saw it. An old vicarage with a For Sale sign outside.

He pulled over and I opened the door and jumped out. There was a large front garden with a gravel path up to the doorway. The left side of the house was covered in red ivy. On both sides of the gate were some very tall and fluffy reeds. I jerked the gate open and peered through a window. There was a garage at the side. Johnnie simply stood there, rolling his eyes, as he wrote down the number of the estate agent and the address. Without saying anything, we got back into the car and drove directly to the agent.

As we walked into the office, a young man sprang up from his chair. 'How can I help you good people today?'

'I want to buy 363 Ditchling Road,' I announced.

He gave me an indulgent smile. 'You and nineteen other people, madam,' he said. 'The Church is quite adamant that the successful buyer will not be whoever pays the most money, but the most suitable occupants, as the house has been a vicarage for many, many years.'

I sat down, crossed my legs and lit a cigarette (in those days, you could!). 'I'll tell you why they will choose me,' I explained. 'First of all, I have four children and the schools are just around the corner from the house.' He looked at me as if to say, *And what makes you any different from anyone else?* 'And secondly,' I continued, 'because I *want* that house and I trust you to make sure I get it!'

He looked a bit shocked for a second or two, and then began to bellow with laughter. 'Well, you're certainly adamant it's the house for you, aren't you? But don't you think it might be a good idea if you viewed the interior first?'

It was hysterical, we hadn't even seen the kitchen, but I had a good imagination. We'd been looking for a new house for ages; this one felt right and I knew we would get it. We told him we were more sure than we had ever been about anything, and with a chuckle and a disbelieving shake of his head, he picked up the phone and put in a good word for us. It was only a short while later that we received a phone call from him saying we had got the house – ahead of nineteen other people.

We grabbed the kids and jumped into our car to drive round to the property immediately, meeting the agent at the door. As soon as I walked in, I had a good feeling about the place. It was a huge house, with three big reception rooms, including a lovely sunny lounge, three bedrooms on the first floor, and a huge room that ran the entire length of the building on the second floor. It needed a complete overhaul, a top-to-toe make-over, but I knew it was perfect for us. And Johnnie was just the man to fix it up. Together, we could make the property into our own Shangri-La. We fell in love with it immediately.

On the day we moved in, the removal men, behind my back, asked the children if they'd like a pet rabbit. In the back garden there was a chicken pen, and anyone who knew me would know there was no chance I'd be putting any chickens in there, after my experience as a young girl, looking after the chicken farm my father won in a game of cards! Anyway, the removal men had suggested to the children that the pen was ideal to use as a rabbit hutch and they even had a rabbit to give them. They had sold them on the idea even before I'd heard about it, and the following day a removal man came to the front door holding a white rabbit with caramel markings, which Claire promptly named Mr Fluffy.

I had no choice, as she was obviously in love. 'Go and show it its new home,' I said. 'Get it out of the house.' I glared at the removal man. 'How dare you do that without asking my permission first,' I growled.

'But your husband said yes,' he said defensively.

I knew he was probably right, so I simply said, 'Well, you can't take it away now anyway. She's obviously besotted.'

Johnnie had gone out to buy some timber. 'God help him when he gets back,' I thought. Then, on reflection, I relented. Poor Johnnie, he had so much work to do, I didn't want to upset him. He was such a Libran pushover when it came to the kids, wanting to give them everything he had never had. Johnnie was born in 1930, nine years before the Second World War began, and was only eight years old when he was evacuated and taken away from his parents. He'd left school before he was fourteen and worked on ships, delivering goods, as well as in a ship yard, building boats. He'd never really had a childhood, and his mother, Constance, had died very suddenly of a brain tumour when he was twenty-one. If he wanted to give our children a bit of pleasure and delight in their childhood, I was not going to take that away from him.

The very next morning Mr Fluffy became Mrs Fluffy.

When Johnnie came into the kitchen from the garden to break the news that there were now eight bunnies in the pen, not one, he was full of apologies.

'Well, we're going to have a very stinky garden now,' I said. I looked at him while cooking the breakfast, knowing it was not his fault. 'Better get plenty of carrots in,' I said with a wink.

About a week later, Johnnie came downstairs and told me to keep the children away from the back of the house.

'Why, what on earth's happened?'

'A fox has got into the garden and there are little pieces of bunny rabbit all over. I don't want the children to see it, they'll be devastated, especially my little Claire.' Although I'd never wanted the rabbits, my heart sank, and I suddenly missed them very much indeed. How were we ever going to tell the children? It wasn't as if it was a fish that had died and you could replace it with the explanation that it had changed colour. Eventually, we decided to tell Claire and the boys that the rabbits had gone walkabout, as they were actually of Australian origin and this is what people and animals Down Under sometimes decided to do. We said we were sure they would drop in on our relations up north and hopefully send us a postcard. As the children were of Romany heritage, we explained that they should understand that any person or animal needs to wander.

This went completely over Claire's head, of course, but once she'd started talking about the horse riding lessons that Johnnie had mentioned, things began to calm down. Honestly, he was going from bad to worse with his promises. This time next year he would probably promise her a pet elephant!

To further compensate Claire, he took her to the toy shop and bought her first Sindy doll, with accessories. It marked the beginning of her main childhood passion. On birthdays and at Christmas from there on in it was Sindy, Sindy, Sindy. She would spend hours upon end playing with her dolls. She acquired so many that Johnnie had to build them their own house and even went so far as to use real wallpaper and carpets on the floor.

Before long, the vicarage became known as the Kamikaze Club. We threw a party and Johnnie's secretary, Ruth, was one of the guests. She'd been there an hour or so and came to tell me she was going.

'Ruth, you can't go home yet,' I said. 'This is the Kamikaze Club and you're not allowed to leave until you're pissed!'

She did eventually go home, in a bit of a state, and the name I'd come up with for the house stuck.

When we first moved into Ditchling Road, I surveyed my domain. Outside was my Garden of Eden. We had a huge green space and a well, although the first thing Johnnie did when we moved in was to have it filled in. We didn't want any of our children falling in and, at their ages, they would definitely have gone in head first. Beyond the well, we had apple trees, a pear tree and a Victoria plum tree. Plum jam! I'd been taught how to make jam by Mummy. There was also plenty of room to plant vegetables. I was in absolute heaven. All my life, I'd wanted to have a real garden, and this was a dream come true. All mine!

My burning ambition while travelling had been to grow some nasturtiums. Whenever we used to stop somewhere, Mummy would buy packs of nasturtium seeds which we would plant and after a few days, we would see the heads of the first little shoots start to appear. We never got to see them flower because we were always on the move. So the first thing I did was buy a packet of seeds for each of my children, to fulfil an ambition which had always been with me.

While Johnnie was toiling away building my dream kitchen, I walked to the next block, where there was a wonderful garden centre, and interrogated the head man there, explaining that I'd moved in up the road and wanted roses. White roses. He was very kind and understanding, explaining that the soil in the area was chalky and offering to show me what I had to do.

'First of all,' he said, 'you dig a big hole.' He indicated

a bag of compost. 'You put some of this in first, love.' Then he indicated yet another bag. 'Then you put some of this in, put your roses in and cover them with the earth you've dug out. Give 'em a good old soaking, and you're away.'

I was determined that this was a project I was going to do on my own. I bought fifteen rose bushes and complimented myself when I had them planted. I was a gardener! They looked absolutely beautiful in my Garden of Eden.

Mummy came down to see how we were getting on. When she saw all of the work Johnnie was doing, she said, 'You're working the poor man to death, but what an amazing job he's doing. It's stunning.'

When she saw my rose bushes, she said, 'I want some.'

When Nathan and Sue had bought their house in Peacehaven, just outside of Brighton, they had built a granny flat on the side for Mummy, and she had recently decided to move in. There was a large garden behind the bungalow that she had claimed for her own.

Mummy and I strolled down to the garden centre, me so very confident in my new gardening abilities, now that I had finally got my heart's desire after years of admiring other people's gardens. We were both so excited and full of enthusiasm to be achieving something we had both desired all of our lives. I sought out

Isaac, the man who had so kindly explained to me how to plant my roses.

'Hello, Isaac,' I said. 'I told you my mother would be down here. As soon as she saw my roses, she said she wanted some.' We were like two little girls, Mummy and I, in this wonderland of plants and flowers.

'I think I'll have red roses,' she told Isaac, and ordered an assortment of different plants and flowers, arranging for one of her sons to pick them up. Isaac went through the routine once again, explaining how to plant the roses as, like me, she wanted to do it herself.

As he ran through the rigmarole, he said, 'You dig the hole, then you put some of this in' – pointing at a bag – 'followed by this' – pointing at another bag – 'and then you take the bag off the roots, put the roots into the soil and cover them with the earth you've dug out.'

Well, I just stood there, open-mouthed, as if I'd been struck by a rock, and eventually said, 'You didn't tell me to take the bag off the roots!'

I had planted my lovely white roses with the bags on, assuming they would rot down. What an idiot I was. As soon as we got back to my house, I told Johnnie what I had done. I was wailing. 'He didn't tell me I had to take off the bags.'

Johnnie immediately got on the phone and called a

gardener, to try to undo the damage I had done. Both he and Mummy were in hysterics.

Johnnie said, 'Any planting you want done in the future, darling, just tell the gardener. You just tell him what you want and where, and leave it to him.'

Halfway down our very large back garden, beyond the fruit trees, I had my gardener plant some vegetables and, to separate the vegetable patch, Johnnie built a trellis and I got the gardener to plant honeysuckle and various other climbing plants.

My gardening days were over, apart from tending the herb garden near the back door, where I grew fresh herbs to cook with. Rose bushes were obviously not my forte!

Mummy never let it lie, of course. For years to come, whenever there was a lull in conversation, she would say with a giggle, 'Shall we plant some roses, darling?'

THIRTY

The Bright Lights of Hollywood

My cousin Adeline's eldest child, Russell, was a strikingly handsome boy. He would frequently come to Brighton to stay with me and my family, and we had seen even more of him recently as he had been coming regularly to take Eddie out in a bid to take his mind off Nicky. He and Eddie were great mates and were always there for each other like that, and Russell seemed to be the only one who was able to pull Eddie out of the doldrums. Russell had recently married Angela, a petite, pretty girl who adored him. On one visit, when Russell and Eddie arrived back from a drinking session in Brighton, I noticed that Russell had grown a little beard. I thought it made him look a bit scruffy, which was not in his character.

I looked at Eddie and Russell as they lounged in my garden, getting the last of the sunshine. Both had deep tans and, like many of their generation, were great sun worshippers. I was sitting in the kitchen, talking to Johnnie and Angela.

'Angela,' I turned to her with a quizzical look, 'would you mind if I played a joke on Russell?'

An idea had been buzzing around in my mind. I had already told everyone that I had a meeting lined up with the actress Joan Collins, and that very morning, at breakfast, Russell had been reading the newspaper, with Joan splashed all over it. She was looking for a new leading man for an upcoming film. This had immediately planted a thought in my head. I called my friend Brian Dearson, who was always up for a joke.

'Brian, hi, it's Eva. Would you do me a favour? I want you to call me up at eleven tomorrow morning and pretend to be a man called Mr Divortsky.' I went on to explain in detail what I needed him to say and do. He laughed, as he too was always up for a prank.

'I love it, Eva. I'm in.'

Sure enough, at eleven o'clock on the dot, when everyone was around the dining table, ushered in by me on the pretext of tea and snacks, the phone rang. It was Brian.

'Oh, Mr Divortsky, how nice to hear from you,' I said, aiming a confident smile at the others in the room. I pretended that we were having a business chat, and ended with, 'Give Joan my love. Oh, by the way, I hear she's looking for a leading man for her next film. Has she found anyone yet?' I was watching Russell out of the corner of my eye as I said, 'Do you think she'd be interested in a very good-looking Romany boy?'

Russell dropped his knife and fork and his Adam's apple went up and down as he tried desperately to swallow the food he'd just put into his mouth.

I'd now turned my head and was looking at Russell's face, which was staring back at me with a look of utter shock. Brian, alias Mr Divortsky, was giggling on the other end of the phone. 'Ask him how old he is,' he said.

I checked with Russell.

'I'm twenty-five,' he responded in a husky tone.

'Now ask him if he's got any experience,' Brian directed.

To this, I replied, 'Well, actually, he happens to be in my house right now.' I put my hand over the mouth-piece and whispered to Russell, 'He wants to speak to you.' Russell rose from the table unsteadily and walked over to take the phone from my hand, and I noticed that he was shaking.

Brian/Mr Divortsky must have repeated the same question to Russell. 'No,' Russell told him, 'but I believe I have an aptitude for it.' I turned my back to Russell and looked directly at Eddie, Angela and Johnnie, who were all in on the secret and had been sworn to silence. I could see Eddie's shoulders moving up and down slightly as he clasped his hand over his mouth, desperately trying to suppress his laughter. He was on the verge of giving the game away so I mouthed the words, 'If you can't be quiet get out of the room,' pointing firmly to the door. I was not ready to stop the fun yet.

They could see I was serious and very quickly pulled themselves together, not wanting to miss out on whatever was about to happen next. I sat down at the table, watching Russell's face. We were all staring at him to see his reaction. When he put the receiver down, he said, 'Jesus Christ, he's coming to see me next week. He wants us to meet him in the Grand Hotel at seven o'clock.'

The date was set for six days' time. He explained that the 'agent' had said what good publicity it could be to have a Romany in the film.

I was rather annoyed that Brian had not made the date for the following day, as this meant we had to continue this prank for six more days and I wasn't sure if the rest of the gang would give in before then and let me down. I looked Russell firmly in the eye and said, 'Now look, Russell, these are very important people and, quite frankly, if you present yourself looking the way you're looking at the moment, you won't stand a snowball's chance in hell and it will also make me look ridiculous. You've got to smarten yourself up, lad, and you've got to knock all this drinking on the head.'

'I totally agree with you,' he replied.

'And get rid of that beard,' I added.

He went out that very same day and came back clean-shaven, with a new haircut and a new suit and tie. He wasn't short of money, so I didn't feel guilty. It was June and the weather was beautiful, and he spent all of his time sitting in the garden, topping up his tan and getting ready for his big day.

Eddie, Johnnie, Angela and I would watch him through the window. 'Do you want me to really go through with this or should I just tell him?' Russell was a real practical joker and was always up for a laugh, but even so I was now beginning to feel a slight pang of guilt.

'Not on your life,' Angela beamed at me. 'It can't do him any harm, can it? I'm glad he's not out boozing with Eddie every day for a change. Have you told my mother-in-law what we're up to?'

'Good God, no,' I said. Aunt Adeline would have given it away in a shot. 'Have you told anybody else?'

'Not a soul,' she promised.

'OK.' We were in agreement. 'Let's see it through.'

'Just look at him,' Eddie said. 'He's actually lying

out there dreaming of Hollywood. He's got his eyes closed with a big grin on his face.'

The meeting was held on the following Sunday, at seven. I dressed up, and so did Russell, who looked absolutely handsome and smart as a carrot. He actually did look like a Hollywood movie star.

'What time are we leaving?' he enquired.

'Well, Johnnie can drop us off at the Grand, so if we leave at twenty to seven, we'll be perfectly on time.'

He rubbed his hands together and at the agreed time we were all in the car and were dropped at the Grand Hotel.

'Good luck,' Johnnie said, with such a straight face that even I was impressed.

'Come on, let's wait in the bar,' I said.

We sat there, not talking, just waiting for the action to begin. At three minutes past seven, I turned to the barman and asked, 'Have there been any messages for Eva Petulengro or has anyone been enquiring for me?' Nobody had. It then got to twenty past seven and I said, 'Russell, darling, I think you should have a large gin and tonic. I'm certainly having one.'

He looked at me and his eyes widened as the penny dropped. 'Oh my God, this is a wind-up, isn't it?'

'I couldn't resist it. I'm sorry.'

'Do Angela, Eddie and Johnnie know?'

I decided to keep the charade going a little longer. 'Oh no, because they'd have told you, wouldn't they?'

'Can you do me a favour then,' he pleaded. 'Please don't tell them. I want to make an excuse, so they don't find out.'

The devil in me came out and I found myself saying, 'All right then, what do you want me to do?'

'Just follow my lead when we see them. I'll think of something.' With that, we phoned for a taxi and headed home to the unfolding drama.

Thankfully, no one let the cat out of the bag when we got in.

'What happened, darling?' Angela asked.

Russell held his ground. 'Well, darling, they wanted me to start working with them at the same time as we're going on our skiing holiday, so I've turned it down.' With that, we all burst out laughing and realization hit Russell. 'You bastards, you've given me a double whammy, haven't you?'

'Now, shall we have a drink, Russell?'

'Give me the phone first. I'm going to phone my mother – she's going to kill you.'

He was, as I had hoped he would be, very good-natured about it. I hadn't meant for things to go so far, but it had all ended well.

'You look fabulous for it though, Russell. Now stay

that way,' I told him. 'You look like you've been to a health spa.'

A few months later, I was actually in Hollywood and couldn't stop myself from buying a card to send him. Of course, I signed it from Joan!

THIRTY-ONE

Troubled Waters

'Well, Jules, you haven't had any dramas or adventures yet. I've been waiting for something to happen every day,' Johnnie said teasingly. He should have known better!

We were on holiday in Florida, a trip Johnnie had booked without telling me, as he knew I was petrified of flying and had never flown long-haul before. Just before I'd left for a trip to Scotland, the children had been talking about Disneyland and how some of their friends had been to this magical place. I found, on my return, that Johnnie and the children had made a large calendar on which they were crossing the days off because in one week we would be flying to America and Disneyland. Thinking about the flight ahead, I was not happy! Still, I realized I could not disappoint the children.

When the day of our flight dawned, we set off to Heathrow Airport, with the children and Johnnie ecstatically happy and me in fear for our lives. But the fear of the unknown is always more frightening than the reality and, to my surprise, I thoroughly enjoyed the flight to Florida, long though it was.

We were staying at the Contemporary Resort in Disneyland itself where, needless to say, the children had an absolute ball. We all got beautiful suntans and we had a really relaxing time. It was wonderful to see the children so carefree and happy. Then, one day, they begged me to go in the sea with them. I had never told them that when I was a little girl and couldn't swim, my father had thrown me into the sea. I can remember to this day the salt water going in my eyes, up inside my nose and into my mouth. So I never learned to swim and kept well away from the sea from then on.

But the children were so enthusiastic I couldn't talk my way out of it, and I said, 'Maybe I'll have a paddle with you tomorrow.' I was hoping their own excitement would make them focus on the fun they could have with me watching from a safe distance, while Johnnie played lifeguard and splash mate.

Early the next morning, we were woken up by the children trying to drag us both out of our beds.

'We're all going in the sea. Come on, Mummy!'

Johnnie gave me a wry grin and said, 'There's no getting out of this, girl.'

As we headed towards the water, me wearing a

swimsuit with my bathrobe over the top, it felt strange that there were no other people on the beach. At the same time, I was relieved that I would not have an audience for my second experience in the sea, which I was not sure how I was going to handle. The children dived into the waves immediately. They quite clearly had no fear of the water, as we had been taking them to swimming lessons at a country club twice a week, but I had never had to venture in with them, until now.

Warren, Bradley, Gregory and Claire came out of the sea and walked towards me. 'Come on, Mummy, in you go.'

In the distance, I saw a man walking along the water's edge. I used him as an excuse. 'I'm waiting until that man's gone past. I don't want him to see me in my bathing costume,' I protested.

We all sat on the sand, my children eager for the man to pass by so they could get their way with me, and me petrified, knowing I was going to have to go in.

'Good morning,' the man said, as he walked past.

'Good morning,' we all chimed back.

I half hoped he would sit down with us, just to give me more time to acclimatize to the situation. But, alas, he walked past and headed off the beach. I had no choice. I slipped off my bathrobe and gingerly walked towards the sea. I tried to tell myself this was a new experience which had nothing to do with the fear of the sea my father had instilled in me. I dipped my toe in the water, which was lovely and warm. Closing my eyes, I cautiously moved forwards, intending just to get in up to my waist, certainly no more. This was not to be though, and suddenly I had gone too far out and found myself with my head under the water and my nose and mouth filling up. My arms began flailing and I panicked. 'I'm dead,' I thought. 'This is it.'

Just as I'd stopped taking breaths, I found myself being pulled up and gently lifted onto the warm sand. I was still spluttering for breath as I jumped to my feet, scrabbling to get away from the sea before it swallowed me up again. Johnnie looked at me with worried eyes and, pulling the children into his arms, he bundled them towards me.

'Let's get your mother back to the hotel. Come on.'

He guided me straight into the bar and sat me down. There was a man sitting opposite, the same man who had walked past us all on the beach. Rather than look with pity at me, in my drenched and panic-stricken state, he simply shouted, 'Are you all raving mad? What are you doing taking your family into the sea? Why do you think there are no people in the water? Didn't you see the flag?'

'What?' I asked, astonished by this outburst. 'What do you mean?'

'An alligator has swum up from the Keys and the warning flag is a danger signal that it's in the water here.'

I addressed the barman first of all. 'A large brandy,' I said. Then I turned to Johnnie. 'Enough adventure for you? How would you have explained this away to my mother, if the alligator had eaten me?'

The children all looked bemused. I suddenly saw the hilarity in the situation and started to laugh, and so did Johnnie, then the boys, then Claire, not really knowing what they were laughing at, but finding it impossible not to join in with the joviality of their very unpredictable parents.

The man from the beach got up and shook his head. 'You're all mad!' He walked out, shaking his head in disbelief, which only prompted us to laugh even louder.

'I wouldn't change us for the world,' I said to Johnnie.

'And I *couldn't* change you if I tried, Jules,' he replied.

Later that evening, Johnnie announced to me and the children that he had hired a babysitter and was taking me out. We'd had early nights with the children ever since we'd arrived in America, and he felt that after my 'adventure' I deserved a night off.

'Where are we going? I asked.

'Apparently there's some good jazz in Disneyland, and we're going to find it!'

Sure enough, we were directed to the jazz quarter and we sat in amazement, listening to the jazz idols playing. We got into conversation with some of them when they were on their break. They had toured with the greats: Ella Fitzgerald, Satchmo, Count Basie and even Billie Holiday. All of a sudden, Johnnie got out his wallet and produced a business card.

'Do you remember those people I got a table for at the dog stadium?' he said.

A few weeks before, we had been sitting in the Cricketers pub in Black Lion Street and a couple next to us had asked us what the food was like at the dog stadium.

'Very good,' we told them.

We frequented the place often, as we had two racing dogs. The man went to phone to make a booking and came back disappointed. 'I can't get a table,' he complained.

'Hang on a minute,' Johnnie said. He went to the phone and came back a few minutes later. 'Your table's booked. I'm a dog owner and have priority. You can have my table.'

During the conversation, the man had told us he was in charge of all the electrics in Disneyland and Johnnie told him that he planned to go there one day.

The man gave Johnnie a card and said, 'Give me a ring when you get there and we'll all have a drink together.'

Little did I know that a few weeks later Johnnie would surprise me with the news that we were going to Florida for real, and now we were in this same couple's home territory.

'What do you think, Jules, shall we call them?' Johnnie asked, turning the card around in his fingers.

'Call them,' I smiled.

Before I knew it, Johnnie had returned from a phone booth. 'He said not to move and he also told me not to pay the bill, as he gets a special concession.'

A bad day was turning into a great night and the taste of salt was finally beginning to disappear from my mouth. My clairvoyance had told me that this was a very useful contact to have and it proved to be so.

Within the hour, the couple had joined us. We had a great evening, with added humour in that the man's wife could not keep herself from trying to paw Johnnie. Every time her back was turned, my husband would mouth the words, 'Help me.' My response was raucous laughter, partly as a release after the stress of the day and partly due to the large number of gin and tonics Johnnie had plied me with to get me over my ordeal.

The next day we were with the children at a ball park, which Claire revelled in. There was a pool filled to the brim with different coloured balls, the size of tennis balls. We had never seen anything like this in England and, of course, I loved it, as there was no water involved and no danger of anyone drowning!

Two days later we were on a plane on our way back to Heathrow Airport. When we landed, we were met by Brian Dearson. Brian was the most reckless driver I had ever met. My heart sank when I saw him standing there, for although I loved him very much and we all had many laughs together, being in a car with him at a wheel could not help but unnerve me. He whizzed along the motorway as if his life depended on it. I leaned forward and said to him in as calm a voice as I could muster, 'Brian, we've just flown thousands of miles in a plane and I felt safer up there than I feel with you in this car. Slow down.'

He ignored me. A few minutes later, a truck came past, so close we were sure it would hit us. Instinctively, the children and I all leaned over to the far side of the car, as if this would make a difference as to whether the truck hit us or not! Luckily, all it did was take the wing mirror off the passenger side, but it was still far too close for comfort! We pulled up behind the truck and Brian and Johnnie went to talk to the driver, while I sat inside the car completely in shock. I vowed never to get in a car, or let my children get in a car, with Brian again.

*

I'd enjoyed my first trip to America so much I was happy to go again not long afterwards. An actress who had recently returned to England from LA related to me how she had been telling actors and actresses about her visits to me in Brighton for readings and how my predictions had all come true.

'When will you be going over to America, Eva, as I've got at least a dozen people over there who are all asking to see you?'

'I'll ring you if I do ever get over there and you can let them know,' I told her. That night I turned round to Johnnie in the kitchen, as we were making dinner, and made an announcement I hadn't even realized I was going to make. 'Johnnie,' I said, 'I'm going to America.' Again, my mouth had run away with me.

I was always blurting things out to family, friends and clients before my brain had processed whether or not the words should be spoken out loud. Every now and then I got the Romany urge to get away and, thank God, Johnnie recognized that it was nothing to do with wanting to get away from him, but simply the way I was.

'I can't go with you, Jules,' he said with an arm around my shoulder. 'One of us has to be here for the children. But you go, darling. Why don't you take Eddie with you? He'd love it and he'll look after you.'

If I ever forgot how lucky I was to be married to

Johnnie, moments like that would always remind me. Not only did he encourage me to follow my dreams, but he was always busy helping me in other ways. When we first moved into the vicarage in Ditchling Road, Johnnie had concentrated on decorating the children's rooms first and this is where his skills as a carpenter came in. Now he was concentrating on the kitchen. The house had a huge kitchen, with a very high ceiling. 'I don't like the high ceiling. I want oak beams,' I had said to him.

'You want oak beams, you shall have oak beams,' Johnnie had said.

'I want it to look like an old country pub.'

'Does that mean you want a bar?' he asked.

'Oh, why not?' I exclaimed.

Johnnie sat down with a pad and a pencil and began to make notes.

'I want optics above the bar and my appliances under it. I also want stools, so the children can sit up at the bar.'

We stayed up well into that night, excitedly planning our new home. Lo and behold, the high ceiling became a low one, and Johnnie installed my requested oak beams.

I confidently made my plans for the trip, feeling safe in my mind that my children would be well cared for. With Johnnie and our nanny Linda coping with the house and the children so well, I knew I had nothing to worry about.

Before I knew it, the day for Eddie and me to fly to America had come. We flew from Gatwick very early in the morning. Eddie knew better than to attempt to talk to me because he knew I didn't do mornings and also that I was afraid of flying. We were five hours into the journey when he turned to me and said, 'Good morning. I trust you're ready to have a conversation now, my dear.'

'Good morning to you too, Edward,' I said with a smile.

'They're going to serve us lunch in an hour,' he commented.

'Oh God,' I said, exasperated. The last three times I had flown, they'd always served chicken. I hated chicken, due to my childhood chicken farm experience, courtesy of my father. Now I couldn't go near even the meat. 'I'm one step ahead of them this time,' I whispered, and pulled out a package of tin foil from my bag. 'Bacon sandwiches,' I smiled, triumphant.

When the meal arrived, it was not chicken, but beef in gravy, much to my delight and surprise. Not a piece of chicken in sight.

Then came the moment I had been dreading, as the captain's voice came over the tannoy. 'Ladies and gentlemen, we are now making our descent to LAX. We will be landing in forty minutes.'

My heart began to pound, my stomach turned over and my fear of flying gripped me at once. I couldn't help myself, and grabbed Eddie's hand. We'd both always had a wicked sense of humour, and Eddie's kicked in right then, as he turned to me and calmly said, 'What's all this about? You can't be scared. We're only entombed in metal, hurtling towards the earth at 5,000 miles an hour. What's there to be scared about?'

We both started to laugh out loud.

Once we'd landed, we had to go through customs. I watched my handbag go through the scanner and, as I did, I saw the frown on the face of an official. Before I knew it, there were six armed policemen and an Alsatian dog alongside me. The official pointed at my bag and demanded, 'What's in that?'

For a moment, I couldn't speak. Then I opened my mouth and muttered the immortal words: 'Bacon, lettuce and tomato sandwiches.' At least I tried to, but I didn't hear anything come out, I was so terrified. I turned to look at Eddie, who had tears of laughter running down his cheeks. He'd guessed they'd found my packed lunch.

He was still laughing when he said to me, 'You've started already, look, and we haven't even got out of the airport yet.'

Once we'd satisfied the officials that my BLT sand-wiches weren't going to endanger any lives and had seen them taken away to be disposed of, we headed for our hotel. LA was vast, exactly as it appeared in all the films I had seen.

When we arrived at the Beverly Wilshire Hotel, there were already lots of messages waiting for us from several friends and clients who wanted to book in and see me. This was beginning to get exciting. The hotel was luxurious, and I felt like I was in a movie. We were shown up to the double room we had booked and Eddie duly tipped the porter. We'd never seen a hotel room like this. The beds were both doubles – in fact, you could have got my whole family into just one of them. This was the first time I had seen a king-size bed, and I made a mental note to myself that I would get one once they became available in England.

I picked up the room service menu on the bedside table: the food sounded amazing.

'Do you want something to eat, Eddie?' I asked.

'No, you have something,' he replied.

I ordered a fillet steak and a salad. I'd never seen anything like it. The steak was as big as the plate and the salad would have fed ten people. There was a whole French loaf cut into fifteen slices. I took in the generous portions and said, 'When we order on this trip, we only need to order for one.'

Now, one of my favourite television shows was an American series called *Hart to Hart*, and I discovered that the wife of the producer had been calling the hotel to try to book in for a reading with me. I was invited to their home to give her the reading. The Americans certainly seemed to be a very friendly lot. I'd also been invited for lunch by Shakira Caine, wife of the actor Michael Caine, the next day.

I'd bought myself a shoulder-length curly wig, because in the heat of the LA sunshine my thin hair got damp and would not hold a curl, so I couldn't have my usual French plait, and I was having great fun experimenting with my new look. Wearing a very smart black designer dress with very high black patent shoes, a matching handbag and all my gold jewellery, I made my way to the bar with Eddie.

'How long will you be out to lunch, do you think?' asked Eddie.

'How long's a piece of string?' I replied. I had three-quarters of an hour before I had to be at the restaurant, which was only fifteen minutes away by taxi, so Eddie ordered a bottle of lager and I ordered a tomato juice. We discovered that the barman was English, from Worthing, which was only twenty minutes from Brighton. He and Eddie were about the same age and hit it off immediately. Eddie asked, 'What time do you close?'

'Half past two,' he replied.

Looking at his watch, Eddie said to me, 'That gives me three hours. I'll stay here.'

I smiled to myself as I left the bar to get my taxi, thinking Eddie was in good hands. He'd found a pal.

When I walked into the restaurant, I was directed to Shakira's table. She was with six other women. I greeted her with a kiss on the cheek and she motioned for me to sit down. At first I thought I was seeing double, but on further inspection, it could have been quadruple, for four of the women looked as if they had identical faces. It was later revealed to me that they had all been to the same plastic surgeon.

We had a very pleasant lunch, and I had two glasses of wine and yet another glorious steak. I was certainly going to be heading back to England a little heavier than when I'd left. The other women all had salads with water. No wonder they all looked to be size zero.

Shakira turned to me and said, 'I want you to come over to the house tomorrow night for dinner, Eva. It will be nice for you to relax and have a home-cooked meal. I'd like you to meet Michael.'

Of course, I accepted. We said our goodbyes and, as I glanced down at the card she had given me – which read: 6 Benedict Drive, Beverly Hills – I revelled in the stories I would be able to tell Mummy and Johnnie when I got home, and repeated the address over and over to myself, to check it was real. It was all very surreal for a girl from a painted caravan.

At the hotel, I headed for the bar, but stopped in my tracks because I remembered the barman saying it shut at two thirty. However, it was still open, so he had obviously meant they closed in the early hours of the morning. I thought, 'Good job Eddie doesn't know that.' I took the elevator up to our floor and opened the door to our room. Eddie was nowhere to be seen. Where could he be? I made my way back down to the bar, and there he was, all right, or a very drunk version of him anyway. The barman also looked a little worse for wear.

'My friend Alec here is trying to get me drunk. He's been making me every cocktail on the list, but it's not working,' Eddie said. With this, he gave a very loud hic and they both started giggling.

'You'll get the sack if the manager sees you,' I warned the barman.

'Don't think so,' he replied with a slur. 'Dad wouldn't do that to me.'

With this, he proceeded to pour me the biggest glass of wine I had ever seen. Eddie revealed that he hadn't paid a penny, as all the drinks had been on the house.

I made my way up to the room, removing myself from what looked like a car crash waiting to happen. A couple of hours later, the door handle turned and in walked Eddie – or rather, he zig-zagged across the room, stumbled onto the bed and fell asleep. A few hours later, we were both awake, our body clocks still set on English time. The cocktails had begun to wear off and Eddie was relaying the stories and jokes the barman had been telling him. We dozed for a while, but I was woken up at midnight by Eddie getting changed and putting on a clean shirt. I could smell the aftershave wafting in from the bathroom. I had promised Mummy I would look after him, so I jumped out of bed and said, in my big-sister voice, 'What are you doing?'

'I've got a date.' He beamed back at me like a proud schoolboy.

Apparently, the barman had met two girls who had come into the bar earlier in the afternoon, and they'd all arranged to meet at the poolside at midnight.

'Alec's bringing the drinks, the girls are bringing themselves and I'm bringing, well, me.'

'But, Eddie,' I cautioned, 'you can't even swim.'

'I'm not going in the pool, silly. It's a pool party, not a swimathon.'

'Just watch yourself,' I warned.

Eddie grinned. 'Go to bed, girl,' he replied, and set off for his pool party.

I ran over to the window, praying the pool could be seen from there, so I could keep a watchful eye on him. Yes, at least I could see him. I settled down by the window, keeping one eye on the pool and another on the television, and then the hotel alarms suddenly went off. I was wide awake, knowing it had to have something to do with my brother – and, yes, I was right. Eddie had, I learned later, tried to open a door that was alarmed. I was sure my brother thought he could walk through walls, but clearly he couldn't, and instead managed to wake up everyone, as the hotel had to be evacuated.

It was a very short pool party, to say the least.

We were up bright and early the next morning, and decided to hire a car and have a look at the place. We drove around and found ourselves cruising past Warner Brothers Studios. We were listening to the news, and all of a sudden the voice on the radio said, 'I'm standing outside Warner Brothers Studios, and there are hundreds of people waving banners.'

'But, Eddie,' I pointed out, 'look, there are only four people, and only one of them has a banner! Talk about exaggeration! Americans certainly don't do anything by halves.'

We drove on, amused.

'Find me a supermarket, Ed, I want to buy some presents for the kids. The next few days will be busy and if we do it now, then I won't have to worry about it.'

We pulled up outside a huge supermarket and, once inside, must have spent over two hours there. Finally, Eddie called an abrupt halt to the shopping spree.

'You've done enough shopping. We'll need another plane if you buy any more. Plus you've got dinner tonight and you'll want to get some rest before you put your Polyfilla on.'

I gave in. He was right. I didn't know how we'd get it all in the car, let alone how we were going to get it home, but the thought of the looks on the children's faces spurred me on.

Back at the hotel, after a long, leisurely soak in an enormous bath that was like my own small swimming pool, I tried to do something with my hair, but with the humidity of the day, failed miserably. I pulled the wig out of its bag. 'Thank God I bought this,' I thought to myself. I put on one of the outfits I had bought especially for the trip, a brandy-coloured satin shirt and a pencil skirt. I was pleased with the effect. Right, ready for action.

'Ready?' I asked Eddie.

'There's a cigarette machine in the foyer,' he said. 'Would you go and get me some while I have my bath?'

In the foyer, next to the cigarette machine, was a row of telephones. Speaking on one of them was a little fat man in a suit that was a ghastly shade of green.

He was puffing on a very large cigar and screaming down the phone at some poor bastard.

'Get me out of this goddamn place,' he demanded. Then, noticing me, he looked me up and down from head to toe and, staring right at me, said, 'This place is full of goddamn dogs.'

I rushed back upstairs and, throwing the cigarettes at Eddie, said, 'Out of my way, I've got to get changed.'

I put on a green silk shirt and fitted skirt and off we went.

We set off for 6 Benedict Drive, which we found quite easily, having been instructed by Eddie's by now good friend Alec. Upon arrival, we were greeted warmly by Michael Caine, who was in a pair of shorts and a T-shirt, and his wife Shakira, who was dressed in a similar style. I thought Shakira was lovely and very down-to-earth, and it turned out her famous husband was just the same. Michael was holding a very large brandy glass.

'Welcome to my humble abode,' he said. 'Hope you like curry, I've made you one.'

They showed us to what they called 'the den', where we spent a fantastic evening, eating the best curry I'd ever tasted and hearing the most delightful stories. Michael really was one of the nicest people I'd ever met, as was Shakira, and it was clear that they were very much in love, which was really nice to see for someone of my race, having been brought up to believe that marriage was for life.

After we came back from America, we had a lot of catching up to do with the family. Eddie turned up one afternoon with a tale to tell. He could hardly speak for laughing. 'I walked into the Druid's Head and one of my mates was sat in the corner, looking very ill and sorry for himself, so I asked Greg, the landlord, what was going on with him. Greg looked worried. "Ted's been like that for three days, Eddie. Sitting right there from the moment I open until the moment I close, but he's not drinking. Any more customers like that and I'll have to close up and change trades."'

Eddie walked up to Ted. 'Would you like a drink, mate?' He could see, on closer inspection, that Ted looked terrible. Red-rimmed eyes stared back at him. He looked absolutely awful. Eddie looked Ted straight in the eye and asked, 'Ted, why won't you have a drink?'

Ted replied, 'I haven't told anyone, Eddie, for fear of everyone taking the mickey out of me, but I got my penis caught up in the zip of my jeans, and it's so painful, I daren't drink in case it makes me go to the loo.'

Without further ado, Eddie called for an ambulance and accompanied his friend to the hospital. The doctor informed Eddie that had things been left a few more hours, it would have been very serious. Ted already had an infection. The next pint was most definitely on him, but that wouldn't be until the antibiotics had kicked in!

THIRTY-TWO

Christmas Shop

Johnnie was always very good when I wanted to do a big shop at the supermarket. He would ask me what I needed and would write a list, in aisle order, so as not to waste time. Then he would go through the food cupboards to check the list, turning to say, 'Oh, we're collecting dried peas now, are we?' This item would be crossed off the list. 'Black pepper again? We've only got six boxes.' The pepper would be struck off too. You could guarantee this would happen every time.

Coming up to Christmas, we decided, stupidly, to take the children shopping with us, and on our arrival at the supermarket, looked at each other in dismay. They'd changed the order of the aisles. I suppose this was done to confuse the shopper, so that instead of avoiding certain aisles, we had to go down them all, and, as you do, we would pick up items we didn't need or want.

Anyway, with the children needing toilets and drinks and getting really bored, we too were getting fed up. After filling up six trolleys, we joined the very long queue for the checkout. After about half an hour or so, we were at the front of the checkout and next to be served. We were eagerly anticipating being able to go home and have a cup of PG Tips. When the checkout job was finally finished, I pulled out my cheque book. The young lady serving us pointed to a sign that said, 'No Cheques, Cash Only'. With this, Johnnie looked at me and said, 'Go get 'em, Tiger. I'll take the kids to the car.'

I said to the girl, 'Get me the manager.'

Instead, a senior checkout attendant came along. 'It's a new policy. We're not to take cheques,' she said.

I repeated, 'Where is the manager?'

'He's downstairs,' she said, pointing to a door.

'What's his name?' I demanded. By now, I was browned off, cheesed off, hungry and aggravated. I ran down the flight of stairs, to be met by a young man in a very badly ironed white shirt. He must have been all of seventeen or eighteen.

'Where's the manager?' I asked.

'I am the manager,' he said.

'And I'm the lady with the cheque book.'

'But you're Eva, the star lady in the *Evening Argus*.'

He had obviously seen the picture that accompanied

my nightly column in the paper. 'So?' I said, wondering what difference it made who I was.

'You should have said,' he replied. '*You* can pay with a cheque.'

'And *you* can come with me to the cash desk.'

He followed me and when we got there, I turned to the very big queue and said, 'I hope none of you is going to try to pay with a cheque.' Several people said they were. I put my hand on the young man's shoulder. 'Well, this gentleman is the manager and simply because I work for a newspaper, he is going to allow me to pay by cheque. I suggest you tell him what your jobs are!'

I then turned to the manager. 'Get me some help, please, to get these trolleys to my car. I have wasted enough time in this store and I shall not be coming again. Putting this policy in place at Christmas is an outrage.'

When I first married Johnnie, he was totally useless in the kitchen, but he had watched me cook, and while I was stuck behind my desk, he would prepare the vegetables, as he'd seen me do them, and put them on a low light on the cooker. He would also prepare the meat, covering the lamb in rosemary, black pepper and salt, putting it into a hot oven to seal it and then turning it down low, so that it would be thoroughly cooked, as we didn't like pink meat. I suppose this had much to do with the men catching fresh meat when I was a child and my mother always making sure it was cooked well, so as not to risk any sort of food poisoning. It was a habit I found hard to break.

When I was cooking I would tell the boys to watch how it was done and, when they were old enough, every Sunday, I would get one of them to help me in the kitchen. I was thinking how awful it would have been for Johnnie if he hadn't had a wife that could cook, and I wanted my boys to be able to hold their own and cook for themselves if they had to.

Some of the dishes I cooked had been passed down through the generations. The 'Joey Grey' was a firm favourite. I'd fry two or three large onions in olive oil with a tablespoon of butter and add mixed herbs and sliced potatoes. I'd add water and cauliflower or cabbage, which gave a wonderful flavour, and then an Oxo cube. Once the potatoes were cooked, I'd stir in some Bisto. It was great with chops or steak. I was also known for my bacon dish of the week. It was customary in my family to always cook more than was needed, especially potatoes and cabbage, so we always had some left over for bubble and squeak. I did it Mummy's way, with cabbage topped with mashed potato and fried onions, then topped with grilled bacon and grated Cheddar cheese. It was finished under the grill and was delicious.

Once, in Blackpool, I had to cater for relatives at short notice and made do with what I had in the house. The dish became known as fish and fingernail pie. I found frozen prawns, some fresh smoked haddock, cod, two bags of spinach, parsley and potatoes. I cooked the fish in milk, drained it and saved the milk, then checked the fish and removed any bones. I cooked the spinach and tossed it in butter. I chopped the parsley and added it to the milk, then mixed some cornflour with a little more milk and used it to thicken the sauce, then added the fish back into the mixture. In a dish, I placed the cooked spinach, added the fish with its sauce on top, mashed the potato with butter and cream and layered that on top of it all. I sprinkled it with grated cheese and cooked it in the oven until the top was brown. It was only at the end of the cooking process that I noticed that two of my lovely red false nails, which I had just had done that day, were missing . . . presumably inside the pie! Do not make this if wearing false nails.

The boys particularly enjoyed helping me to make spaghetti Bolognese, beef Bourguignon and roasts, all dishes I'd learned to make since moving out of the vardo. The type of foods we had when I was young were dishes that had been handed down from mother to daughter through the centuries. Once I'd settled down in Brighton, and into a life of bricks and mortar,

I wanted to experiment with dishes that weren't on the Romany menu, and Johnnie was more than happy to be my guinea pig.

Gregory's particular forte was an English breakfast, which proved to be very handy and popular later in life. One of my own creations is what I call cherry delight, a variation on banoffee pie. It's easy, as there's no cooking required. Just bash up some biscuits, or grind them in a blender, add half a bar of melted chocolate and two tablespoons of melted butter and mix well. Put this base into a baking dish, top with a tin or carton of black morello cherries, place in the fridge until set and add fresh cream.

Johnnie taught the boys woodwork, a skill at which he excelled. Electrical work and painting were also talents he passed on to them. We wanted our boys to be able to look after themselves and to be capable in lots of ways. When it got to the time I thought was about right, I suggested to Johnnie that he talked to the boys about the facts of life. He gathered them all together in the lounge and closed the door behind him. Within five minutes, he emerged and came to find me, with a sheepish look on his face.

'I've been told they know more about it than I do. They laughed at me. Apparently, they've been taught it at school.'

They'd never told us they'd had sex education lessons. I suddenly realized the reason why my cousins' children were all taken away from school early: it was to avoid this very thing happening. My cousins didn't believe it was anyone else's place to teach their children about such things, and I agreed. I believed this was why there was so much promiscuity, because children were encouraged to think about it at such an early age. Johnnie had admitted he'd learned a lot during the war years, but because it was such a sensitive subject, it was not always brought out into the open. This, he said, had made it all the more exciting. Personally, I would have preferred to have kept the boys' minds innocent of such things for as long as possible. As it turned out, though, that was one aspect of their education over which Johnnie and I had no control!

THIRTY-THREE

On a Mission

As well as Aunt Vera's family, who had settled in Blackpool, we had family who had stayed in Skegness, where decades earlier Billy Butlin had invited Granny to set up a booth at his new amusement park. One day Eddie decided it was time he visited his friends and cousins there. One of his old friends, Tommy, a travelling man who had amusements in the big park, told Eddie it was his birthday. 'I want to go out and celebrate,' he declared.

'Who else is coming?' enquired Eddie.

'Nobody, mate, it's just you and me. Let's have a little pub crawl,' Tommy said. 'We've got a lot of catching up to do. I want you to tell me what's going on down in Brighton.'

Eddie told me they had a great time and each pub they went into, they met someone he knew. They made their excuses after a while though, as they were on a mission of their own and didn't want any other company.

'We ended up in a club and danced ourselves silly,' Eddie said. 'The club turned out at about two thirty.'

'What did you do after that then?' I asked.

'Well, Eva,' he said, with a cheeky grin, 'that's just it. We'd both run out of cigarettes, and by now there were no shops open and the clubs and bars had all turned out. There was no way, though, that we were going to go home without our ciggies . . .'

'You're flogging a dead horse here, Eddie,' Tommy said, convinced they were out of luck.

However, Eddie had spotted a hotel. 'Ah, but that's where you're wrong, Tommy, old mate. There's a cigarette machine in the foyer of that hotel over the road. Follow me.'

Exasperated, Tommy told him, 'They're closed up for the night. You can't get in.'

Looking up, Eddie noticed that one of the bedroom windows was open. In his inebriated state, he saw this as the answer to their problems. 'There's my way in,' he smiled, looking up at the window.

'Don't you dare,' Tommy whispered sternly. 'You'll get us both locked up. They'll think we're trying to rob the place or something.'

But Eddie had already made up his mind and nimbly began to shin his way up the drainpipe.

As Eddie was animatedly relating this part of the story to me, he began chuckling to himself.

'It must have been the livner [drink], as you know I'd never do that sort of thing normally. But to me, I was simply going to buy some cigarettes. I put my head through the window, and there was a man and woman, sound asleep in bed, bless them. I thought the best thing I could do was creep through their room quietly, so as not to wake them.

'I carefully climbed through the window, proud that I was being so quiet, and tiptoed to the door. I unlocked it and crept through the hallway and down the stairs. There in front of me, like a beautiful vision, was the cigarette machine. "A perfect end to a perfect night," I thought to myself. "Tommy won't believe how clever I am."'

Eddie put his money in the machine and, pleased with himself, retrieved two packets of cigarettes.

'I crept back to the room, closed the door and turned the lock,' he said. 'The lock went *click*, and as I turned to go back to the window, the lady sat bolt upright in bed, looking at me in horror. I tried to ignore her and made my way across the room, thinking she was probably about to scream and beginning to realize the silliness of my actions. She didn't scream though. Without thinking, I just turned to her and said, "It's all right, my dear, I've just been to get my cigarettes," and I held them up with a smile. "Now go back to sleep." She was still sitting bolt upright, not moving, and simply blinked, maybe wondering if it was a dream.

'I shinned my way back down the drainpipe and, as I reached the pavement, I said to Tommy, "Don't ask, just run!" And we ran like hell down the street, stopping every couple of minutes to double up in laughter.'

I stared at Eddie and knew that every word he said had been true. I tried to imagine what the poor woman must have been thinking. Did she think it was a dream? Did she wake her husband up to tell him about the man using their room as a thoroughfare for his cigarette call? We would never know.

If, by any chance, the lady concerned is reading this story, I would love to know what happened, and I would also like to offer my apologies on behalf of my brother, who really was only trying to get a packet of cigarettes.

THIRTY-FOUR

The Wheel of Fortune

Among other newspapers, I was working for the *Leicester Mercury*, and was forwarded a letter to the editor in which a Mr Ted Jones Fenley had asked, 'Is Eva Petulengro a real person? If so, can you put me in touch with her, please?'

I phoned the gentleman and introduced myself.

'I would love to meet with you, Eva,' he said. 'I have a proposition for you.'

We arranged a meeting in Leicester for the following week. My curiosity had got the better of me for some reason that I could not quite put my finger on. He picked me up from the Grand Hotel in Granby Street, after, I must add, some research on my part, to make sure that he was indeed a reputable businessman. I had found out that he made board games under the name of Invicta Plastics, the most successful one being Mastermind, which we actually had at home. He had manufactured and sold over forty million of these games, so this was one stranger's car I was willing to get into and listen to what he had to say. He drove us to a fabulous Greek restaurant, and the waiters fawned over him. When I got a better look at him in the light of the restaurant, he was a dead ringer for Omar Sharif.

'Eva,' he said, 'I've designed a game, which is called Osiris, and I need a good name to publicize it and wondered if you'd be willing to put your name to it?'

He'd brought the game with him and had no hesitation in laying it out on the table of the restaurant, to show me how it worked. I was not impressed, I have to say.

'Mr Fenley, I have to be honest, I have a feeling this is not for me.' I always followed my instincts and was expressing my true feelings. 'But,' I added, 'I have a game which I have designed called the Eva Petulengro Wheel of Fortune. I'll send you all the details when I get back to Brighton.'

'I'll have a look, Eva, but I'm sorry that you won't take me up on my game. However, I respect your decision and I am willing to do some business with you.' With this, we parted company. As soon as I got home, I packaged up my game and sent it off to him – and before I knew it, he was on the phone.

'I love your game,' he said, gushing with enthusiasm.

'I also have some ideas of my own, which will add to the fascination of it.'

I had been contacted by the producers of the popular TV show *Jim'll Fix It*. They had a young lady who wanted to have her palms read, and it was arranged that I would do this, but I had a condition. I wanted to show my Wheel of Fortune game on the show, as I felt it would be great advertising for when it came out in the shops, since Jimmy Savile's show was watched by millions. When we arrived at the studio, we were greeted by the host and the lovely Toyah Wilcox. Both were very interested in what I did for a living and were fascinated by my Wheel of Fortune.

The programme went well and my children were invited to sit at the other end of the stage, on beanbags. It was quite an adventure for them to be on the set of the show, as they always watched the programme at home.

The week before, Lord Boothby and his wife Wanda had been in Brighton, and came to see us. When I told them I was going to be in London for a show, they insisted I visit them at their flat in Eaton Square afterwards, where they would make dinner for us all.

When we arrived at their flat, Bob was relaxing in his big armchair, as usual in a gorgeous dressing gown, and he beckoned me over discreetly.

'Eva,' he whispered, 'in the hall cupboard, there are some bottles of whisky. Go and get me one.'

When I glanced at the table beside him, I noticed a half-full bottle of whisky. 'But, Bob, you've got half a bottle next to you, darling.'

'No,' he replied, keeping his voice down. 'Wanda waters it down. Go and get me a new bottle out of the cupboard.'

Not quite knowing what to do, I slipped into the kitchen where Wanda was putting the finishing touches to our dinner and told her what he had asked me to do. After all, who was I to override his wife? Plus I didn't want to make poor Bob ill.

Rather than looking surprised, Wanda simply laughed gaily. 'Do as he asks you, Eva. They're all watered down before they arrive here, but for God's sake, don't tell him I told you so.'

It turned out that Wanda had made arrangements with the whisky company to have the contents watered down before the bottles were sealed, something you might have thought was hard to arrange, but, after all, in his younger days Bob had been secretary to Winston Churchill and a man of important standing.

'He does this to everyone, Eva,' Wanda said, 'but I have to look after my Bob's health.'

I couldn't help but laugh. She clearly loved her

husband and I think he secretly loved the fact that she was looking out for his best interests.

When I returned to the lounge, it seemed Bob had forgotten his whisky quest and instead had my children transfixed by a story about his life.

'So, then there's the time I met Hitler,' he said, and their eyes widened, waiting to see what this charismatic man with a twinkly expression would say next. 'I was ushered into a very big and very long room, at the end of which sat the Führer. I could tell that the setting was meant to make me feel inferior. As soon as I stepped into the room, Adolf Hitler jumped up, raised his arm in the air, clicked his heels and shouted, "Heil Hitler."'

'What did you do?' asked Bradley, his mouth gaping open in awe.

'Well, Bradley, I raised my arm, clicked my heels and shouted, "Boothby!"'

He started chuckling, and the children chuckled too. Claire, by now, was on his lap. He had the spellbinding aura of Father Christmas or some other magical character. Anyone, of any age, could not help but be drawn by this charismatic man.

Meanwhile, another good friend of mine, Tudor Gates, a playwright who had become famous for writing *Barbarella*, starring Jane Fonda, as well as episodes of the popular TV show *Z Cars*, showed a strong interest when I told him about the Wheel of Fortune game and my dealings with Ted Fenley. Tudor got very excited and wanted to become involved as well. So Ted, Tudor and I got together in a hotel room in Leicester, where we sat round and planned out the game in detail.

Ted and Tudor hit it off straightaway. Ted was a man who didn't let the grass grow under his feet, and he made a perfect team with Tudor, who had all the contacts in the industry that anyone could desire.

On the drive back to Brighton, Tudor was very excited. 'I've got a friend in the States who helped Pat Reid devise the game *Colditz*, which was a bestseller. Can I introduce you to him?'

'Of course,' I replied. I saw no harm in that at all, and after stopping for Tudor to make a phone call, we drove on and he said, 'Are you doing anything Sunday?'

'Nothing I can't get out of, Tudor.'

'Then let's go pay a visit to a Colditz escapee. He's invited you and the children for lunch at his house, and I'll get my friend to fly over from the States to join us. We'll have a meeting. Let's get things moving.'

I tried not to show my excitement, but I know I did anyway, thinking about how far things had gone for me in recent years. However, there was a little warning bell ringing. Too many people were now keen to get involved. They were all good and experienced people, but still I felt I couldn't allow it. It would ruin things. I also had a premonition that, as good as things seemed, something was going to go really wrong. Being clairvoyant isn't easy: although you can read for other people, you cannot read for yourself because what you want gets in the way of what you see.

We drove up to Pat Reid's picturesque house on the outskirts of London the following Sunday. It was an olde worlde property, with leaded windows and lots of chintz inside. Pat Reid was truly a heroic character. The boys were so impressed because, of course, they'd studied the war at school, and to meet someone who was a real hero was such a thrill. Ignoring everyone else present, Pat Reid said to the children, 'Follow me.'

He led them into the garden, with everyone else following. 'Watch this,' he said. He picked up a small silver bell next to a fish pond and, as if by magic, when he swung the bell to and fro, a shoal of goldfish raised their heads above the water. 'Quickly, children,' he said, holding out a bowl of fish food, 'sprinkle it on the water.'

He had trained the goldfish to come to be fed at the sound of the bell. The children's faces were joyous, and Claire clapped her hands with excitement as the heads of the fish kept popping up. But who was most enthralled? Pat Reid.

'We'll save the business talk until after lunch,' he said, as he turned towards me.

We were served one of the best Sunday roasts I've ever had. My children were very well behaved. I had brought them up to talk to adults only if the adult spoke to them first. I was always getting complimented in restaurants, both here and abroad, on their manners, something which, coming from a Romany family, was very important to me. We had a reputation to keep up. I knew that the boys were burning to ask Pat all about his time in the Colditz prisoner-of-war camp. When the housekeeper saw we had finished eating, she came to collect the plates and returned with a very large cheese-board and some desserts for the children.

'You may notice that the cheese is very mouldy,' Pat said. There was indeed mould on every piece of cheese on the board. 'Now, you may be disgusted, but that's the way we used to receive it in Colditz. Our families would send us food parcels and by the time they got to us, they'd be full of mould. But, my friends, let me assure you that cheese is at its best when it is like this. You just cut the mould away and the cheese underneath has really matured. Tell me what you think.'

Indeed, it was delicious. After tasting it and realizing how good it was, it became a habit from then on with me not to throw away cheese that was past its sell-by date. I would simply cut the mould away and, as Pat said, it tasted at its best.

Once lunch was over, Pat settled the children with games and books on some cushions on the floor, and we sat around the table to talk business. I was rather unwilling to divulge the workings of my game to these men of influence, power and know-how without some kind of reassurance that my ideas would not be copied. You might call it paranoia; I call it the Romany in me. I suppose my father's words came back to me, from the day I jumped from the steps of our vardo and he promised to catch me and then let me fall. As I lay in the mud, he had instructed me to 'trust no one'. When a man you love lets you down, it does give you a hard shell and makes you suspicious of those you barely know, however famous or well connected they may be.

The men were discussing things like advertising, distribution and various other matters which, quite honestly, went over my head. I could not get rid of the feeling of doom I had about the project. And I was to be proved right.

Two days later, I received a parcel from Ted Jones Fenley, with a prototype of my Wheel of Fortune, which was very impressive. I was then called to a board meeting in London with Ted, which I took Johnnie along to. I had a feeling I would need him there for the decisions that were going to be made. When we arrived, there were six men sitting around a table, including Ted, and they proceeded to have some sort of discussion between them which I didn't understand and didn't want to. It turned out they were receivers. Ted had gone ahead with the Osiris game, using another clairvoyant, and had lost a great deal of money. If only he'd heeded my words. It had cost him £35,000 to make the prototype of the Wheel of Fortune, and he was trying to get the receivers to lay off, so that he could market the product and make the money back, but they stubbornly refused.

It was going to cost a fortune to produce and market the game, and Johnnie and I looked at each other across the table. The look said it all. We were not willing to part with our assets to get involved in something we did not fully understand or know enough about. The game was packed into a suitcase, with all the instructions, and was put away in my office. Ted, Tudor and Pat have all passed over since. Perhaps, one day, the game will come to light again. If fate intends.

This wasn't the only time a project failed before it began. One day Johnnie drove me up to London, to an important meeting with a TV producer who wanted me to appear on his show. On the way, I asked him to stop at a shop, so I could buy some cigarettes. Johnnie didn't smoke, but he did like a bit of chocolate, so I bought him a packet of chocolate mints. I opened them for him and put them on the bench seat between us, so he could reach them easily. Johnnie was wearing a brand-new grey Jaeger suit, which he had purchased the day before, and, with his suede trilby on his head, looked very smart indeed. He smelled nice too: he was wearing his trade-mark aftershave, Ho Hang by Balenciaga.

I had to make a quick call at one of the news-papers in Fleet Street to drop off some photographs first. When I came out of the newspaper office, Johnnie was leaning against the far side of the car with his arms folded on the roof, a very worried and uncom-fortable look on his face.

'What's wrong? Are you all right?' I asked.

'Not really, come round here and look,' he replied.

I quickly skirted round the car. 'Johnnie, you've shit yourself!' I said, aghast.

'It's your bloody chocolate mints. They must have slid out of the packet and gone underneath me while I was driving, so they're nice and melted.'

Sure enough, a big brown stain that looked like something it wasn't was on the seat of his trousers. We climbed back into the car and stared at one another.

'I know, let's find a chemist,' I suggested.

We did and, once inside, I told the assistant what had happened. 'Is there anything I can get it out with?' I pleaded.

She went and had a word with the pharmacist and came back carrying a bottle of white liquid. 'This should do the job,' she smiled.

'I'll also have a couple of white flannels, please,' I said. We drove on and found a secluded street, where I had to make him lean over the back seat, bum up in the air, while I drenched one of the flannels and rubbed away at the stain on his bottom. All the chocolate came off onto the flannel. Handing Johnnie the other flannel, I said, 'Now take this, get out the car and rub it until it's dry.'

After rubbing for several minutes, he turned around and said, 'What's it look like now, Jules?'

To my absolute horror, although the chocolate was gone, it had left a big white stain, which I took to be the mint inside the sweets. It must have got caught in the fibres of the material. He sat back in the driver's seat and we looked at each other again.

'What are we going to do now?' I asked.

'I know,' he said, putting the car into gear, and he parked up as close as he could to the Café de Paris. 'Come on.'

I followed him, not able to stop myself from bursting out with laugher. He held the beautiful suede hat over his bottom, looking like he'd done a murder. He disappeared into the gents and was gone ages. I sat waiting, wondering what on earth was happening. Had he taken his trousers off? Was he running them under the hot tap? I seemed to be sitting there for an eternity before he eventually emerged from the toilets.

'Well? Turn around then,' I said. The stain was gone! Thank goodness for that.

'It's all right for you,' Johnnie said, 'but I feel like a right wally. Let's get out of here quick.'

When we got outside, he doubled up laughing.

'What happened in there?' I asked.

'Well, there were some white basins to wash your hands in, so I filled one up with water and sat in it, which was fine until someone came in. A man walked in, took one look at me and turned round smartish and left. He must have thought I was using the basin as a toilet!'

I looked at my watch. We were far too late to get across town for our meeting with the TV producer.

Fate, in the form of chocolate mints, had intervened again!

THIRTY-FIVE

Gypsy Magic

'Come on, Jules, the cab's just pulled up,' Johnnie announced.

We were getting ready to go to a birthday party, and were watching out for the taxi that was bringing our babysitter. The idea was that we'd jump in and take it from there. But when Johnnie spoke, I suddenly found myself rooted firmly to the spot.

'I can't go out, Johnnie.'

He walked into the lounge with a look of disappointment on his face. 'If you're not going, I'm not going.'

'Don't be silly,' I said to him. 'You go and enjoy yourself, really. Drop the babysitter off back home and pay her for the night's work. I'm going to stay in.'

With that, Johnnie agreed to go, and I put the children to bed and settled down for a night in front of the television. Two hours later, my eldest son, Warren, came flying down the stairs.

'Mum, Mum,' he screamed, 'the light in the ceiling is on fire!'

'Go next door and get Bob,' I said, keeping very calm.

I knew that Bob, our neighbour, would be in and could take the children. I flew upstairs, got Gregory, Bradley and Claire out of bed and rushed downstairs with them as quickly as possible.

'What's going on, Mum?' Gregory said sleepily.

'Just do as I say, darling. You've got to get yourselves next door. Now go on and don't ask any questions.'

Gregory looked bewildered and stood scratching his head, still not quite awake. As I ushered the children out of the front door, I met Bob coming towards the door with Warren. No words needed to be exchanged.

'I'll get the kids safely next door and be back in a jiffy,' he assured me.

I ran for the phone and dialled 999. 'Help, help, I live at 363 Ditchling Road and it looks like there's a fire starting in one of the bedrooms. A light fitting has burst into flames.'

The lady on the other end of the phone firmly told me to stay calm and that they were getting someone out to us. She asked if there was anyone else in the house and told me to vacate the premises.

Bob appeared at my side and said, 'Go next door, Eva.'

He grabbed the fire extinguisher from the wall in my kitchen and headed up the stairs. I turned back to the phone and dialled the number for the Cricketers public house, where I knew Johnnie was. Winnie answered the phone and recognized my voice immediately when I asked for Johnnie.

'Oh, they're having a lovely time, dear. The party is going with a swing,' Winnie said. 'Alan is playing the keyboard.'

'Winnie,' I shouted, 'tell Johnnie the house is on fire!'

Johnnie came to the phone. 'Are you coming down, Jules?' he said, sounding jolly.

'Johnnie, the house is on fire!'

'Are the children safe? Are you OK?' he asked, the panic in his voice disappearing as I told him we were all fine and the children were next door. 'I'll be there as soon as possible,' he said, hanging up the phone.

The firemen arrived and ran straight up the stairs. Bob met them at the top of the first flight and, with a simple sentence exchanged, stepped back for them to get past and do their job.

Before I knew it, my house, which was on fire, had been invaded, not only by Bob and the firemen, but by Johnnie and half a dozen people from the party, all looking as if they were ready to carry on drinking, and obviously already the worse for wear. Johnnie ran straight up the stairs to the children's rooms. The sight of the fire engines outside had obviously sobered him up, if not the other revellers, and he went to see exactly what was going on.

Sammy, whose birthday it was, put his arm round me and said, 'Don't worry, Eva.' He then went behind the bar in my kitchen and poured me a large brandy.

I looked at the other guests rather blankly and said, 'Help yourselves.'

The chief fireman came down the stairs. 'It was only a small fire, madam. You've got faulty wiring,' he said. 'It's all out now. My boys are just checking everything over.'

With that, Sammy cut in. 'You couldn't come to my party, so we're bringing the party to you.' He picked up the phone in the kitchen and dialled the pub. 'Winnie, close up, the party's moved venue!'

'Well, if you don't laugh, you cry,' I said with a weak chuckle.

Johnnie came downstairs, with half a grin and a sheepish look.

'Go and bring our babies home.' I spoke softly to him. He knew that, once again, my instincts had been right, but neither one of us could have known what a blaze Sammy's party would end on.

*

After several weeks of discussing the pros and cons of starting another magazine like the one I had given up when Claire was born, the first thing we did was make an appointment to go to London to see the main man at WHSmith, who had previously been one of our main distributors. He gave us a warm welcome.

'Yes, it was a good little seller, your horoscope guide,' he said. 'However, times have changed, Eva, and you wouldn't be able to do the distribution yourself, as you did before. It has to go through the correct channels now, and you have to have a distributor who is already supplying us with other magazines.'

This came to a blow to Johnnie and me, and we looked at each other in dismay. The two of us went out to lunch. Time for a board meeting.

'If we do it this way, other people would be in control of our money,' I said.

Johnnie looked at me, with his finger on chin. 'On the other hand, these people know what they're doing and they're all big companies. We'll probably be able to sell a lot more than we managed to on our own, even though we did extremely well with it.'

The waiter came over with menus, but we weren't ready to eat, not the way our stomachs were churning. Johnnie put his menu down. 'If we're going to continue in the market, Jules, maybe you should look at a different format? The horoscope guide was a one-man band, with you doing all the writing and the layouts, while I did the distribution. I think it would be sensible to make it a bigger magazine, if we're going to do it.'

I stopped him in mid-flow and said, 'I've just had a flash: herbs, health and horoscopes.'

I pulled my notebook and pen out of my bag – two things I was never without – and began scribbling away as ideas came into my head. Our hunger finally began to kick in and we ordered our food. I must have scribbled my way through our first and second courses, and Johnnie didn't interrupt, as he could see I was on a roll.

I leaned back and threw my pen onto the table, just as the waiter was bringing dessert. 'Right, I've had enough for one day. Let's get home to our babies.'

We called a cab and went home, both our brains buzzing. Over the following weeks, ideas accumulated in my mind and I made lots of enquiries to see if there were any similar magazines on the market, but couldn't find any. As my column in the Scottish *Sunday Mail* was so popular, I decided a similar 'Dear Eva' column in my own magazine should prove just as successful.

Soon the idea had solidified in my mind and we began making concrete plans for my new magazine, which would be released on a monthly basis and called *Romany*. Johnnie, as ever, was behind me every step of the way, supporting me in every way he could, from helping me pick staff to checking out distributors. I felt a huge sense of pride when the first issue arrived from the printers, and all our efforts paid off as it went on to be a huge success for many years to come.

One of the most interesting people I met around this time was Barbara Cartland. She had contacted me and said, 'I'd love to meet you. I think we have a lot in common.' She invited Johnnie and me to have tea at Camfield Place near Hatfield. Her house was fabulous, as was she. Dressed in fluffy pink clothes, face made up immaculately, she showed us into a room and indicated a table. 'If you look through the window, this is the view which Beatrix Potter would see when she was writing at this very table.'

Of course, I was impressed. Beatrix Potter was famous for bringing the likes of Peter Rabbit, Jemima Puddle-Duck, Benjamin Bunny and Mrs Tiggy-Winkle to life.

'Now, Johnnie dear,' she said, 'would you be a darling and pour us a drink?' She indicated a big sea chest which stood near the wall. 'They're in there.'

Johnnie lifted the lid and it was set out like a bar, with glasses and bottles.

'I'll have a gin and tonic, dear,' she instructed.

'I'll have the same, please.' I winked at Johnnie.

She also winked. 'You'd like a beer, Johnnie, I bet.

There's some in there, you know.' We sat down with our drinks. 'Now, I understand you know a lot about herbs,' Barbara said.

'It's the way of my people,' I explained. I told her how I used to gather herbs and watch my grandmother and mother prepare remedies for different ailments. Barbara explained how she had campaigned since the early 1960s for Romany rights. I suddenly realized why she had invited me over. Herbal recipes were a passion with her, and she told me how she supplied the royal family with herbal recipes and remedies. We talked for what seemed like hours, and I was mesmerized by this larger-than-life character who was a fountain of knowledge.

'I must ask you,' I said, 'do you find it hard work writing all your books?'

'No, dear,' she said. 'You see, I talk very fast when I'm on a flow and I have three shorthand typists whom I dictate to.'

'Not all at once?' I asked.

'Oh yes. That way, I am sure that every word I say is written down. These girls, you know, have other things on their minds.'

'Men?'

'Yes,' she laughed. 'This way, I am sure nothing is missed out and, believe me, when you compare the three typed chapters, you can be sure that each one of them will have missed a word or two.'

'Anyway, shall we have tea now?' She rang a bell and a lady soon appeared with a huge tray. 'I've had Cook make Johnnie his favourite cakes,' she said.

Just who had she been talking to, to find this out? She knew he liked beer, she knew his favourite cakes . . . She'd obviously been talking to someone who knew us well. Laid out on the tray were the most beautiful cucumber sandwiches with the crusts cut off, smoked salmon and beef and mustard sandwiches, and meringue cakes, all beautifully presented.

We talked as we ate, about herbs and about the royal family. As I took in the beautiful room, I noticed that there were lots of photographs of Lord Mountbatten, who I knew was a very close friend of Barbara's. After tea, she said, 'I've got a present for you, Eva, as I know you said you're launching your magazine shortly.' From her pocket she produced a slim gold chain with a gold acorn. 'Follow me,' she said.

We followed her into the garden, where stood a beautiful old oak tree.

'Queen Elizabeth I shot her very first deer while standing beside this tree, and I have these acorns dipped in gold to give to my friends as a gift, to wish them luck. I'm giving this to you to wish you well with your new magazine.'

Then all of a sudden a thought came to me. 'You know what, Barbara?' I said. 'I would love to serialize your book in my magazine.'

'What a great idea!' she replied. 'I know, I'll sell it to you for a penny!' So that's how a Barbara Cartland novel came to feature in the first issue of *Romany* magazine! I didn't know how much money a magazine would normally pay to serialize such a well-known author's work, but I knew it was in the tens of thousands of pounds, meaning that she was doing me a great honour selling it to me for a penny. But as the idea settled in my mind, I began to worry a little – what on earth had possessed me? What made me think that her novel would be a good fit for a magazine about Romany life?! But I needn't have worried as it went down a treat; all my readers seemed to love it.

I was deeply moved by how lovely and welcoming she had been. 'Thank you so much for a really interesting afternoon, a lovely tea and especially for my acorn.'

'We must meet up again,' she said. 'I've enjoyed talking to you immensely.'

We waved our goodbyes and hit the road. I found out afterwards that later that same evening she had called her publisher to say that she had thought of a title for her new book – it was to be called *Gypsy Magic*.

THIRTY-SIX

Happy Times

I was in the garden of the vicarage with Mummy, breathing in the scent of honeysuckle and admiring the plants that were flourishing. Our moment of reflection was broken by Johnnie calling to me, 'Daisy's on the telephone.'

I ran to the house and picked up the phone. 'What's the matter?' I asked. We always ask this when we phone each other.

'Everybody's OK,' she reassured me. 'We're all going to America, but we're coming to stay with you to-morrow night before we go.'

'Wonderful,' I said, delighted. 'Now, tell me who's coming.' I was so excited.

'Honour and Eric and their children, Kay, Muzzer and Baby Honour. Then there's me and Sonny Boy and our children, Julie, Debra, Kelly and Leah,' said Daisy.

It may seem strange that my family always decided

to travel on holiday together, in groups of twenty or more most of the time. But this was the way things had always been. In fact, they were so used to being with one another that when Daisy, Sonny Boy and the rest of the gang all decided to move into houses, they settled on the same road and, to this day, practically the entire street where they live in Blackpool is inhabited by their relations. I guess you can't shake the habits of a lifetime!

All my family had no choice but to settle down in houses, for travelling on the open road had become a thing of the past. As best they could, they kept their traditions alive. Each house had a garden, where they had their stick fires, and many of the elders of the family had a caravan in the garden or on the driveway, which they used more as a base than as an actual home. And although they all had toilets in their houses, they had also each built an outside toilet and never used the one inside the house, as it was considered unhygienic.

Most Romany children were sent to school for a while as it was felt that it was good for children to have a rudimentary gorger education; learning to read and write was important, as was maths. But no other academic subjects were given any significance in our culture. So children were taken out when they got to the age of eight to be home-schooled and were all trained by professionals in their own homes, under the watchful eyes of their parents, in vocational subjects that were chosen by the family all together. And it was assumed that this would not be an issue for the children when they grew up as they would go on to marry other Romanies, who would have been taught in the same way and would have the same skills to help them make a living. I was an exception, but traditionally Romanies believed they should marry one another and keep the bloodline going. After all, we were a dying race.

The most important thing as far as Daisy and Sonny Boy were concerned was music. All of them could play the piano, accordion and guitar, and they also took singing lessons. Unbelievable as it sounds, one of Daisy's grandchildren was a brilliant drummer and actually played a gig with Ozzy Osbourne at the age of five! She was phenomenal. Another child, William, played the piano accordion and was ranked number six in the world's best players, and he was booked regularly to perform in Las Vegas.

I was thrilled at the idea of them coming to stay. In my heart, I had never truly left my old way of life, and still kept to the old beliefs and traditions. Johnnie and I would often take the children to the country and I'd show them the things that were important to me. They had a mixed upbringing and went to school, a luxury I had never had, but had always wanted. From what I learned from their experiences though, I'm glad I didn't go.

I began to think of what I would cook and Johnnie entered the kitchen. 'Tools down, boy, we need to build a stick fire,' I said. 'We're having a party – the Black-poolers are on their way!'

'OK, boss,' he said with a wink. Johnnie had grown to love the stick fires as much as I and the rest of my family did.

Mummy chimed in, 'Don't go buying anything. I'm going to the shops. I'll buy the vittles.'

'Vittles' was an old English word meaning food or provisions that my Granny had used, and Mummy continued to use it. 'Tell Nathan, Sue and Eddie, and make sure you tell them to bring their guitars.'

'Yes, Mummy,' I replied and headed back to the phone to round up the troops. Luckily, it was Friday – no school for the children the next day – so we could really make a night of it.

On their arrival, Johnnie went out and got the fire started. We all greeted each other warmly and I ushered them out into the garden, where we had placed chairs and cushions and blankets. Honour and Daisy helped me to make cups of tea and coffee and soft drinks for the children, and I had an old-fashioned gramo-phone with a horn on it which we took out into the garden, with a collection of records I knew they would like.

The other women and I settled down to 'crease', have a good old talk. Honour and Daisy's children were in heaven, running free in the garden with my children. Warren, Bradley, Gregory and Claire were also in their element, being with the relations they had not seen in ages. Claire took the girls up to her bedroom to show them her collection of Sindy dolls and the house her father had built her, and they returned to the garden with dolls and clothes spilling out of their arms. The boys came down with a fort, which Johnnie had also made, and tiny green soldiers and Indians. It was like Christmas Day, with all the laughter and banter.

It was now about seven in the evening, and the men decided to go up the road and buy some beers to bring back. The party was really going with a swing. Mummy, Nathan and Eddie arrived laden with boxes of food which, without a word being spoken, the women automatically started to unpack and prepare. Daisy had brought with her an array of amazing herbs from her garden, which she started to scatter over the various meats. Black pepper and salt were brought from the kitchen and thrown over the food, and I busied myself bringing out nibbles for the now very hungry children to devour.

Memories of being on the road in days gone by and

sitting around a fire in the open, sharing food and laughter with my family, came flooding back. It was at times like these that I was truly content.

As it began to get a little bit dark, Eddie and Nathan started to strum their guitars. Sonny Boy and Eric took it in turns to sing and we were really having a ball. Sonny Boy grabbed some spoons from a tray on the grass and started making music with them. We had our own live show in the back garden.

'Why don't we let the children stay up late tonight?' I said. 'That way, they'll be tired and sleep on the train tomorrow. They're on their hoildays now, anyway.'

We were running out of fuel for the fire. Johnnie went to the end of the garden and shouted, 'Come on, boys.' He started to dismantle the chicken run, which, after the departure of the rabbits, we now had no use for. The men ferried the wood over and piled it next to the fire, as Johnnie dismantled the whole thing (thank goodness!).

As the night wore on, the whole group of us, including the children, was relaxed and happy. My boys and Kelly, Daisy's son, kept themselves busy going to the end of the garden, where they continued to collect loads and loads of wood, piling it up next to the timber the men had already stacked. As the night wore on, the pile was getting bigger and bigger. The adults were so engrossed in talking and singing along to the music that we failed to notice how big the woodpile was getting. It wasn't until the next morning that we noticed our back fence was completely missing and there was a huge pile of logs as well as pieces of fencing next to the fire!

'So where did the logs come from?' Johnnie asked.

The boys, thinking they had done a good thing, said, 'Well, when we took the fence down for the fire we saw a pile of logs in the garden next door and we thought you could use it.'

Johnnie immediately went next door to explain to the neighbour, saying that he would have a load of logs delivered the same day and also would have a new fence put up.

'We heard you all. Sounded like you were having a really good time,' our neighbour said.

'Next time, come and join us,' Johnnie offered. 'You'll be welcome anytime.'

We didn't usually encourage our neighbours to become friends, apart from Pat and Brian in Ship Street Gardens, as we liked to keep ourselves to ourselves, but Johnnie felt they needed some thanks after putting up with all of us.

Before our visitors left, I ran upstairs and beckoned Daisy to follow me. 'Here, try this on.' I gave her my jumpsuit, which was the latest trend. 'They're so comfortable, and perfect for an aeroplane.'

Being married to a gorger for so long, it had gone out of my head that Romany women didn't wear trousers. She looked fabulous in it though, and started to go downstairs. She did not get even halfway down before Sonny Boy stopped her in her tracks, horrified.

'Daisy, get those trousers off.'

She ran back up the stairs. She had known that trousers were not the done thing among Romany women, and that the jumpsuit was like a red rag to a bull. Daisy was not upset though, as she knew that Sonny Boy couldn't help his beliefs and upbringing. Besides, you only had to look at the two of them together to see they were deeply in love. He still serenaded her and worshipped the ground she walked on . . . as long as it wasn't in a pair of trousers!

After they had gone, I told Johnnie about Honour's daughter, Baby Honour. She had been born with a disorder and Honour and Eric had taken her to doctors all over the country to try to get to the bottom of it. They had been told by numerous doctors that there was nothing wrong with her, but they knew there was. It wasn't until she was sixteen years of age, after numerous tests, that she was diagnosed with a dysfunctional kidney. She would need a transplant. Honour donated one of her own kidneys to her daughter, but her body rejected it. Baby Honour went on to have two more transplants, neither of which took. This amazing young girl had tremendous courage and never complained about the illness which would eventually take her life.

As the sun went down, I stood with my mother in the garden of my dream home, joyful scenes from the night before running through my mind. Music wafted out from the house, the strains of Nat King Cole singing 'Unforgettable'. I smiled. It was one of Johnnie's favourites. He always liked to play music when he worked. As I thought about our journey in life together and how far we had come, it was as if time stood still. Vivid scenes of a painted Romany caravan merged into family gatherings in a field, with food cooking on an open fire and laughter ringing out. So many happy memories, and so much laughter.

Right then, at that moment, with my beloved mother next to me, my four beautiful children and my dear husband, Johnnie – my best friend, my lover and my confidant – I felt my life was complete.

Acknowledgements

I would like to say a special thank you to my editors at Pan Macmillan, Ingrid Connell and Lorraine Green, and to Maria Malone, for their help with the text – the only people I've ever met who could read my handwriting.

I am also very grateful to my brother Nathan for tirelessly searching through piles of photographs, and to my cousin Honour Boswell for remembering places and names I couldn't.

And the biggest thank you of all must go to my daughter Claire Petulengro, who managed to help me write this book, all the while juggling her own big workload and looking after her four wonderful children, Paris, Carmen, Lucy and Honey. They remind us daily that the most important thing in life is never to lose your sense of humour. This book is also for you, my darlings.

extracts reading groups
competitions books new
discounts extracts
competitions
books new
events books
extracts new titles reading groups
interviews
events extracts
discounts
new books events
events new events
discounts extracts discounts

www.panmacmillan.com

extracts events reading groups
competitions books extracts new